THE LIVING EARTH BOOK OF
DESERTS

THE LIVING EARTH BOOK OF

DESERTS

SUSAN ARRITT

THE READER'S DIGEST ASSOCIATION, INC.
Pleasantville, New York/Montreal

The Living Earth Book of Deserts

A Reader's Digest Living Earth Book

Produced for The Reader's Digest Association, Inc.,
by Redefinition, Inc.

The credits that appear on page 223 are hereby made a part of
this copyright page.

Library of Congress Cataloging in Publication Data

Arritt, Susan.
        The living earth book of deserts / Susan Arritt.
            p.   cm—(A Reader's Digest living earth book)
        Includes index.
        ISBN 0-89577-519-0
        1. Deserts.   I. Title.   II. Series: Reader's Digest living earth.
GB611.A77 1993
508.315'4—dc20   93-28902

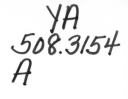

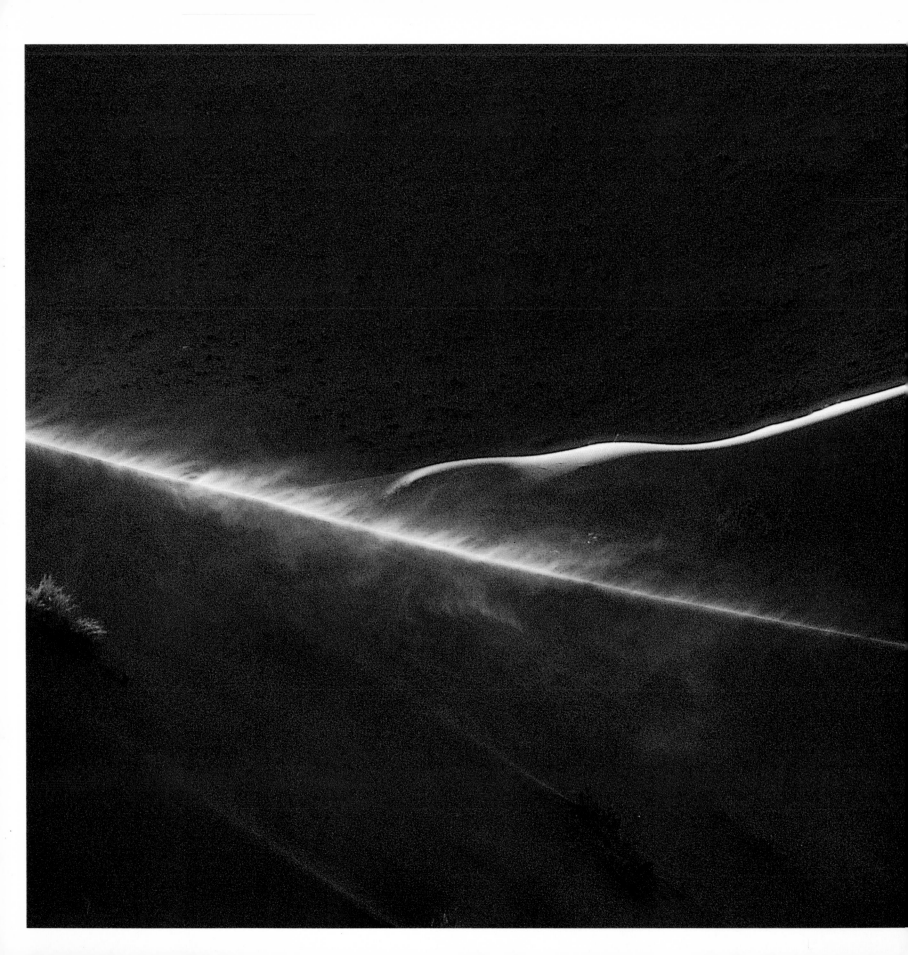

DECIPHERING DESERTS

WITHOUT WARNING, A SPELLBINDING SOUND akin to far-off violins pierces the silence of the desert. High-pitched and shrill, yet gravelly and deep, it skims across sunlit dune crests and swoops down into shadowed valleys of sand. Little is stirring in this wilderness today—no thunderheads loom above the horizon, nor is the wind howling or especially uproarious. At most, shimmering ripples from the heat are all that distort the fine line where the chalky blue sky and scorching amber sand converge. No earthly creature could let loose such a far-reaching cry. What culprit, then, could fill the desert air with this plaintive, resonating wail?

Few and far between are the desert lands where sand itself orchestrates the rare music of the dunes. Tiny grains dislodged by wind and other movements create avalanches—large and small—that cascade downward, producing sounds of the most unpredictable nature and magnitude. The phenomenon is called "booming dunes" by today's scientists, but tales passed down for centuries by desert travelers and indigenous peoples liken

A constant sea breeze sculpts dunes of the Namib Desert (*left*), along the southwestern coast of Africa, keeping them in perpetual motion. A massive sand mountain in the Gobi desert (*above*) was formed of angular grains eroded from nearby rock.

the bizarre sounds of sand to cannons, foghorns, rumbling cavalry hooves, incessant barking, cart wheels—even the music of zithers, bells, tambourines, or pipe organs or the melodious voices of frogs or humans.

More than 1,200 years ago, in one of the earliest accounts of desert acoustics, Chinese scribes reported "strange noises" spewing from a sand hill deep in a vast desert region in Asia called the Gobi. Time and again, local festival-goers would scale the face of the 500-foot-high (150-m) dune to incite the rumbling of thunder during their celebrations. Marco Polo, who journeyed to China in the late Middle Ages, wrote that a desert traveler separated from his caravan may hear "drums and the clash of arms," the work of "spirits talking in such a way that they seem to be his companions." Humbling tales of these supernatural forces, he recounted, forced many en route across the Gobi "to close their line of march and to proceed in more compact order." Thousands of miles away, in the deserts of Arabia, legend attributes the sounds to the banging of gongs in a convent long buried in the sand—or to the moaning of one of the spirit entities known as *jinn*.

The rare, resonating sands have been heard emanating from about 30 duned sites in arid parts of Africa, Asia, the Middle East, and North and South America. Exactly why such sounds occur remains one of the mysteries of the multifaceted world of deserts. Where dry lands exist, so do other quirks of nature as awe-inspiring as the elusive virtuosos of the dunes. The unique identities of the world's deserts are shaped as much by elements and unseen forces as by all that the naked eye can behold within these seemingly endless domains.

DRY AS A BONE

A desert is a land so wanting in water that its very essence is its aridity. Dryness is the most powerful determinant of whether or not a region of the Earth is truly a desert. The scant availability of water influences the lay of the land and the quality of the soil, besides dictating which plant and animal species flourish. It is also the hinge upon which life or death swings for humans, who do not have highly evolved, natural mechanisms to survive in waterless lands.

Once, scientists defined deserts as places that receive 10 inches (254 mm) or less of rainfall each year. That was misleading, because not all precipitation is actually available for use by plants and animals. In deserts, heat from the sun and dry winds cause more water to evaporate over a year's time than falls from the clouds as rain. Sometimes during light showers, raindrops dry up long before they hit the earth. But occasionally, enormous downpours pelt the sun-dried earth with so much water that most is carried away in flash-flood runoffs. Finally, in the coldest deserts on Earth, what little precipitation there is may be frozen as ice or snow, and therefore not a source of moisture for flora and fauna.

While all deserts are intrinsically dry, slight variations in rainfall from one region to the next can create vastly diverse microenvironments within a single desert. Within an hour's walking distance one may encounter naked sand dunes, then round a bend and happen upon a protected niche where tiny animals take shelter from the sun amongst an abundance of green-leaved desert plants. Although the term *arid* broadly describes all desert lands of the world, elaborations of the word categorize places that fall at opposite ends of the spectrum of aridity, and thus have different climates and biological communities.

Hyperarid desert regions are the driest spots on the planet and support a limited variety of species; these areas receive less than 4 inches (102 mm) of precipitation per year. Because rainfall measurement alone does not take into account either runoff or evaporation, scientists quantify the actual dryness of a locality with an "aridity index,"

Fog—formed when warm onshore wind meets the cold Benguela Current of the South Atlantic—is the chief water source for much of the Namib, enabling hundreds of species to inhabit the dunes.

A herd of springbok, a type of antelope, bounds through a national park in the Kalahari Desert of South Africa. Highly adapted to the dry savanna, springbok get much of their moisture from the vegetation they eat, drinking only when water is available.

which considers the ratio of precipitation received to solar energy received. Some places in the Sahara, for example, have an aridity index of 200, indicating that energy from the sun is capable of evaporating 200 times the amount of rain that falls there. Semiarid lands get about 10 to 15 inches (254–381 mm) of rain a year, yet may lose more than that amount to evaporation. Where these semiarid places line the fringes of more arid deserts, they may serve as ecological transition zones between the flora and fauna of extremely dry lands and those of Earth's more humid, non-desert regions.

Global Desert Bands

Deserts encompass nearly one-third of Earth's 58 million square miles (150 million sq km) of land surface. That is such an immense parcel of planetary real estate that if all these arid and semiarid regions were interlocked like jigsaw puzzle pieces, the resulting landmass would be large enough, in theory, to blanket the entire surface of the moon. In actuality, deserts are solidly linked here on Earth—not necessarily by adjacent geographical borders but by their physical inclusion in one of six arid bands that encircle the globe.

"Put a girdle round about the earth," wrote William Shakespeare, more than 14 centuries after Greco-Roman cartographers devised a grid system to make two-dimensional sense of our spherical planet. They early envisioned an imaginary line called the Equator, wrapped around the globe midway between the planet's two icy Poles and intersecting the steamiest jungles, the rain forests, and the warmest of oceans. This 24,902-mile-long (40,165-km)

circle—where the sun's rays strike most directly—is the 0° latitude line, which divides the planet into its Northern and Southern hemispheres.

The desert bands that girdle the globe run parallel to the Equator in each of the hemispheres. In the north, the largest chain of deserts lies along the Tropic of Cancer, which circles the planet along the 23°27' latitude line. These are the subtropical deserts—the hottest lands of all. With an area of 3.5 million square miles (9 million sq km), the Sahara in northern Africa reigns supreme. Eastward along the band is the arid Arabian Peninsula, which, like the Sahara and other massive arid zones, includes numerous individually named desert regions within its boundaries. Beyond that, stretching from a corner of Pakistan into the plateaus of northwestern India, lies the Thar, or Great Indian Desert. And halfway around the world, more or less along the same subtropical latitudes, are the hottest deserts of North America: the Sonoran, Chihuahuan, and Mojave.

Another band of subtropical deserts lies in the Southern Hemisphere, at the same distance from the Equator as the deserts to its north. The Kalahari Desert encompasses a huge part of southern Africa, along the Tropic of Capricorn, at latitude 23°27' S. And in the arid interior of Australia there are five subtropical deserts: the Great Victoria, Gibson, Great Sandy, and the Simpson, which includes Sturt Stony.

WHERE DESERTS FORM

The world's deserts lie on all seven continents. But their locations are far from random. Other than the highest deserts in the world, which lie on the tallest and most frigid mountain peaks, deserts are distributed along six vast belts of aridity that wrap around the Earth parallel to the Equator—three to the Equator's north, three to its south. Within each band lie deserts created by similar forces where climates are strikingly similar. All four desert types are grouped by color in the map at right.

The hottest deserts are the subtropical deserts, which straddle the Tropic of Cancer or the Tropic of Capricorn—23 degrees north or south of the Equator, respectively. High-pressure systems that wrap around the Earth at these latitudes keep the lands perpetually dry. There, too, lie the rare coastal deserts, where cooler climates result from frigid offshore ocean currents.

Between 35 and 50 degrees latitude in both the northern and southern hemispheres are cold-winter deserts. Hot in summer, bitter in winter, these lands remain dry either because they are too far inland to be reached by ocean-born moisture or because they lie in the arid "rain shadow" of mountain ranges that effectively block precipitation.

Encircling the top and bottom of the Earth are polar deserts. There is plenty of moisture in these ice-covered lands, but they are considered arid because frozen water is not available for plant or animal use.

Great Basin Desert
Colorado Plateau
Mojave Desert
Sonoran Desert
Chihuahuan Desert

Atacama Desert

Patagonian Desert

Subtropical
Polar
Cold Winter
Cool Coastal

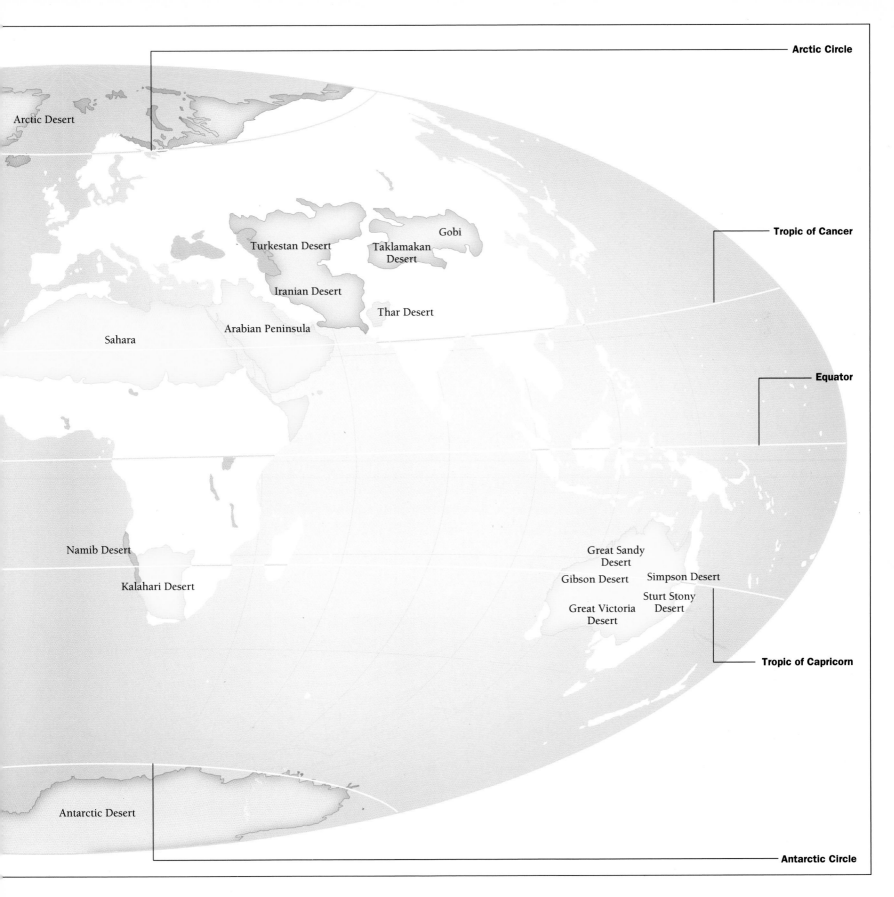

Arctic Circle

Arctic Desert

Tropic of Cancer

Turkestan Desert

Gobi

Taklamakan
Desert

Iranian Desert

Thar Desert

Sahara

Arabian Peninsula

Equator

Namib Desert

Great Sandy
Desert

Gibson Desert

Simpson Desert

Kalahari Desert

Sturt Stony
Desert

Great Victoria
Desert

Tropic of Capricorn

Antarctic Desert

Antarctic Circle

Subtropical deserts on both sides of the Equator are primarily formed by a never-ending cycle of air movement in the atmosphere. Hot air masses rise and drop rain over the verdant equatorial zone, then travel over the subtropical latitudes, virtually depleted of moisture. There the desert lands sit, hostages of high-pressure systems and the scorching sun.

At subtropical latitudes in both hemispheres, another kind of arid land exists—the coastal deserts. Few in number, they are anomalies in that they are frequently blanketed in fog created by temperature inversions, which in turn are products of cold offshore ocean currents that arrive from the frigid polar regions. Since nearly all moisture is bound up in the cloaks of fog, these rare deserts are some of the driest and most uninhabitable places on Earth—for plants, animals, and humans.

Farther from the Equator, bands of cold-winter deserts straddle the zones between 35° and 50° in both the Northern and Southern hemispheres. In these windswept lands, late spring, summer, and early autumn days may be warm, but nights are chilly. During winter months, temperatures plunge below freezing, and snowfalls on the high plateaus, gravel plains, interior basins, and even sandy dune fields are not unusual. Temperature extremes vacillate dramatically because of the high latitudes as well as the often high elevations of these deserts; aridity is caused by the fact that distance or mountain barriers prevent moisture from the ocean from reaching these lands.

Asia contains the largest of the world's cold-winter deserts—the Taklamakan, Turkestan, Iranian Plateau, and

Polar regions, where precipitation is scarce and most fresh water is frozen, qualify as deserts. Huge chunks of glaciers dominate Iceberg Alley in the Labrador Sea near the Arctic Circle.

the Gobi. The Colorado Plateau and Great Basin deserts lie in western North America, and below the Equator the Patagonian Desert sits at the southernmost tip of South America.

Farthest from the Equator are two arid bands that cap both ends of the Earth with polar deserts. Most areas north of the Arctic Circle (at 66°33' N) and all of Antarctica—the "bottom of the world"—are, because of extreme aridity, every bit as deserving of the term desert as is a hot wilderness with scorching sands. The North and South poles, which lie at 90° N and S, respectively, are the highest latitude points on Earth. There, dry air from ever-circulating high-pressure systems means scant precipitation. What little moisture reaches the earth is in the form of ice or snow and is inaccessible to most plants and animals. Much about these frigid environments is mimicked elsewhere in the world on the tallest mountaintops and along alpine slopes at extremely high elevations, where aridity, strong winds, and intense solar energy are forceful deterrants to life.

Part of the Planet

Clearly, there is order to the arrangement of deserts across the face of the globe. They are not randomly scattered lands that nature forgot. Rather, deserts are the work of numerous forces that converge in well-defined zones around the Earth to create richly diverse lands—lands in which aridity is the most common thread. Much of a desert's overall character is predestined by its latitude: temperature, solar energy levels, and availability of moisture, to name a few. These qualities, in turn, help dictate the scope of plant and animal diversity as well as soil quality. Yet at both global and local levels, nature has countless ways of otherwise influencing desert environments—regardless of latitude. The collective workings of Earth's single grand ecosystem continually shape and reshape every region of the globe.

The arid lands of the world are ever-fluctuating environments in which significant changes can take place over the course of millennia—or within split seconds. Earthquakes and volcanoes can remodel a desert vista in an afternoon, just as torrential downpours can reconfigure the banks of gullies and riverbeds in a matter of hours. Global climatic changes, too—causing widespread glaciation or, conversely, the swelling of oceans—have repeatedly orchestrated the role of desert lands, which have emerged time and again over the past half-billion years in places where great oceans once teemed with life.

About 250 million years ago, when tropical waters covered much of what is now the arid American Southwest, algae, sponges, and organisms that secrete calcium carbonate conglomerated on the sea bottom to form the 400-mile-long (645-km) Capitan Reef. As the global climate became drier, the warm waters gradually evaporated, and the limestone reef became buried under layer upon layer of the sediment, which forms the foundation of today's Chihuahuan Desert. Millions of years later, massive shifts in the Earth's crust caused such geologic upheaval that three large portions of the horseshoe-shaped fossil reef were pushed up above the present ground level. Today, on the high peaks of the Guadalupe, Glass, and Apache mountain ranges, which loom above the scrub-covered desert in southern New Mexico and western Texas, fossilized seashell fragments are commonplace mountaintop evidence that this territory was once the site of an ancient ocean.

The North African region where the sweeping Sahara now lies has experienced three periods of predominantly wet climate in the most recent 60,000 years. Huge portions of the area were covered by ocean 40 million to 50 million years ago; in the dunes southwest of Cairo, Egypt, paleontologists have found complete skeletons of early whales—some of which had small hind legs. As the waters subsided, the lush green land abounded in animal life, and swamps and rivers were equally prolific. When humans arrived, about 10,000 years ago, wildlife populations—

Orange flowers of a desert mallow (*top*) bloom in a sandstone alcove of the Mojave Desert in southern Nevada. Iron deposited here some 150 million years ago gives the rock its reddish hue.

This brightly marked chameleon (*above*) basks in the warmth of the sun. Chameleons change color in response to temperature and light variations rather than to camouflage themselves.

including hippopotamuses, elephants, antelopes, and lions—were similar to those in some central African regions now. But by 2000 B.C. the climate of northern Africa had changed so severely that it was the bona fide desert it is today. Beneath its surface, however, vast underground reserves of potentially tappable "fossil" water, remnants of wetter times, still lie in wait.

UNRAVELING DESERT MYSTERIES

In 1839, after his voyage on the *Beagle* to the southern-most reaches of the Americas, Charles Darwin was confounded by his own fascination with the region's dry, "boundless" wilderness: "I find that the plains of Patagonia frequently cross before my eyes . . . . They can be described only by negative possessions; without habitations, without water, without trees . . . they support merely a few dwarf plants," he wrote. "Why then . . . have these arid wastes taken so firm possession of my mind?"

These limestone outcroppings at Pinnacles Desert (*left*) in south-western Australia began forming when calcium carbonate leached through dunes and was exposed in recent centuries as sand gradually blew away.

Flat-topped basaltic mesas (*above*), remnants of ancient lava flows, rise from a low area in the central Patagonian Desert of Argentina. Eons ago, this area was a dense forest.

Countless people have likewise been intrigued—and perplexed—by deserts. By the very nature of their arid ambiance—expansive, desolate, windswept places engulfed in solitude—deserts assume a beguiling air of intrigue. The word *desert* itself derives from the Latin *deserere*, "to abandon, or forsake." And *wilderness* may have given rise to the verb *wilder*, meaning "to bewilder, or cause to be perplexed or lost." Many a novice has been lured by the desert's unknown, drawn into zones whose names, at best, portend danger: Skeleton Coast, Empty Quarter, Last Chance Range, Devil's Playground, and Tug-of-War Canyon. That which is most foreign often holds the most allure for people—be they thrill seekers, the science-minded, or merely inquisitive lovers of nature.

It is because of the mystery inherent in deserts that preconceived notions about them should be cast aside. All deserts are not, for example, covered with sand dunes; in fact less than 20 percent of the arid lands of the world are blanketed with sand. The rest may be rolling plains peppered with gravel; deeply carved, rock-faced canyons; dry basins of cracked clay; ice fields a mile or more thick; even gritty layers of salt-encrusted soil.

Nothing about deserts can be taken for granted. Spanish explorers in the 18th century could not imagine that the Great Basin Desert of North America had no waterway link to the Pacific Ocean. They believed there had to be a river passageway; such "reasonable" geographic design was their only frame of reference. Tales of the supposed Buenaventura River were handed on to American hopefuls, who after a hundred years of scouring the dusty sagebrush desert, came up empty-handed as well. During the same decade, British explorer Charles Sturt was convinced by all his early notions of geology and topography that Australia's uncharted, arid interior contained a huge body of water, the "new Australian Caspian Sea." Time and again, in vain, he struck out on torturous inland journeys over thousands of miles of hot scrubland, sand dunes, and a region carpeted with rocks, which is now called the Sturt Stony Desert.

Another whose high hopes were dashed by the sobering realities of the desert environment was Saudi Arabian Prince Muhammad ibn Faisal. In 1977 he proposed towing a 90-million-ton iceberg from Antarctica to the Red Sea, where it could be melted to provide his parched country with fresh water. The logistics of transport, however, and the difficulty of keeping the berg from melting on its voyage through the warm northerly waters caused the ungainly and impractical project to be abandoned in the early 1980's.

Despite centuries of exploring deserts, exploiting their natural resources, and determined attempts at taming them, deserts remain among the most misunderstood environments on the planet. In many cases, there is little consensus about how and why these arid environments function as they do—even among those who spend lifetimes studying these realms. Our collective knowledge about these wild places is still in the fledgling stage.

Nature's Ebb and Flow

Deserts are integral components of Earth's massive ecosystem, or biosphere, which comprises all the physical environments on this planet and the organisms that live within them. This grand ecosystem functions like a massive machine that runs primarily on energy from the sun. And nothing occurs within the huge system without its affecting something else along the way; so much so, in fact, that incalculable chains of events are happening on the global and local, as well as the microscopic, levels at any given moment.

Desert environments are in a continuous state of flux and are intimately related to other parts of Earth's ecosystem in myriad ways. One link begins with dust particles smaller than the head of a pin. When water or wind erodes the soil surface of scantily vegetated arid lands, nitrogen and other valuable minerals and nutrients are flushed away in runoff water or lifted into the sky on airborne particles of dust from rocks or organic matter. These rich specks of dust, called *aerosols,* may travel many thousands of miles before settling to the ground. Some scientists estimate that up to 70 percent of the nitrate in the air over the North Pacific comes from dust particles kicked up from the deserts of China, as does 95 percent of the available iron in that same ocean—iron that may encourage the growth of underwater plankton. In some parts of the rain forest of South America—known as the "black water" regions—soils are of such poor quality that plant survival depends upon nutrients blown in on phosphate-laden dust from the Sahara. One tropical meteorologist likens storms over the Amazon to "huge vacuum cleaners," which, in one year, may suck up 12 million tons of atmospheric dust blown in from the Sahara and deposit nearly a pound (.5 kg) of phosphate on every acre of rain forest in the northeastern and central black-water regions of the Amazon basin.

Since the 1970's, repeated droughts and ensuing famines have brought Africa's Sahel region—along the southern fringe of the Sahara—into the world spotlight. This has given rise to some of the most debatable topics among scientists involved with arid lands: Are the deserts of the world truly encroaching at an alarming rate on now-fertile land? If so, are there measures that can be taken to halt this massive drying-up process, or desertification? If air pollution causes a global warming trend, as many predict, will desert borders advance in the heat? Or will they contract, as lush equatorial areas become moister and move in on the dry subtropics?

In Utah, the meandering San Juan River lays bare layers of sedimentary rocks, revealing different fossilized life forms in each cross section.

Lessons from Desert Peoples

Globally, such questions about deserts may seem beyond the scope of the individual. But nothing could be further from the truth. Grass-roots research has shed promising new light on some long-held notions about deserts. Where once-fertile lands are drying up, hope is arriving where it is needed most—not in high-tech laboratories, but on farms and rangelands where individuals can see results with their own eyes. Land that once seemed destined for desertification under the scorching sun in times of drought can be returned to health.

Nomadic herders have long been blamed for the destruction of pasturelands; overgrazing and overtrampling were thought to be responsible for turning productive lands into deserts. Now, however, fresh ways of looking at how desert environments function have enlightened scientists, agricultural scholars, and ranchers alike. The notion of making deserts and their fringe lands off-limits to animals is being dispelled as a new generation of agriculturalists discovers that the best lessons come from the most traditional herders of the deserts—indigenous nomads.

It is the ancient wisdom of desert peoples that is bringing new life to parched or severely degraded lands in countries such as Zimbabwe, Canada, and the United States. Many traditional desert nomads run their herds of camels, cattle, goats, or sheep over pastureland for brief periods of time, then move them on so that the herds mimic the habits of natural grazers, such as the buffalo that once flourished on the North American plains. Much like the work of many fast-digging plowshares, the short-term but concentrated impact of animal hooves breaks up the thin crust that often forms on sandy desert ground surfaces. Water—as well as nutrients from dung and dust particles—has a chance to percolate beneath the broken soil, rather than roll off of it, and seeds can get a start on life beneath the freshly churned earth. Crushed under the weight of the animals, uneaten plant stalks do not go to waste but rather become mulch and a coolant for the soil. When herds are ushered along quickly, there is little chance for browsers to cause much root damage. As desert nomads have long been aware—and today's progressive agriculturalists are learning—new and often more prolific plant growth will in time grace the land and beckon the return of the animals.

These complex questions are raised continually, but there are no hard and fast answers when it comes to deciphering deserts. Satellite surveys have shown that the line of vegetation along the southern—Sahelian—edge of the Sahara ebbed and flowed by dozens of miles during a recent 11-year period, rather than marching progressively southward. Many scientists see that as proof that the desert margin is not advancing; others claim that the longer-term fluctuations are the only reliable indicators.

The activities of indigenous peoples in deserts are unquestionably fated by the nature of the environment—be it a searing sand desert where dunes billow like waves enveloped in golden silk, or ice-encrusted tundra where frigid, dry winds rarely cease. Yet in coping with such hostile environments—no matter how diverse—indigenous desert peoples are unwittingly tied to one another, whether they are Karandashli nomads who herd animals on the arid steppes of Asia's Turkestan Desert, or Havasupai Indians in villages within North America's mile-deep (1.6-km) Grand Canyon. The Chileans who earn a living as copper miners in the highlands of the fog-shrouded Atacama Desert have more in common than they know with the Ethiopians who pry salt slabs from a dry lake bed in the parched Sahel.

Many people—whether native to arid lands or not—have chosen to spend an hour, or a lifetime, within a desert because of its power to stir the senses and foster introspection. "Deserts and plateaus and canyons are not a country of big returns," wrote American novelist Wallace Stegner, "but a country of spiritual healing, incomparable for contemplation, meditation, solitude, quiet, awe, peace of mind and body."

The arid lands of the world are places of diverse beauty, and in one way or another each of our lives is touched by them. We may eat fruits and vegetables grown in their warm, irrigated soils; drive automobiles fueled by gasoline tapped from deep within their sands; or admire paintings of sun-streaked desert vistas. Appreciating their beauty, versatility, and even menacing nature, while maintaining a keen awareness of the powerful role of the deserts in Earth's ecosystem—none of this is a call to the frontline. Rather, it is the unimposing mark of an informed and responsible citizen of this planet.

"We were born of wilderness and we respond to it more than we sometimes realize," wrote Wallace Stegner. "Factories, power plants, resorts, we can make anywhere. Wilderness, once we have given it up, is beyond our reconstruction."

Hundreds of thousands flock to the yearly Pushkar Fair in the Thar Desert of India to trade camels and bathe in Pushkar Lake, sacred to the Hindus.

SCORCHED EARTH

Embracing the northern- and southernmost reaches of the Earth's steamy, equatorial regions are two sweeping, parallel bands of aridity that encircle the globe. There, within these discontinuous and irregularly shaped belts, lie the hottest, driest places on the planet—the subtropical deserts.

On five continents, these desert lands at some point intersect either the Tropic of Cancer in the north or the Tropic of Capricorn in the south. Their fate determined by latitude, these wilderness regions include the Sahara and Kalahari in Africa, the deserts of the Arabian Peninsula, and the Thar Desert of northeastern India. In North America the Sonoran, Chihuahuan, and Mojave deserts lie along the subtropical band, as do the desert expanses—such as the Great Victoria, the Gibson, the Simpson, and the Great Sandy—that cover most of the continent of Australia.

Globally, subtropical deserts have much in common. That they are hot and dry is a given, considering their latitude, but other features and characteristics set them apart from the rest of the world's deserts. Because daylight hours are longer in subtropical deserts than in any others, these arid lands receive more exposure to sunlight—hence their parched terrains, rapid evaporation rates, and the necessity for life-forms to be well equipped to withstand the sun's scorching rays and the lack of water. Night is a time of respite, when clear skies allow heat trapped by the land to escape into the atmosphere. It is a cooling-off time, when plants carry on physiological activities with little risk of moisture loss and when many animals can safely go about their business of finding food and drink without assault from the sun. Although altitude and distance from the equator influence the climates of individual localities, daytime temperatures in subtropical deserts routinely rise well above 100° F (38° C) during summer months. Without cloud cover to hold the warmth of winter days near the ground, the mercury may dip near or below freezing on an occasional winter night. Crisp, star-studded hours before dawn give way to daytimes of pleasant temperatures, even in the heart of the coldest season.

People have long been drawn to the world's subtropical deserts for myriad reasons, not the least of which are spiritual inspiration, religious fervor, adventure, and opportunities to commercially exploit the natural resources tucked within these hot, barren environments. For miners and prospectors, wide-open, hot desert plains and craggy mountains have yielded a wealth of valuable commodities in the form of metallic ores—gold, silver, lead, copper, and tin. Other than petroleum, which in recent times has become the number-one profit-making asset of arid lands, the subtropical deserts are also the main sources of other valuable energy resources such as uranium, coal, and borax—the source of boron, which is an element used in nuclear reactors. Other minerals also abound beneath these deserts: manganese, gypsum, and fertilizer ingredients including phosphates, potash, and nitrates. Salt, which is drawn to the surface by the swift evaporation typical of the world's hottest arid places, is abundant and has been harvested by countless generations of people.

Plants growing wild in subtropical deserts are also valuable resources, and native peoples have harvested them for centuries as sources of food, water, and medicine. One desert cactus, for example—the Lophophora williamsii—yields peyote, or mescal, from which the hallucinogen mescaline is derived. For about 10,000 years, the plant has been used by the indigenous peoples of the American Southwest in their religious ceremonies.

Subtropical irrigation has made possible the cultivation of both edible crops and a number of desert-thriving plants that have consumer and industrial uses. The seed of the jojoba, a wild shrub native to the deserts of Mexico and the southwestern United States, produces an oil used in making shampoos, polishing waxes, smokeless candles, and even chewing gum. It is also an effective replacement for precious sperm whale oil, which had long been used to lubricate high-speed industrial equipment. Another desert shrub, the guayule, produces rubber. Native to the Chihuahuan Desert, it was used extensively in the United States during World War II, when foreign rubber sources were not accessible. Despite the development of synthetic rubber, scientists have recently turned their attention to the guayule again because of the discovery of a chemical that can double the plant's rubber production.

In addition to making the hottest places on Earth fit for habitation by large numbers of people, modern technology has made it possible to access new arenas of once-untappable desert wealth. With their vast horizons and clear skies, subtropical deserts are ideal locations for solar-energy collection stations as well as for vast satellite tracking and communication centers.

Far from their reputation as scorching, sandy wastelands fit only for outcasts, the world's subtropical deserts are brimming with riches. Their ecosystems are complex and endowed with curious flora and fauna that, to the human eye, can appear at once both elegant and odd. But indestructible they are not; the more we discover about them, in fact, the more fragile they prove to be.

"Where and how did we gain the idea that the desert was merely a sea of sand?" wrote historian John C. Van Dyke after his turn-of-the-century travels in subtropical deserts. "The deserts should never be reclaimed. They are breathing-spaces and should be preserved forever."

No one traveled the old Devil's Highway across the Sonoran Desert without flirting with death. Still, thousands took the gamble on the trail before realizing, often too late, that in this wicked and almost waterless waste the sun calls the shots. Mile after mile, alongside the deadly ribbon of dust, stone-shrouded graves with makeshift crosses testified to the perilous journeys undertaken by countless travelers of centuries past.

Until the beginning of the 20th century the 200-mile (320-km) trail known to the Spanish as El Camino del Diablo was the shortest route crossing the American Southwest from Quitobaquito, a tiny settlement just a few yards north of the Mexican border, and the town of Yuma, Arizona. Originally etched into the arid land by the feet of pre-Columbian Indians, the trail became a vital east-west link between the centuries-old royal roads of western Mexico and California's El Camino Real, along which 18th-century Spanish padres built their adobe-walled missions. In the 19th century the highway became the most treacherous stretch of the Old Yuma Trail, the southernmost passageway for thousands of American settlers bound for California.

The Devil's Highway crossed a landscape so dry and desolate that only one dependable water source existed along its entire route—at Tinajas Altas, or High Tanks, about 75 miles (120 km) southeast of Yuma. Otherwise, the trail wound around gulches frequented by coyotes and wild burros, and traversed vast belts of black lava called *malpais*. Along the way, tussocks of desert grasses and stands of prickly pear cactus, mesquite, and creosote bush were abundant. In late spring, if a sudden rainstorm came, the 15-foot (4.5-m) branches of the ocotillo bushes suddenly produced clusters of flame-red blossoms and thousands of minute leaves; but when dry times came again, both quickly dropped off to conserve moisture. Not even the Sonoran Desert's indigenous Papago Indians were year-round residents. During winter these semi-nomads lived in "well villages" on mountain slopes where water and wild game were more plentiful. They moved to their desert "field villages" only during summer, when flash floods occasionally brought moisture and when the red, green, or yellow fruits of the organ-pipe and saguaro cacti were juicy and ripe for harvest.

Under the searing desert sun, the going was never easy. Often, the Devil's Highway was little more than two deeply carved parallel ruts; in other places, it nearly faded from sight under layers of freshly blown sand. Weary mules pulled ramshackle wagons loaded with families heading for new lives on the other side of the sun-scorched wilds. Parties of *aventureros*, or prospectors, traveled by horseback, lured by the smell of fortune blowing in the westerly winds. And every so often the occasional lone soul would pass along the dusty trail, equipped, perhaps, with little more than a bit of nourishment and high hopes.

In this part of the Sonoran Desert, where legend has it that one can fry an egg on a rocky ledge in less than a minute in summertime, desert travelers were unusually

A crumbling wooden post (*above*) marks the grave of a traveler who perished trudging the Devil's Highway, the ancient, desolate trail that crosses the Sonoran Desert in America's Southwest.

At dusk, an aerial view of Arizona's Mount Ajo in the Sonoran Desert (*left*) captures the desolate beauty and heroic grandeur that make the Sonoran America's greatest subtropical desert.

lucky to feel a drop of rain on their perspiring bodies. Dust devils—miniature tornadolike wind frenzies—came from out of nowhere, kicking up dust and gravel and causing horses to rear up in fright. An inferno in disguise, the Devil's Highway could snatch the life from anyone who was not careful.

AN AMERICAN DESERT TALE

Tales of peril and death on the Devil's Highway did little to deter Mexicans or Americans from heading west along it, especially during the great 19th-century California Gold Rush. Nor did the trail's grim history stop an adventurous and determined scientist named W J McGee (his given names were *William John,* but he always signed himself *W J*—without periods), who was one of the first to systematically study the Sonoran Desert and its wildlife. McGee, a director of the St. Louis Public Museum and an associate editor for the National Geographic Society, first traveled the trail in 1900 with an expedition from the Bureau of American Ethnology. "Most of this ancient way is peopled only by graves, enriched but by memories, nearly as lost to labor and to thought as the sand-tombed cities of Arabia and farther Turkestan," he wrote.

Returning five years later, McGee set up a small camp and research station along the old highway near the water at Tinajas Altas and for three months studied weather patterns and observed the effects of sunlight on the desert's flora and fauna. It was during this time that he met a Mexican prospector named Pablo Valencia. McGee's account of Valencia's struggle to survive despite extreme dehydration would go down as a minor classic in the annals of human endurance.

The tale began in the predawn stillness of August 23, 1905, as McGee lay sleeping on the desert floor not far from the pockets of water hidden among the rocky cliffsides of Tinajas Altas. Gila monsters and coyotes prowled silently near McGee's camp, while free-roaming cattle meandered in and out of his dreams; a "stalwart bull," he later wrote, led an imaginary herd across the range. Suddenly, the bull let out a great roar, an "ear-piercing bellow of challenge and defiance," and McGee awoke with a start. He realized the scream was not part of his dream but the agonized cry of someone close by.

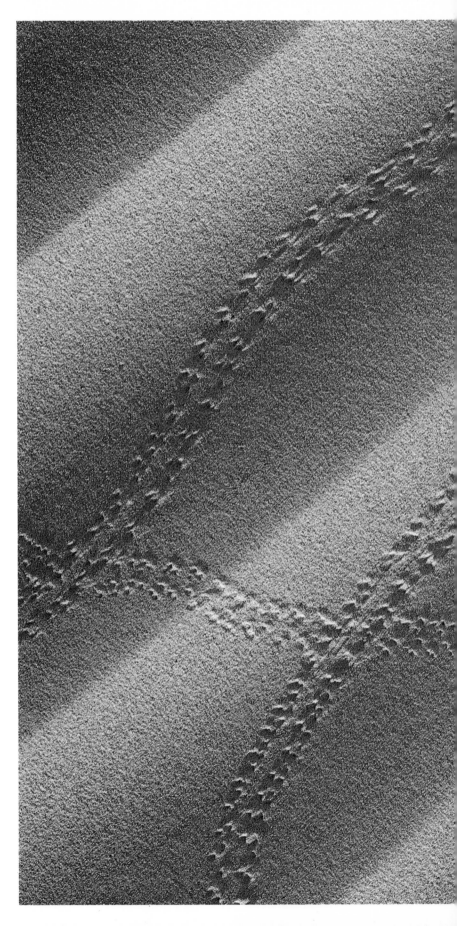

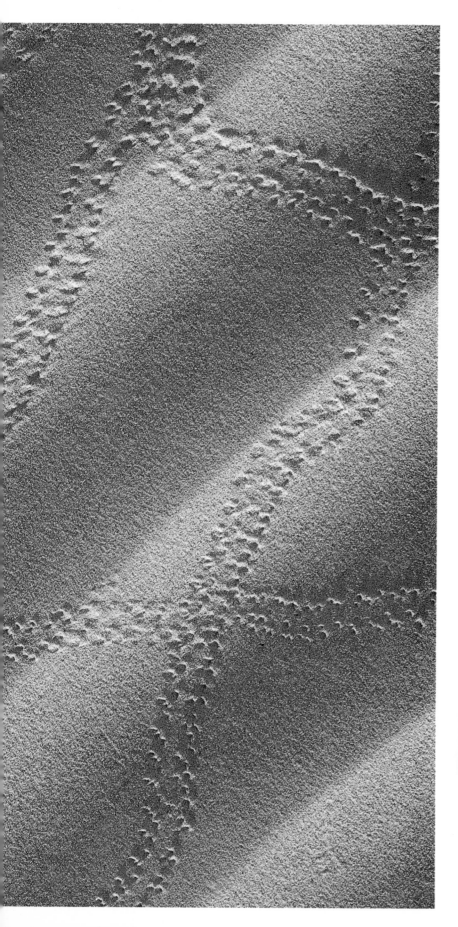

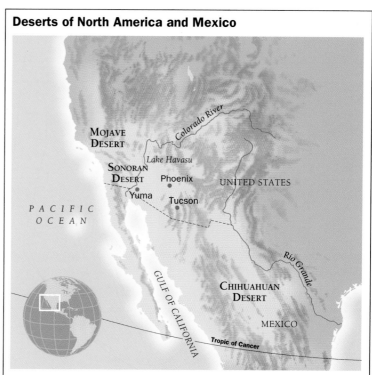

Deserts of North America and Mexico

The Mojave, Sonoran, and Chihuahuan deserts stretch across states of the American southwest and northern Mexico. Interconnected, the deserts are defined by differences in vegetation and animal life. Orange areas signify higher elevations.

Tracks of 1-inch-long (2.5-cm) pinacate beetles (*left*) make tiny, grid-like patterns across a sandy waste in the Mexican portion of the Sonoran Desert. Like the brittlebush (*above*)—growing from a bed of lava and ash—the beetles have evolved to survive in the harsh desert environment.

Picture Rocks in the Tucson Mountains show humans and animals flourishing in the Sonoran Desert. The petroglyphs were carved during the first millennium A.D. by the Hohokam, an Indian people who used sophisticated irrigation techniques to farm the otherwise arid region.

Just over the edge of a nearby canyon McGee came upon the naked body of the once-robust Pablo Valencia, who had camped overnight at the watering hole only eight days before. McGee recalled his previous impression of the Mexican's "remarkably fine and vigorous physique." But in the early morning light Valencia's "ribs ridged out like those of a starveling horse," while "his joints and bones stood out like those of a wasted sickling though the skin clung to them in a way suggesting shrunken rawhide."

McGee and a guide named Jose sloshed water over the man's withered body. They poured diluted whiskey into his mouth, without help from Valencia, who could neither swallow nor talk. "His lips had disappeared as if amputated, leaving low edges of blackened tissue," wrote McGee; "his teeth and gums projected like those of a skinned animal, but the flesh was dry as a hank of jerky, his nose was withered and shrunken to half its length."

Valencia and a fellow prospector named Jesus Rios, it turned out, had—despite the parching summer heat—set off into the desert with high hopes of striking it rich at an old gold mine. But the two had soon become separated: Rios had possession of their horses and supplies, and Valencia was left stranded deep in the desert with only a canteen's worth of water.

As McGee later pieced together the Mexican's confused recollections, he estimated Valencia had been only 35 miles (56 km) or so from Tinajas Altas when his ordeal began. But disoriented by heat and thirst, he had wandered an additional hundred miles or more. "His lower legs and feet, with forearms and hands, were torn and scratched by contact with thorns and sharp rocks," wrote McGee, "yet even the freshest cuts were as so many scratches in dry leather, without trace of blood."

Valencia's canteen was empty within a day of his losing contact with Rios. Tormented by thirst, he scrounged for anything that might bring relief, chewing on mescal plants, on twigs from the spindly palos verde tree, on spiders, on flies, and on calabacitas—bitter wild gourds—that made him sick. Buzzards circled above by day and coyotes lingered nearby at night, waiting for Valencia to die.

On his seventh and final full day alone in the wilderness, Valencia could barely hear or focus his eyes. He had lost nearly 40 pounds (18 kg); his tongue had "shrunken to a mere bunch of black integument." Still, he walked another 7 miles (11 km). Then, certain of death, he prayed, and lay down in a dry arroyo at the foot of the Mesa of the Forty Graves to let fate run its course. Finally, although convinced he was already dead, Valencia wailed a dreadful howl that brought McGee and Jose to his rescue. Revived somewhat by their water showers and whiskey, Valencia was transported to Yuma in a miner's wagon, and he eventually recovered.

Finishing his work shortly afterward, McGee bade farewell to the Sonoran Desert and to the Devil's Highway and returned to St. Louis, where he wrote extensively about desert thirst—including his classic tale of Valencia's

A desert tortoise (*left*), which can live in the baked Sonoran Desert by eating water–storing plants, nibbles the fruit of a prickly pear cactus.

Escaping the heat, a female tarantula (*bottom left*) burrows into the desert floor. Tarantulas, ancient members of the spider family, survive by remaining underground.

Prowling the desert at dusk, a coyote (*below*) hunts for the mice and other small game that supply its food.

FORCES THAT CREATE SUBTROPICAL DESERTS

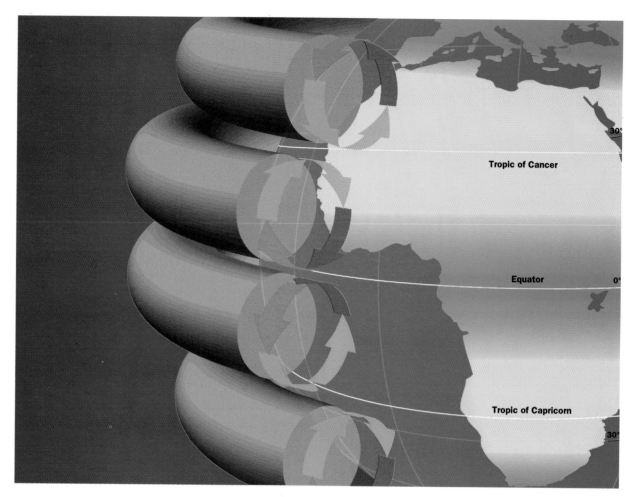

Giant rotating atmospheric cells, driven by heat from the tropics, circulate around the Earth and contribute to the creation of the world's deserts. The four cells that effect subtropical deserts are shown in simplified detail above—two above and two below Earth's equatorial regions.

Moist equatorial air is heated by the Sun, which causes it to become lighter and to rise (*red arrows at middle two cells above*). A low-pressure zone forms throughout the region. The rising air (*blue arrows over middle two cells*) becomes cooler, increasingly dense, and unable to hold moisture. The moisture condenses, clouds form, and rain falls, creating lush tropics below. The warm air ascends until the air above is of equal temperature. This occurs at the tropopause, some 10 miles (16 km) above the surface of the planet. There the air reaches the apex of its cycle and begins to sink back to the earth (*purple arrows over middle two cells*).

As the air drops, it is warmed. Because warm air can hold more moisture than cool air, it draws in rather than releases moisture. As a result, the land below—at about 30° N and S latitude—becomes parched; this accounts for many of the deserts in Africa, Arabia, Australia, and the United States that straddle these latitudes at the Tropics of Cancer and Capricorn. The warm dry air (*orange arrows over middle two cells*) is then drawn along Earth's surface to repeat the cycle.

Some air, however, flows into the adjacent mid-latitude cells (*top and bottom cells above*) in the temperate regions of each hemisphere. These cells, which operate in the same way as the equatorial cells, create arid zones around 60° N and S latitude. And at the top and bottom of the planet, a pair of polar cells circulate air in the same manner, producing the polar deserts.

ordeal. It was hailed, in the words of one scientist, as one of the "most remarkable historic cases of desert survival ever recorded."

The Most Precious Resource

Pablo Valencia managed to beat the odds in the pitilessly dry and searing climate of the Sonoran Desert. But untold thousands have perished in this supremely inhospitable part of the southwestern United States and in other subtropical deserts around the world. Even local inhabitants accustomed to such aridity have met grisly ends, especially when trusted wells and water holes have suddenly dried up. At times, certain spots in these lands have been strewn with human skeletons bleached like alabaster by the sun. In one caravan alone, at the beginning of the 19th century, 2,000 people and 1,800 camels perished en route across the southern Sahara after discovering that a usually reliable oasis had turned to dust.

In subtropical deserts, where daytime temperatures routinely soar to 110° and 120° F (43°–49° C) in the summer, literally sucking the moisture from all living things, water is the most prized resource of all—and the most elusive. Moisture-bearing clouds are a rarity in these high-pressure bands of dry air that encircle the planet. In parts of Australia's arid interior, for example, such rain clouds may show up only once in a decade.

Indigenous peoples in the world's hottest deserts

One of the pools at Tinajas Altas in Arizona—the only water along the old Devil's Highway—sits in a hollow atop a rocky bluff.

make water their chief priority day in and day out: it is their lifeblood. They must be able to find it, collect it, and conserve it however they can. Water must take precedence over food and other basic needs because without it raging temperatures and aridity go hand in hand with dehydration, or death. The bone-dry winds that sweep through the subtropical desert can soak up moisture like a dry sponge—from the soil, from animal and plant life, even from the human body.

Unlike well-equipped desert plants and animals, humans have evolved only slightly in order to cope with extreme aridity. Perspiration is their built-in cooling system, and in some cases desert inhabitants develop extra sweat glands to cope with their climates. But the loss of fluids and salts through the skin cannot be slowed down. Without internal reservoirs, people can adapt to heat and aridity only by modifying their dress, food, and lifestyle to conserve water.

Using words borrowed from classical Greek, physiologists distinguish among the various degrees of thirst. *Eudipsia* is a term signifying "ordinary thirst," *hyperdipsia* means "temporary intense thirst," and *polydipsia* refers to "sustained, excessive thirst," in which the victim grabs at anything to find relief. Pablo Valencia's last-ditch effort to quench his thirst was *uriposia,* or "the drinking of urine." Parching

An isolated Arizona watering hole (*left*) provides welcome relief for a flock of sheep tended by Navajo shepherds.

agony has compelled many a stranded desert traveler to drink camel urine, their own blood, or even radiator coolant and gasoline. Others, in a state of thirst-induced delirium, have unwittingly sucked on poisonous scorpions.

Many a foolhardy adventurer, in search of fortune in the desert, has deliberately ventured into its hot, barren stretches with neither an ample supply of water nor a sense of where to find it. Eagerness is little match for the body's basic need for moisture.

Even resting in the shade in a hot desert, a naked person can lose more than a gallon (4 L) of water through perspiration in a few hours. With any physical exertion, that quantity can double. Water makes up more than half of the human body—about 14 gallons (53 L) in a 160-pound (72-kg) adult. Without replenishment, there is danger of kidney failure after the loss of only one gallon. Body tissues start to shrivel and drying skin begins to wrinkle. If 2 to 3 gallons (7.6–11 L) of water are lost, fever develops, the eyeballs begin to soften and shrink, and the blood thickens. Delirium may set in, and as water loss approaches 4 gallons (15 L) a skyrocketing body temperature brings death.

Piping Life to the Desert

Air conditioners, swimming pools, and—most vitally—large-scale water supply systems have made living in deserts possible and even pleasant for millions. The desert environment is a formidable adversary, however. Sophisticated technologies that enable people to inhabit and exploit dry lands may be costly to the environment, as well

as the economy, and—like all human-made devices—subject to malfunction. Consider the impact of a long-term power failure or water system breakdown on subtropical desert metropolises such as Riyadh, Saudi Arabia, and Tucson, Arizona, or on a resort community like Palm Springs, California, where more than 10,000 swimming pools dot the Mojave Desert. Touch-of-a-button relief from the heat has clouded 20th-century perceptions of the inherent harshness of arid environments. It is a mistake to assume that, in the long run, the desert can be tamed.

Air-conditioned homes cluster in a tract set down in the desert near Albuquerque, New Mexico. Only modern technology and irrigation systems make such developments possible.

There are other uncertainties involved in peopling the desert. When politics and economic factors are involved, even the best-laid plans can backfire, as witnessed by the water feud that is brewing between Arizona's farmers and the state's growing urban population. In 1991, construction was completed on a 336-mile (541-km) water pipeline system called the Central Arizona Project (CAP).

DRIED UP

When the indigenous Hausa of southern Niger say *kasar mu, ta gaji*—"the land is tired"—they echo the sentiments of many farmers and ranchers in arid lands throughout the world. In more than 100 countries where rainfall is seasonal and minimal, pasture and cropland are succumbing to *desertification*—serious land degradation that can follow on the heels of drought, land misuse, or sand encroachment.

On the coast of Somalia, at right, offshore winds from the Indian Ocean have blown thousands of acres of sand into dunes, which are edging their way across the landscape south of the port city of Mogadishu. Roads, villages, and the scant cultivable land are in danger of being engulfed by sand there; the Somalis have planted cacti and casuarina trees to stabilize the dunes and, they hope, keep the coastal dunes at bay. Theirs is one of many land reclamation projects along the southern borders of the Sahara where catastrophic droughts have caused severe desertification of once-arable and grazable lands.

Desertification is much more, however, than a product of drought or the invasion of fertile lands by blowing sand. It is most often a process in which lands gradually lose their ability to sustain life. Grasses become sparse. Without ample vegetation to feed upon, many wild animals move elsewhere, and their predators follow. Since the soil now lacks a hardy ground cover or good root network, it becomes more compact and thus less porous. Both wind and water are then free to transport particles of soil and organic matter far and wide, gradually denuding the area.

What few grasses still cling to life in these desertified lands are eventually replaced by widely spaced desert shrubs—creosote bush, saltbush, and sagebrush, for example—which provide food for far fewer animal species than do grasses. The region has by this time been transformed into a true desert, where—as is common in almost all deserts—more precipitation is lost to runoff or evaporation than remains available to sustain life in the area.

Blown inland by ocean winds, sand dunes creep across the Somali coast (above). Once enveloped in sand, the desertified land cannot sustain life.

People in this Iranian desert village (left) near the city of Yazd wage a constant battle against tormenting sand that surrounds them.

Algerians construct palm branch fences (right) to protect crops, dwellings, and highways against blowing Saharan sands.

The complex network of steel and concrete aqueducts, tunnels, and dams is able to pump nearly 489 trillion gallons (18.5 trillion hl) annually from Lake Havasu, situated on the Colorado River where it winds along the border between California and Arizona. From Lake Havasu, the water flows through a tunnel in the Buckskin Mountains and then across the cactus-studded desert to irrigate cropland near Phoenix and Tucson.

Red pipes of a pivot-point sprinkler snake across an arid stretch of eastern New Mexico. Such irrigation devices are often the only way to bring water to the desert.

The U.S. $3.6 billion project, financed by loans from the federal government, was conceived in the 1940's and seemed sure to benefit the economy of Arizona—and of the United States as a whole—during the decades when the desert state's dominant industries would be agriculture (including cotton farming), mining, and ranching. But downturns in the economy, compounded by a plunge in cotton prices, crop damage by insects, and other setbacks have left most of central Arizona's farmers unable to afford the exorbitant cost of the diverted water. It is sold by the acre-foot—the amount of water that will cover an acre of land to a one-foot depth. One acre-foot of CAP water, or 325,851 gallons (12,343 hl), can cost U.S. $25 to U.S. $52. For farmers with large tracts of land to irrigate, the desert's lifeblood can seem like liquid gold.

Arizona's city and town dwellers—90 percent of the state's total population—do not need much of the CAP water as yet because most of their supply comes from underground aquifers and in-state river water. Nor do they wish to bail out the farmers who, in an agreement approved by the U.S. Congress, were earmarked as the primary purchasers of the Colorado River water for the first four decades or so, until urban demand should increase during the 21st century. The folks in Phoenix, in short, have no intention of chipping in to help repay the loans made by the government, which begin to come due in 1994 to the tune of more than U.S. $50 million a year.

The result of all this is a great deal of tension in Arizona among farmers, townspeople, and politicians. To make things more complicated, many Arizonans fear that if the state does not take full advantage of its rights to the Colorado River water, California's desert agriculturalists may claim it. "We'd be fools to think all the water Arizona is not using can stay in the Colorado River forever," said one state official in Phoenix.

If the people of Arizona cannot find a solution to the debt they owe for the CAP, U.S. taxpayers will ultimately foot the bill for the state's large-scale attempt to green the

Part of the vast, recently completed irrigation network called the Central Arizona Project, a concrete aqueduct zigzags across desolate Sonoran scrubland, carrying Colorado River water to irrigated fields in the Phoenix area.

desert. So far, the multibillion-dollar project has not made the desert anywhere near as profitable for the Sonoran farmers as they had hoped. The CAP dilemma exemplifies the problems that may arise if people pin their hopes of desert survival on costly, high-tech solutions.

Marvels of Adaptation

Compared with people, who almost totally lack the physiological means of contending with harsh desert living, many plants and animals are remarkably outfitted for the heat and aridity found in subtropical deserts. Otherwise, they could not survive.

Some subtropical desert birds, like the turtle dove of the Sahara, must consume water on a daily basis. The adult dove is capable of flying nearly 50 miles (81 km) for a drink and, unlike most birds who merely let drops trickle down their throats, can suck and swallow the water, as mammals do. In flight, or when feeding their young, they regurgitate and recycle the liquid. The sandgrouse of southern Africa's Kalahari can fly just as far for its daily water ration. But before returning to its nest, the brown-speckled bird submerges its breast feathers until they are soaked like a sponge, then flies back to its waiting young who draw water from the feathers with their tiny beaks.

Some of the smallest of all desert mammals, kangaroo rats, are adaptive marvels. They can survive without drinking a drop of water during their entire lifetime. Instead, they get by primarily on dry seeds, which contain about 4 percent water, as well as occasional bites of leaves and insects. Other than the rare sip from a puddle of rainwater—which some kangaroo rats shun—the animals depend upon a complex moisture-conservation process to protect them from dehydration. Their kidneys operate a highly efficient recycling system, which allows the body to retain metabolic water and eliminate very little urine. What does pass out of the body as waste is so highly concentrated that it looks more like paste or crystals.

Further, kangaroo rats, like most small desert mammals, have no sweat glands. Their respiratory systems, too, are specially equipped to retain moisture. In humans and large mammals,

Using its powerful hind legs, a tiny kangaroo rat (*left*) hops across the Sonoran Desert in the American West on a nighttime food-finding expedition. The strikingly similar jerboa (*above*), a native of Asian and African deserts, darts along in the same way but is not related—the two rodents evolved independently but survive in similar conditions.

moist, warm air escapes from the lungs through the nostrils; some carnivorous desert mammals, like the sand cat and the black-backed jackal of the southern Sahara, pant to allow moisture to evaporate from the mouth. But the nasal passages of the kangaroo rat cool the breath before it can be exhaled. The cooled moisture condenses into minuscule droplets, most of which are then reabsorbed by the rats' bodies.

The various species of kangaroo rat—the banner-tailed, chisel-toothed, Panamint, and others—all have small, drawn-up front legs, oversized hind legs, and huge feet. They look strikingly like miniature kangaroos, and like those bounding Australian marsupials, kangaroo rats are bipedal animals—meaning that they travel on their hind legs. Like some subtropical desert lizards that also run on their hind legs, kangaroo rats do so with astonishing speed when threatened by other desert creatures, such as kit foxes, coyotes, and hawks, that prey on the tiny rodents. Moving in 2-foot (60-cm) hops, zigzag fashion, kangaroo rats can zip along at 20 feet per second (6 m/sec)—more than 13 miles an hour (20 kph). If a predator catches up, the rat can use its long, tufted tail as a rudder, turning left or right—at 90° angles—in midair. Kangaroo rats can also escape from face-to-face confrontations by using their hind feet and tail to shoot straight up about 2 feet (60 cm) from a standing start. Once in the

Protecting a Popular Cactus

People have long been attracted by the saguaro, the tall, branching cactus that is the statuesque symbol of the American Southwest. Pima Indians marked their new year by the harvest each July of the saguaro's juicy red fruit, which they ate fresh or dried and fermented into a potent wine. More recently, the saguaro has become a fashionable addition to home gardens, particularly in water-scarce regions.

High demand—met legally by nursery-raised cacti and limited harvesting—has led to an underground trade in poached saguaros, which are protected under federal law. Cactus rustlers can dig the giants out by their shallow roots in minutes and typically get U.S. $1,200 for an 18-foot (5.5-m) specimen, plus a U.S. $50 bonus for each arm. Rare cristate saguaros, which grow sideways in a fan shape, have fetched U.S. $15,000. Black-market saguaros have turned up in private homes in the Netherlands and Japan.

Unique to the rocky soils of the Sonoran Desert, the saguaro cactus can grow to 50 feet (15 m) or more and can live 200 years. Saguaros require as little as 5 inches (13 cm) annual rainfall and can withstand heat of 120° F (49° C).

Poaching penalties are as high as 10 years in jail and a U.S. $250,000 fine, and Arizona has a full-time law-enforcement officer devoted to the cactus beat. But with nearly 114,000 square miles (295,260 sq km) to patrol, catching cactus thieves red handed is mighty tough. After all, it's hard to fingerprint a saguaro cactus.

air, the rat can perform an abrupt about-face and surprise its enemy with a swift exit.

To survive in subtropical deserts, where there is relatively little ground cover for hiding, many animals other than kangaroo rats are specially adapted for lightning-pace speed. In Mexico's Chihuahuan Desert, a hare known as Allen's jackrabbit fairly flies across the bleak desert in leaps and bounds; its huge, heat-radiating ears flatten up against its back so as not to create wind resistance. The roadrunner of the American Southwest, a member of the cuckoo family, and Le Conte's thrasher are among desert birds that prefer running over flying; the strong-legged roadrunner can run 15 miles an hour (24 kph).

The kangaroo rats' swift, energetic activities occur at night, when they hunt for seeds in the relative coolness of dark. After daybreak, when desert temperatures soar, the animals retreat to underground burrows, plug up the entrances with soil, and curl up to sleep. Remarkably, they conserve moisture even while they snooze next to their caches of seeds. Temperatures in the nests are cool, and the relative humidity ranges between 30 and 50 percent— far damper than above ground. As the curled-up animals rest, nestled in their ground pockets, moisture that escapes from their noses and mouths while they breathe is trapped there. The dry seeds nearby soak up a good portion of that moisture, and later provide additional water when it is time for the rodents to dine.

Kangaroo rats thrive in the subtropical deserts of North America—the Sonoran, the Mojave, and the Chihuahuan—as well as in the Colorado Plateau and the Great Basin, farther north. Far away, in arid regions of Asia and Africa, another rodent, the jerboa, provides an example of a startling phenomenon known as "convergent evolution." Jerboas look like kangaroo rats, hop like kangaroo rats, and physiologically conserve water in many of the same ways. The two diminutive creatures, however, are not closely related. They share parallel evolutionary histories because both have adapted to the same sort of desert environment.

Subtropical desert plants also cope with arid conditions through remarkable adaptive structures and mechanisms. They generally grow far away from each other, to cut down on root competition for moisture; some even secrete a toxic substance from their roots to keep other plants at a distance. Many have innate methods of sheltering their leaf and stem surfaces from the scorching rays of the desert sun. The eucalyptus, or gum, trees that grow in Australia's desolate interior produce white bark and a light, waxy leaf coating that reflect more than fifty percent of the sunlight that strikes them; their leaves also droop away from direct rays during the daytime. Other plants, such as the desert broom of the Middle East, have minuscule leaves—or none at all—giving them relatively few pores through which moisture can escape.

Succulents are desert plants that store water in the soft tissues of their leaves, branches, or trunks. These highly absorptive plants have waxy coatings that hold in moisture and protect the plants from dehydrating in the desert sun. Among the subtropical succulents are aloes, such as the kokerboom tree lily of the Kalahari Desert; certain *Euphorbias* of the Sahara and North American deserts; and cacti and yuccas from deserts in the Western Hemisphere. The trunks and armlike branches of the huge saguaro cactus, which grows in the Sonoran Desert, are pleated like an accordion, so they can contract and expand depending upon water supply. In a natural race against evaporation, their extensive root systems rapidly draw in water after a rainfall. The largest saguaros, found near Tucson, Arizona, may tower 50 feet (15 m) above the desert floor and weigh 8 tons at 150 years of age. At that stage, the massive prickly water tanks can absorb 200 gallons (almost 760 L) of water during a single rainstorm—and survive on that for a year. The saguaro and other succulents have also evolved the ability to store some of the carbon used in photosynthesis and food metabolism for use during sunlight hours. Because they are so equipped and do not need to take in carbon dioxide around the clock, as do other plants, succulents can keep their pores mostly closed until nighttime—when relative humidity is higher than during daylight hours—and until after rainfalls, when they can collect moisture from the ground and air.

Producing a lavish flower display, a yucca plant (*above*) lives up to its nickname of Our Lord's Candle. A yucca moth (*inset*) lays eggs in the ovary of a yucca in an example of mutually adaptive evolution. The moth gathers pollen from the flowers and fertilizes the plant, which in turn nourishes the moth larvae.

Slow-growing and stately, saguaro cacti tower above the scrub-covered floor of Arizona's Saguaro National Monument. The saguaro, largest member of the cactus family, can host an entire ecological system.

AUSTRALIA'S ARID INTERIOR

Lacking internal reservoirs and other adaptive mechanisms such as those of the kangaroo rat and the saguaro, people can survive desert heat and aridity only by modifying the environment with air conditioners and huge water-diversion projects like the CAP in Arizona—or by the age-old modifications in clothing, diet, and ways of life developed by the world's ancient desert-dwelling peoples. Among the most remarkable of these desert survivors are the aboriginal inhabitants of Australia, who have lived in the island continent's vast and hostile interior for many millennia—ever since, apparently, they migrated there when the ocean level was much lower and travel relatively easy from northerly islands, such as Papua New Guinea, and the Southeast Asian mainland.

Some of the Aborigines inhabited parts of Australia's coastal areas before Europeans began arriving in numbers in the late 18th century. But the natives were soon shoved inland to join others dwelling in the arid and semiarid plains that cover two-thirds of Australia's landmass—more than 1 million square miles (2.6 million sq km) of desert where rain is rare and rivers few and far between.

The extreme aridity of interior Australia is caused by geography as well as latitude. The Great Dividing Range runs north-south along the eastern side of Australia, and its mountain peaks prevent much Pacific-born moist air from reaching the heart of the continent. The interior's subtropical deserts, lying along the Tropic of Capricorn with its chronic high-pressure weather systems, also miss out on the two main sources of rains that keep some of the continent's coastal bands green. The moist summer monsoons pass too far to the north; the rain-rich, winter westerlies blow by too far to the south.

The result is a land so dry and barren that it seems impossible the aboriginal people could have succeeded in living there for tens of thousands of years. But they did, subsisting in their traditional manner, until very recent times. Although many Aborigines work as miners, railroad laborers, or as stockmen on Australia's remote sheep-raising ranches, large numbers live in impoverished areas of towns and cities outside the desert. The few, if any, who still cling tenaciously to their ancient way of life have survived by hunting and by making use of every edible tuber and berry. They have survived as well because they have

Heaving in treeless ridges and deep waterless gullies, a range of ancient, eroded mountains undulates across Australia's desolate interior in this aerial photograph (*far left*). Much of Australia is flat; what mountains there are have been ground down over eons by wind and water.

A descendant of Australia's indigenous inhabitants, an Aborigine leans on his spear while resting in a cross-legged stance often assumed by the men of this ancient people. The Aborigines had inhabited Australia for at least 40,000 years before the first Europeans arrived.

Australia's Deserts

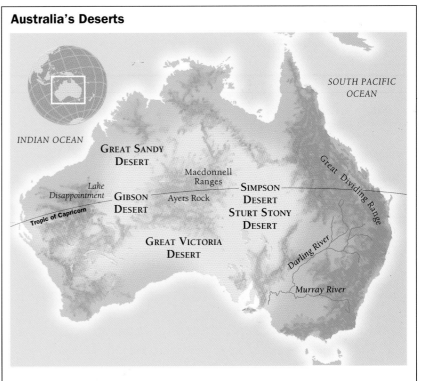

Australia's interior is comprised of several deserts surrounding the higher area known as the Red Centre (*orange above*). The continent's interior hosts animal and plant varieties that, because of isolation, are uniquely adapted to their desert environment.

Wrapped in blankets against a chill desert night, the members of an Aborigine family sit for a photograph taken about 1900, when many thousands of these nomadic people still roamed the Australian interior, hunting game and gathering the sparse berries and tubers of their desiccated homeland.

Spiky, pale green spinifex grass, common in Australia's central and western deserts, grows in clumps from the red, sandy soil that gives part of the continent the nickname "Red Centre."

learned that life-sustaining sources of water can wear a multitude of disguises.

One unexpected source of water—although well known to many traditional Aborigines—is a frog that stores moisture in its body and then digs itself a cool refuge a foot or more in the earth. A visitor exploring Australia's forlorn interior, where barely a handful of raindrops had fallen in months, observed the curious strategy of an aboriginal father and son on the hunt: The boy's bare foot hit the ground with a thud and churned up a small cloud of reddish-orange dust. Again and again he stamped the soil, taking cues from his father, who was causing a dull ruckus by pounding his own feet nearby.

A foot-long lizard, a blue-tongued skink, hissed loudly to stave off its noisy enemies, then bloated its brown belly to give the illusion of mighty size. The father and son were not interested in lizards, though, and continued to stomp the desert while the skink made a swift getaway across the heat-stricken scrubland.

But soon the father and son heard what they had been waiting for: the muffled, distant croak of a frog. The foot stomping had been designed to mimic the rumble of thunder—which would, if all went as planned, fool a desert frog or two into thinking rain was on the way. Suddenly, as if from nowhere, more muffled croaks could be

Hissing ferociously, a blue-tongued skink tries to frighten off interlopers. These repellent-looking dragons are among the largest of Australia's 240 species of lizards, growing to a length of 2 feet (.6 m). They have survived because of their resistance to drought and their ability to intimidate predators.

heard emanating from the ground. The man and the boy stepped up the pace of their stomping to be sure their ears were not playing tricks. Then, as the croaks continued, they both grabbed wooden digging sticks and gouged feverishly in the earth. Within minutes they found several frogs, alive and well, buried beneath the surface. Father and son each picked up one of the water-holding frogs, held them just above their mouths, and squeezed the bloated amphibians firmly until a stream of tasty liquid poured down their parched throats.

Resourceful Survivors

Many aboriginal methods of surviving involved a similar watchfulness and knowledge of the land and the life that thrives upon it. The people roamed across loosely defined territories that encompassed thousands of square miles for each nomadic band. For guidance, they relied upon age-old stories called "songlines" that, passed from one generation to the next, preserved the people's knowledge of their environment. The Aborigines could remember how to find a fertile area 100 miles (161 km) away or locate some low-lying sandy catchments where water might remain after a rare rainstorm, when most of the desert had become bone-dry. Moving often about the stony flatlands, dunes, and scrub-dotted wilds, they had no permanent encampments and erected only temporary shelters, usually simple semicircles of acacia branches or clumps of razor-sharp spinifex grass carefully aligned to protect against wind or sun. The Aborigines' wanderings were never random; rather, they were deliberate and based on the mental maps offered by the songlines.

The songline legends also led the Aborigines to abundant hunting grounds and to places where they could find and gather wild foodstuffs. The men of the tribes stalked the game—kangaroos, wallabies, snakes, and the large flightless birds called emus, among others—and did their killing with stone-headed spears, throwing sticks, or heavy boomerangs. The women scoured mile after mile of land for fleshy tubers, berries, and other wild plants, as well as edible beetle grubs and lizards.

Scant as the resources were, the aboriginal tribes did not spend every waking hour on the run, nor were they—except in times of severe drought—doomed to a constant struggle to stay alive. Attuned to their environment and adept at exploiting its meager resources, they often had leisure time at the end of the day to spend in talk and tribal rituals, as well as singing and storytelling.

Like spadefoot toads of the North American deserts—which back into burrows by pushing soil with a spade-shaped hind-foot protrusion—the water-holding frogs sought by thirsty Aborigines are one of only a few amphibian species that survive in subtropical deserts. Most

Emergency water source for Australia's Aborigines, a water-holding frog (*right*) emerges from its underground burrow, its shiny skin bloated with moisture. The frogs can retain water amounting to 50 percent of their body weight.

of the world's amphibious creatures—frogs, toads, and newts—have loose, moist skin that provides little defense against evaporation in arid climates. But Australia's water-holding frogs have adapted to the harsh desert environment in especially remarkable ways. During periods between rains—frequently the better part of a year—the frogs bury themselves inside pocketlike burrows and then shed several layers of skin in rapid succession. Once the sheath of skin has lifted up from the body, it dries out and forms an almost impermeable casing around the frog. The dry, parchmentlike covering allows the frogs to absorb some moisture from the surrounding soil, but lets little escape from the humid air pocket sandwiched between the old and new skin. Thus protected, the frogs remain moist and dormant, looking for all the world like bulging plastic bags with two eyes and a mouth.

When heavy rain falls again, the frogs climb above ground for replenishment, finding food and drink in newly formed ponds or puddles. They mate quickly in the short-lived shallow pools and then lay their eggs. Fortunately for the species, tadpoles develop more quickly in the desert than in other, wetter environments. In the race against evaporation, they have little time to spare.

Lizards and other reptiles have an easier time adapting to deserts than do amphibians.

Cornered by an enemy, an Australian frilled lizard (*below*) unfurls the brightly colored fan around its neck. Predators, startled by the sudden show, usually pause, allowing the fast-moving lizard to escape.

Their scaly skin resists water loss through evaporation. And like other desert creatures, most lizards deal with scorching temperatures by hiding below ground during the hottest part of the day. One curious exception is Australia's dragon lizard, which instead of retreating underground, climbs higher and higher into a shrub as the soil below becomes unbearably hot. By mid-afternoon, the lizard can be found comfortably stretched out, oriented away from the most penetrating rays of the sun, along one of the plant's higher branches.

The 19th-century writer Marcus Clarke, who spoke of "the subtle charm of this fantastic land of monstrosities," had surely seen the likes of these lizards. With names that do justice to their physiques, the frilled lizard, bearded dragon, thorny devil, and shingleback are monstrous-looking creatures that seem well outfitted to face off all but the most persistent of their predators. Rigid defense postures, erect flaps of skin, fanlike collars, spikes, and spiny beards combine with bared teeth and open jaws to give enemies the impression these desert lizards are ferocious antagonists and mean business. Despite their menacing fronts, though, most are confirmed bluffers and retreat from actual skirmishes whenever possible. Some that display great bravado will actually attack only ants, their main source of food.

An Enduring Alliance

After charting much of Australia's coastline in 1770, Captain James Cook, the great 18th-century British explorer and navigator, encountered a number of the Aborigines. "They live in a Tranquility," Cook wrote in his journal, "which is not disturb'd by the Inequality of Condition: The Earth and sea of their own accord furnishes them with all things necessary for life, they covet not Magnificent Houses, Houshold-stuff etc."

What Captain Cook sensed was the profound harmony that the Aborigines felt with their homeland, as do other inhabitants of the world's deserts. Native American peoples feel a similar spiritual connection to all of nature, or "Mother Earth," and "Great Mystery"—to many, the source of all creation. "Great Mystery lives in everything, is everything, and encompasses everything in Creation," said one tribal writer. "Native Americans have been taught through more than 100,000 years of oral history that all of Creation and each individual life form was an expression of and contained Great Mystery."

Like Native Americans, the deeply spiritual Aborigines trace their beginnings to a powerful source, a moment in time called "the Dreaming." It was the period of creation, when ancestral beings roamed Australia's immense spaces in the form of various plants, animals, and even rocks.

Stencils of boomerangs and hands dominate a painting created by Aborigines about 2,500 years ago on the underside of a rocky overhang in northern Australia, where it has been protected from the weather. Aboriginal hunters used boomerangs, as well as spears and throwing sticks, to kill game.

While hunting, fighting, or lovemaking, the Ancestors, as they are called, shaped the land, from the deserts to the seashores and all points in between. The Aborigines sculpted their nomadic existence around an abiding respect for these wise, mythical entities. "We have been here," explained a tribal elder, "since the time before time began," adding that in all those many millennia his people "have lived and kept the earth as it was on the First Day."

The age-old reverence for the sanctity of their environment is expressed in the word *ngurra,* which the Aborigines still use today to refer to their natural surroundings, to the countryside, to their campsites, even to the metaphysical connotations of the concepts of "place" and "space." Humans and *ngurra* are physically and spiritually inseparable. All living things and all natural processes work in harmony with one another. So at one were the Aborigines with their surroundings that the concept of owning land was unheard of. "White man's fences strangle the music of the countryside," remarked one elderly aboriginal tribesman.

THE THIRSTLAND OF AFRICA

Compared to many of the world's other arid lands, the Kalahari is so richly endowed with vegetation and wildlife that, at first glance, it seems not to deserve classification as a true desert; some, in fact, prefer to call it a "thirstland" instead. But a closer look at the southern African region reveals telltale signs that it ultimately measures up to standards of other subtropical deserts. Located mostly in Botswana, the Kalahari is a 220,000-square-mile (569,800-sq-km) sand-covered basin that stretches from the highlands of Zimbabwe in the east to the long barchan dune chains westward, in Namibia. To the south, the desert is bounded by the Orange River in South Africa, and reaches north to the Makgadikgadi salt pans and Okavango Swamp in northern Botswana.

The sandy central Kalahari is marked by dry fossil river beds—their ancient tributaries, winding across the land and gradually fading from sight, now sparsely covered with desert grasses. Surface water, if any, in the Kalahari is seasonal at best. As in other arid regions of the subtropics, rainfall in the region is erratic, varying from year to year and from one point on the map to another. During a

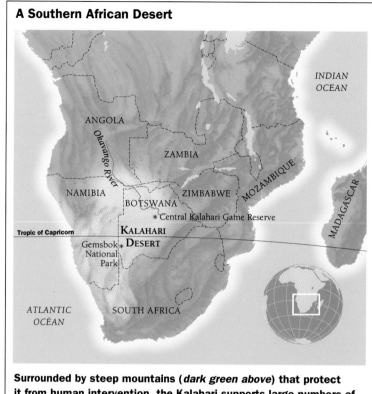

A Southern African Desert

Surrounded by steep mountains (*dark green above*) that protect it from human intervention, the Kalahari supports large numbers of plants and animals. The Tropic of Capricorn bisects the Kalahari, as it does other subtropical deserts in the Southern Hemisphere.

Grasses and acacia thorn thrive in part of Africa's Kalahari Desert where underground water is near the surface. At right, elephants lumber across another relatively fertile section of the Kalahari.

Inhabitants of the Kalahari, a Bushman family group (*left*) gathers around a fire site. The Bushmen, nomadic hunter-gatherers like Australia's Aborigines, camp in one spot until the local game and other edibles become scarce, but they never build anything more substantial than the sort of temporary shelter of branches and grass shown here.

A scrawny male lion and his mate devour a meal of wildebeest on a sandy plain in South Africa's game-rich Kalahari Gemsbok National Park. Apart from fat zebras, lions favor wildebeest because they are slower and easier to catch than swift antelopes and gazelles.

recent 20-month period, for example, barely 4 inches (100 mm) of rain was recorded in the center of the region. Overall, annual precipitation throughout the Kalahari's 220,000 square-mile terrain averages less than 15 inches (381 mm).

The term *desert* is especially apt when the annual summer rains of December and January—which normally supply enough moisture for animals and plants to get by during the rest of the year—unaccountably fail to materialize. Then the Kalahari, with its huge 32,000-square-mile (82,880-sq-km) Central Kalahari Game Reserve, becomes a brittle dust bowl. Temperatures soar to 120° F (50° C) or more, grasses turn to straw in the strong thermal winds, and both animals and humans are doomed to a desperate search for water. Even the Game Reserve's great lions, the world's largest, become gaunt and tattered looking, and there have been tragic die-offs among the dozens of other animals—wildebeest, jackals, giraffes, and hyenas alike—that live in the Reserve.

The people who must survive these dreadful dry times are the Bushmen, whose ancestors have inhabited southern Africa for at least 40,000 years. Like the ancient aboriginal people of Australia and the foraging ancestors of today's Zuni Indians—who established themselves in the American Southwest around 6000 B.C.—the Kalahari Bushmen also live a life on the move. Their seminomadic, family-based bands traditionally roam about in search of game and other edibles, such as wild cucumbers, tsama melons, and dozens of species of berries, fruits, nuts, and other plants and roots. Unlike the Aborigines, however, the Bushmen of the Kalahari stake ownership claims to tracts of land, and set up camps for weeks at a time, before moving on within their territory in search of water and food. Those strictly adhering to their ancient ways plant no crops and have never domesticated any animals. Like the Aborigines, the Bushmen have dark skins and generally go about naked except for loincloths. And like the Aborigines, the Bushmen have developed a knack for finding water in waterless times on the scorching sand pans of the Kalahari.

The "sip well," made of a length of simple hollow reed, is one age-old water collection method used by the Bushmen. When the unpredictable rainy season has long passed and the acacia thickets are dry enough to rattle in the breeze, the men, women, and children dig with their fingers or a stick into the sand of

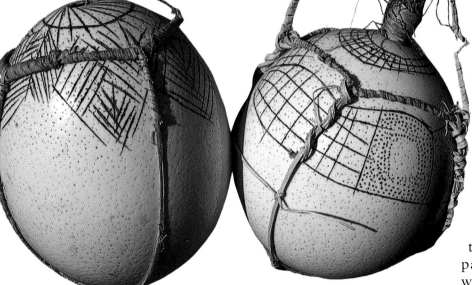

Flightless but amazingly fast—sprinting at 45 miles an hour—ostriches (*top*) high-step across a Kalahari grassland. Their eggs, the largest laid by any bird, provide handy water containers for the Bushmen, who often equip them with handles and plugs like the decorated pair shown above.

a dry riverbed or beneath the soil where wild plant roots intertwine. Then they cover one end of a hollow reed with a clump of matted, dry grass and shove the "filtered" end into the hole. Once sand is firmly packed around the tube, the wait begins. Sometimes half an hour will pass before a bare trickle of water collects below ground around the grass-covered end of the reed. At last, kneeling down, and with lips tightly sealed around the other end of the stalk, the Bushman begins to suck with all his might.

Slowly but surely the tight vacuum within the reed will yield one drop of water, then another, then a brief stream of liquid. When there is more than one thirsty mouth to satisfy, the person drawing the liquid from the tiny sip well may spread the wealth around. The Bushman sucks water into his mouth, then instantly sloshes it out into the waiting half of an ostrich eggshell, from which others can drink.

Ostriches and their eggs form a vital part of the Bushman water-hoarding technique. The world's largest bird, the flightless ostrich abounds in the Kalahari Desert, where it often mingles with herds of antelope.

PLIGHT OF THE WILDEBEEST

During a time of drought in the Kalahari, a black wildebeest reaches water in northern Botswana only after negotiating fences built to control the spread of foot and mouth disease.

When drought has a stranglehold on the Kalahari Desert, hundreds of thousands of animals migrate across its plains toward the lakes and rivers of northern Botswana.

Beginning in 1954, the government of Botswana erected about 1,500 miles (2,400 km) of fencing to keep wildlife from spreading foot and mouth disease to cattle. Yet veterinary experts say the virus can spread past fences and they are not certain that wildlife transmit the organism to cattle.

In the late 1970's, zoologists Mark and Delia Owens came upon one such group, the second largest wildebeest migration on record—260,000 animals in all. They also watched as these husky, horned antelopes were stopped in their tracks by more than 100 miles (160 km) of impenetrable wire fencing.

By the middle of 1979, 80,000 wildebeest, channeled on a long detour around the Botswana fence, died from dehydration. Officials eventually created occasional openings in the fences.

Generally in September, as spring begins in the Southern Hemisphere, the female ostrich lays her clutch of eggs, then abandons them for caretaking by her mate. The male ostrich—which often weighs 300 pounds (135 kg) and stands 8 feet (246 cm) tall—incubates the eggs until they hatch. If Bushman raiders time their approach carefully, they can avoid the wrath of the fierce birds and snatch an egg or two from the ground-level nests.

The off-white eggs—which can weigh 10 pounds (4.5 kg) and have a circumference of 15 inches (38 cm) each—are so enormous that nearly two dozen chicken eggs could fit inside each one. The Bushmen puncture small holes in the ends of the hefty shells, blow out and save the edible contents, then ready the shells for recycling as drinking cups and water storage vessels.

Saving supplies of water in the shells amounts to a prudent rite of frugality. The Kalahari's summer downpours usually furnish the desert's plants and animals with just enough moisture for the remainder of the year. But the Bushmen cannot take chances on the appearance of the fickle clouds and their life-giving rain. Rainfall is not only a cause for rejoicing but also a signal to gear up for the next drought. As soon as pools have formed, Bushman family groups take their precious caches of eggshells and submerge them until bubbles stop rising to the surface. Once they are filled, the shells are carried to strategic points along the Bushmen's migratory routes and buried deep in the sand. As the Bushmen move about, following game and searching for ripe plants, the hidden shells offer reassuring caches of water to be dug up when the desert once again dries up.

Let Dry Lands Bear Fruit

When the furnacelike *khamsin* gusts from the east across Israel's desolate Negev Desert, there can be little doubt about the truth of ancient tales of agonizing treks into this barren part of the Holy Land. Blowing sands have long covered traces of past civilizations, such as the Byzantines and Nabateans, who dared establish themselves in the place known in the Bible as the Negeb, meaning "to dry," or "to wipe dry."

The triangular-shaped desert, which spreads over about 5,400 square miles (13,986 sq km) of rugged mountains, canyon lands, and vast scrub-covered sandy regions in southern Israel, covers about 60 percent of the

Jewish state's total land area. Near the Judaean Hills and Wilderness of Judaea in the north, the Negev spreads out over about one-half of ancient Palestine. Then, bordered on the east by the Jordan River valley and on the west by the Sinai Peninsula, the desert narrows to a point at its southernmost tip, wherein lies the desert tourist town of Elat, on the Gulf of Aqaba.

Since the tiny state of Israel was formed in 1948, much of the bleak and rocky Negev has been transformed into plenteous green hills and valleys. The long-barren wilderness is now dotted with fertile fields and burgeoning groves of trees that belong to Jewish communal settlements called kibbutzim and moshavim. In the center of the Negev lies the hub city of Beersheba, which boasts a population of more than 100,000.

The Negev was anything but green in biblical times. According to the Old Testament, when Moses and his followers, searching for the Promised Land, arrived in the Wilderness of Zin in the heart of the Negev, the people lamented. "Why have you made us come up out of Egypt, to bring us to this evil place? It is no place for grain, or

An orchard of fruit trees flourishes across a valley in Israel's Negev Desert (*top*), transformed into the nation's garden by one of the world's most sophisticated irrigation systems.

A 1981 photograph (*above*) shows a part of the Negev—rocky, sunblasted, and lacking even a blade of grass—as it looked before being reclaimed with water from the Sea of Galilee.

The Sahara and the Arabian Peninsula

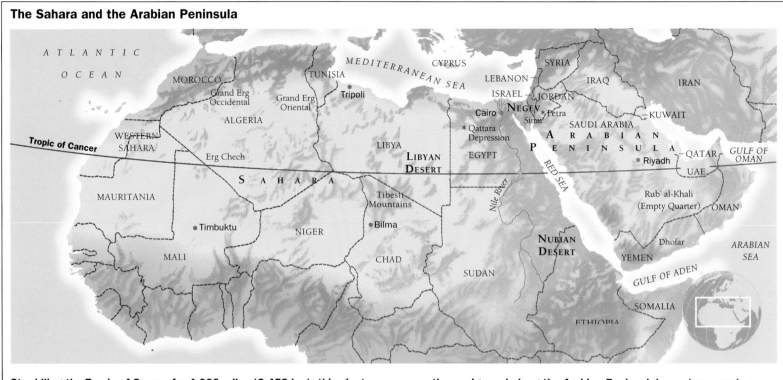

Straddling the Tropic of Cancer for 4,000 miles (6,452 km), this giant region covers almost 1 percent of Earth's entire land surface. Most of the region is low and flat, but mountains exist on the Sahara's far northern edge and along the Arabian Peninsula's western coast, as well as in clusters across both areas (*orange above*). Vast oil deposits are located under each of these deserts.

A dust storm, blown by the *harmattan,* a fierce winter wind, whirls through a Tuareg village in the southern Sahara. The cold northeasterly wind can blow for weeks or even months at a time. The dust it carries is so dense that it obliterates all shadows and any hint of the sun.

figs, or vines, or pomegranates; and there is no water to drink (Numbers 20:5)." Moses, the Book of Numbers reports, had to draw water from a rock so that the Israelites and their cattle could quench their thirst.

The Negev was not much more inviting when Israel's first prime minister, David Ben-Gurion, lived in a kibbutz called Sede Boker on the perimeter of the Wilderness of Zin. But there in the desert Ben-Gurion dreamed that the Negev, where annual rainfall may be as little as 3 to 4 inches (76–102 mm), would someday become the bread-basket of the Jewish state.

Ben-Gurion's vision has become a reality because of irrigation. An 88.5-mile-long (143-km) system of pipelines, canals, and tunnels, called—simply enough—the National Water Carrier, delivers more than 84 billion gallons (3 billion hl) of water each year from the Sea of Galilee to the desert's groves of avocado, citrus, apricot, and other trees, as well as to fields of cotton, grains, and vegetables. The Negev now provides 80 percent of Israel's food and boosts the Israeli economy with profits from winter crops exported to western Europe.

The Negev project has been especially successful because it employs a drip-irrigation system developed by Israeli hydrology experts—modern masters in the art of water conservation. Thousands of miles of thin plastic pipe punched with holes deliver computer-regulated flows of water directly to plant roots in the desert soil. Evaporation is slowed by a covering of plastic mulch that traps moisture. To conserve as much moisture as possible, Israeli agricultural specialists employ a variety of other techniques from trapping droplets that condense on greenhouse walls to using recycled sewage water.

Remarkably, the wrinkled, ancient hills of the Negev were once dappled with flourishing gardens, more than 2,000 years before the modern Israeli projects, by an Arabic-speaking people called the Nabateans. In their earliest days, beginning about seven centuries before Christ, the Nabateans were nomads who raided caravans carrying riches and trade goods between East Africa, India, and Arabia. As their wealth accumulated, so did their power. They carved out a capital city in the red sandstone cliffs at Petra in what is now Jordan, where at the height of the Roman Empire the Nabateans prospered as duty collectors, camel train organizers, and guarantors of safe passage to caravans crossing nearby deserts.

But the Nabateans were also farmers, and at Petra and other mountain towns—including places among the hills of the rocky Negev—they built some of the most sophisti-

The columned facade of a tomb cut in a sandstone cliff in about the second century A.D. by the Nabateans still stands near the site of their capital of Petra. Long before the Israelis, the Nabateans irrigated and farmed the Negev.

cated irrigation systems in the ancient world. They hollowed out cisterns in tabletop plateaus and built dams to keep natural catchments full of water. Along the desert slopes the Nabateans leveled off terraces, where the farmers cultivated fruit trees—almonds, pistachios, peaches, and others—which in turn provided shade so vegetables would thrive in the desert soil below. They channeled water runoff from one terrace garden to the next through stone and masonry aqueducts, which could be opened or closed to control the flow of the precious liquid.

The Nabateans and their desert gardens survived even the conquest of Petra by Roman legions in A.D. 106 and flourished until about the year 700, when their culture was destroyed during the fighting that attended the Muslim attacks on the Christian Byzantine Empire. Then wind and rain slowly obliterated the untended terraces and dams, and the Negev reverted to being a dry, eroded wilderness—until the Israelis began to reclaim it once again.

While the Nabateans were harvesting their figs, dates, barley, and wheat, another people, halfway around the globe, were developing their own irrigation expertise to tame a subtropical desert. By the seventh century A.D., the Hohokam—probably the distant ancestors of the Pima Indians who still live in the Sonoran Desert of the American Southwest—had constructed a sophisticated system of canals to irrigate their farming villages in the Gila, Santa Cruz, and Salt river basins. There in the arid flats around present-day Phoenix, where troubled farmers are now enmeshed in controversy over water piped from the far-off Colorado River, the Hohokam enjoyed more than a thousand years of farming in an otherwise dry and dusty land. In the Salt River valley alone, about 25,000 acres (10,000 ha) were irrigated by more than 500 miles (800 km) of canals. Constructing the canals, archeologists estimate, took the equivalent of 100 people working 12 months a year for 35 years.

Outside their villages, the Hohokam built smaller, sideward-stretching feeder ditches across the flatlands, as well as dams and levees to regulate water flow. They also created irrigated terraces on the slopes of the outlying highlands. The engineering feats of the Hohokam—unsurpassed in pre-Columbian North America—enabled them to raise cotton, tobacco, squash, beans, and corn in the heat of the Sonoran Desert until their culture declined about A.D. 1400, perhaps as the result of a sustained drought that forced them to adopt a nomadic way of life.

Buried Treasure

Pristine deserts are often tricksters in disguise, lands of extremes and contrasts. Shimmering mirages of a sea or an oasis can hover above a morning sandscape and taunt a thirsty traveler unmercifully. Freak winds, like the *zoboas* in the Sahara, appear in seconds, sending spiraling pillars of sand streaking across the wilderness. Dry riverbeds or ravines, often parched for decades, suddenly fill with raging walls of water, then are empty again within hours and stay that way for years to come. In deserts, that which seems eternal may change overnight, and that which is least expected is always a possibility. The barren land wears many faces, both upon its surface and deep in its underworld. What appears to be a wasteland may, in fact, hold a wealth of buried riches: huge lakes of oil, vast deposits of iron and other ores, and incalculable amounts of salt, as well as gypsum, nitrates, and phosphates.

One of many to be deceived was Saudi Arabian king Abd al-Aziz, who came to power in 1932. Looking out at his desolate nation, the king—called Ibn Saud by Westerners—saw only endless stretches of sand bisected not once by a flowing river. His sand- and gravel-strewn kingdom covers the vast majority of the Middle East's imposing Arabian Peninsula and contains numerous distinct desert regions, the largest of which are the Nafud, in the north, the central Dahna, and the forbidding Rub al-Khali, across

the south. In each, the average summer temperature is 111° F (44° C). The country's highest mountain slopes rim its entire western side, which is bounded by the Red Sea. The only undiscovered riches the king dared hope to find beneath the Saudi Arabian wilderness were a few pools of fresh water.

Some venturesome Americans, however, had a hunch that the deserts of the Arabian Peninsula hid untold amounts of oil, and they petitioned Ibn Saud to give them drilling rights. Wooed by promises of chestfuls of gold coins—and of large royalties if oil were struck—the hard-bargaining king finally came to an agreement with the Standard Oil Company of California, or Socal, during the summer of 1933. A down payment of 35,000 gold sovereigns was painstakingly counted out by hand on August 25, and the fate of Ibn Saud's nation was unwittingly sealed. More than a year and a half later, after extensive

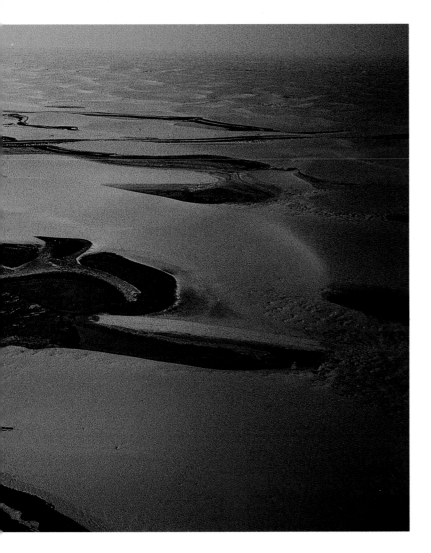

Excess gas burns from a few of the thousand-and-one producing oil wells in Abu Dhabi (*above*), one of the United Arab Emirates. In Saudi Arabia (*left*), huge oil seeps caused by geologic shifts bring underground oil bubbling to the surface.

surveying and preparation, drilling began near Ad Dammam on the Persian Gulf, but it would be another three years before oil was struck. In time the world would learn that the seemingly barren deserts of Saudi Arabia lie atop more than one-quarter of the planet's proven oil and natural gas reserves.

Despite decades of drilling and pumping since the 1930's, the buried treasure of petroleum that lies beneath the entire Persian Gulf region still exceeds 650 billion barrels—at today's oil prices, worth about U.S. $13 trillion. The vast quantity of oil is there, of course, because the now-arid Persian Gulf region was once covered by an ocean, thriving with plankton and other life, that—over millions of years—laid down layer upon layer of rich organic sediments. Hundreds of millions of years of physical pressure converted the decomposed marine animal and plant remains into huge subterranean reservoirs of gaseous

and liquid hydrocarbons known as fossil fuels. Beneath the states of the Persian Gulf are 26 "supergiant" oil fields, each containing more than 5 billion barrels of recoverable—but non-renewable—oil. The Middle East as a whole—most of which is desert—is believed to hold about 40 percent of all the oil deposits in the world. Much of the rest may also be found beneath deserts; there is evidence that huge petroleum reserves still lurk beneath the two polar deserts and within each of the arid bands that wrap around the planet.

It is no wonder, then, that oil has become a major bargaining chip in the global economic arena for the desert nations of the Persian Gulf, where "black gold" is most abundant. It is a resource that has ushered them into a new age of influence and prosperity. It has also, however, added one more source of tension to a region plagued for millennia by political and religious strife.

Duels in the Sun

Recently, the most dramatic flare-up of these tensions was the August 2, 1990, attack on the small desert nation of Kuwait—which sits at the head of the Persian Gulf—by its far larger neighbor Iraq. Kuwait's defense force of only 9,900 troops was no match for the large armies and tanks making up the Iraqi attack force. The Iraqi spearheads had blasted across the border and into Kuwait City before the sun rose on that summer morning.

Under Kuwait's 17,818-square-mile (48,326-sq-km) sliver of desert lie the world's second largest petroleum reserves. And after 50 years of producing and selling the oil, Kuwait had become immensely rich, with a per capita income outstripping that of almost every other nation on Earth. The world's response to Iraq's threat to world oil

supplies in Kuwait was the huge United Nations military effort called Operation Desert Shield. Nearly 800,000 troops from 31 allied countries joined forces on the parched sands of the Gulf region. Most of the first to arrive set up defensive lines along the border in Saudi Arabia along the Kuwaiti border. There they waited for five months—and prepared themselves for the possibility of battle in the desert.

The desert along the Persian Gulf proved to be a formidable adversary for the troops even as they waited to launch the hammer-blow air and land attack, Operation Desert Storm, that would send Iraq's armies reeling back toward Baghdad in January and February, 1991. Although daytime temperatures averaged in the low 80's F (mid 20's C) during those winter months—and nights

Oil-drenched Canadian fire fighters (*far left*) battle to cap a spewing well after the 1991 Gulf War. Huge plumes of oily smoke drift from oil wells in Kuwait (*near left*) set afire by retreating Iraqi troops.

In a meeting of the modern and the ancient, a U.S. Army Bradley troop carrier (*below*) rolls past Arab shepherds and their flock during the U.N. ground offensive that ended the Gulf War.

were cool enough to wear parkas—the troops acclimated themselves to the desert during summer and fall, when temperatures shot above 100° F (38° C) nearly every day. The American men and women—as well as the British, French, and others—assigned to carry out Desert Shield and Desert Storm consumed several gallons of water a day per person for drinking, cooking, and hygiene. And those wearing the 15-pound (7-kg) anti-gas uniforms—to protect against chemical weapons—consumed considerably more water in their bundled-up state. The need for water for all purposes had been grossly underestimated by the U.S. military despite the fact that the army and the marines commonly train for desert action in the Mojave Desert, where the heat, aridity, terrain, and toll on the human body are strikingly similar to those in some parts of the Middle East.

Transporting the water posed additional problems: each gallon (4 L) weighed 8 pounds (4 kg), preventing soldiers from carrying a day's ration and requiring flatbed trucks to transport it in huge bladders.

During wars in subtropical deserts, the heat, the dryness, and the dust also cause numerous problems during combat itself. Heat can cause optical distortions as soldiers peer through sighting devices. It can even bend certain metals, so that the gun barrels of tanks and other pieces of artillery fire off-target. Blowing dust blocks vision and gets into skin pores as well as sensitive parts of motorized equipment. Helicopter blades may wear out more quickly than normal; for tanks, sand shields are a necessity, as are cooling systems and special engine transmissions that reduce maximum speeds over the scorching desert sands. "An armored offensive in desert conditions can be suicidal unless your vehicles are in perfect order," said one Israeli.

Before Desert Storm, the most famous modern war fought in a desert had been the to-and-fro conflict that raged across North Africa during World War II, pitting Germany's famous "Desert Fox," Gen. Erwin Rommel, against a succession of British commanders including the final victor, Lt. Gen. Bernard Law Montgomery. This long series of attacks and retreats was far more harrowing for the troops involved, as well as more destructive of the tanks, aircraft, and other machines, than the U.N. effort in Kuwait. It lasted far longer—in all, from 1940 to 1943. And it was fought in a far more punishing land: the great Sahara, most colossal of all the world's arid places.

The Sprawling Sahara

Embracing nearly one-third of the African continent, the Sahara—its name derived from the Arabic word *sahra'*, meaning "desert"—stretches 3,100 miles (5,000 km) across the entire width of North Africa, from Egypt to the Atlantic shore. Composed of numerous individually named deserts, the sprawling, barren land covers more than 3.5 million square miles (9 million sq km)—an area almost as large as that of all 50 of the United States. It is a tapestry of salt savannas, rocky escarpments, gravel plains called *regs,* and mighty dune-studded sand seas called *erg*s. Deep crevices called *wadis,* carved by long-forgotten flash floods, snake across the seemingly endless Saharan flatlands and plateaus. Some spots in the Sahara's deepest salt basin, the Qattara Depression in western Egypt, lie more than 400 feet (120 m) below sea level. The Sahara's highest peaks reach 11,500 feet (3,450 m), in the Tibesti Mountains in northern Chad.

Vast in size and including some of the globe's roughest terrain, the Sahara is even more forbidding because of its heat and dryness. According to aridity indexes—which take into account precipitation and the amount of solar energy—the eastern Sahara is one of the driest spots on Earth. Along with a portion of the Atacama Desert in South America, it has the maximum aridity rating of 200. In those hyperarid places the sun can evaporate 200 times more water than falls in the form of precipitation. By comparison, the western Sahara has an aridity index of 50, the Sonoran Desert only 10. Some places in the

Called "melons" of the desert, nodules of silica (*below*) sit in the sand in the Egyptian Sahara. The "melons" are deposits left by a prehistoric sea that once covered the Sahara.

Crescent-shaped barchan dunes (*above*) stretch to the horizon across a segment of the western Sahara in Morocco. Barchan dunes form when the wind blows constantly from one direction; when the wind shifts, the original crescent shape is distorted.

Wind-sculpted dunes hundreds of yards high (*left*) flow across the Sahara in Algeria. The Sahara, usually thought of as a sandy desert, is in fact only one-fifth sand; the majority of the area is covered by gravel plains.

FORMING THE EARTH'S DRY WAVES OF SAND

The breathtaking formations of sand found in some of the most arid landscapes on Earth evoke, ironically, images of the sea. Just as wind drives water particles into ocean waves, it also sweeps sand particles into wavelike patterns and geometric forms called dunes. Dune formation begins in a desert transaction called saltation (*illustration below*), which occurs when wind currents fling individual grains of sand across the desert floor. The process continues when irregularities on the surface disrupt wind flow, and sand grains fall and start to accumulate (*right*).

Dunes can occur where there are vast expanses of sand, as in the Sahara and Arabian deserts, or on the bare plains of South America's Atacama Desert, where there is very little sand at all. The shape and size of a dune depends on the amount of sand available as well as on the strength, constancy, and direction of the wind flow. The five most common dune types—and their respective formation processes—are shown on the opposite page.

Saltation

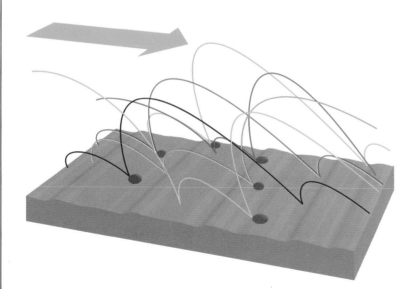

Previously motionless grains of sand are swept into the air by wind currents (blue arrow). The height and speed of their trajectories (colored lines) are determined by wind speed and the hardness of the surface. Rocks and hard spots (brown circles) propel grains higher and farther. When they descend, they launch other grains.

How dunes are formed

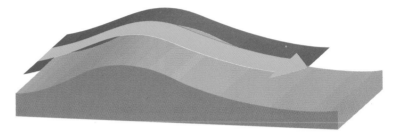

Where the flow of wind-transported sand is interrupted by a boulder, depression, or plant, sand settles and begins to pile up.

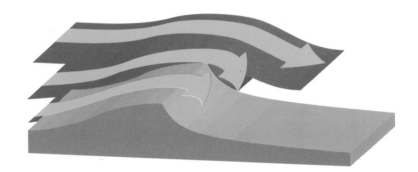

Sand is blown up the windward face and over what eventually becomes the crest of the dune, and spills down out of the wind stream.

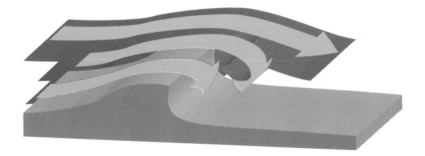

Sand collects on the increasingly steep leeward side of the crest until the sand below collapses and forms a more stable slope.

Types of dunes

Transverse dunes *are formed by moderate winds that sweep up light grains of sand and form ripples perpendicular to the direction of the wind. They have gentle windward—and steep leeward—slopes and occur where there is little or no vegetation.*

Longitudinal dunes *form parallel to strong, steady winds that gouge deep troughs in the desert floor, depositing sand on either side of the trough. Slight changes in wind direction give dune crests a wavy appearance.*

Barchan dunes *have a crescent shape formed by a constant wind coming from one direction. Their horns result from the wind's moving faster around the edges of the dune than over its windward slope. These highly mobile dunes form on rocky surfaces.*

Star dunes *result where winds converge from several directions. Buffeted by the wind from all sides, this dune remains largely immobile. Its arms have sharp ridges, sometimes 262 feet (80 m) high, that radiate from a central point.*

Parabolic dunes *are similar to barchan dunes, but their arms, stabilized by vegetation, face the wind stream. Wind scoops sand from the center of the dune and transports it to the steeper leeward side.*

Sahara receive less than ¼ inch (6 mm) of precipitation annually, often in the form of dew.

Outfoxing the Desert

It was partly the extreme dryness of the blazing desert that made fighting for control of Libya and Egypt a torment for the soldiers of Rommel's Afrika Korps and for the British and Commonwealth troops who opposed the German forces. There never seemed to be enough water to slake the men's chronic thirst. A few desert cisterns provided limited supplies, but the water usually tasted vile and often contained leeches and other unwelcome wildlife. Virtually all the water needed by both armies had to be brought forward in trucks from supply dumps far in the rear, along Libya's main highway—a bumpy track that snaked along the Mediterranean shore. The troops on both sides had to get by on about 3 quarts (2.8 L) of water a day per person, not nearly enough in the Saharan heat. Occasionally when supplies failed, the ration sank to a cup a day. "One's thirst," even the stoic Rommel complained, "becomes almost unquenchable."

Insufficient water, though, was only one of the desert's discomforts. Sudden, violent sandstorms frequently blew out of the depths of the Sahara on 70-mile-an-hour (110-kph) winds, sometimes raising the temperature to 130° F (54° C) and cutting visibility to

nothing. To protect themselves, the soldiers wrapped cloths around their heads until they looked like mummies, wore goggles when they had them, and hunkered down in the lee of a rock or a tank or one of the prickly bushes called camel thorn. When the storm passed, they had to dig out their equipment and shovel the crude tracks they had already laboriously cut to enable tanks and trucks to navigate the sands.

Adding to all these discomforts were the clouds of desert flies that swarmed about the soldiers ceaselessly wherever they camped. Worse were tiny fleas that burrowed into the skin and caused persistent sores. Then there were the larger and uglier yellow scorpions and horned vipers that often sent soldiers on both sides reeling to medical stations to receive first aid for poisonous bites.

The Sahara's sands were also the relentless enemy of all mechanical equipment. During one early battle, in 1941, when Rommel was making his first daring thrust across the eastern part of Libya called Cyrenaica, the British 2d Armored Division found itself losing an average of 1 of its desperately needed tanks to mechanical breakdown for every 10 miles (16 km) the division traveled. To combat the clouds of grit the machines stirred up every time they moved, mechanics fitted all replacement tanks and trucks and aircraft arriving in the desert with special filtering devices for air intakes and other critical parts.

In one way, however, the sands of Libya proved a wonderful place to fight a war for a daring, offensive-minded general like Rommel and for the few British commanders who showed some of the same bold inventiveness. The desert was above all *open,* with no rivers that troops would have to bridge or mountains that would have to be climbed or even—except for the port of Benghazi—any towns that an enemy could fortify and turn into bothersome strong points. The desert, Rommel quickly

A camel caravan loaded with trade goods sets out from Egypt. Camels, capable of crossing deserts that no truck or car can navigate, are still widely used in the Sahara.

perceived, was much like the sea, a largely uncharted expanse that would allow—as does the ocean—the boldest kind of military maneuver. It was the perfect arena, in short, for tanks and for the swift-striking sort of tank warfare of which Rommel was already a master, having led a Nazi panzer division in the blitzkrieg that had invaded and crushed France in 1940 in a matter of weeks.

Ultimately, though, it was the openness and emptiness of the desert that led to Rommel's undoing. His Afrika Korps could in no sense live off the largely barren and uninhabited land. There was no food to be scrounged from farms, no refineries to be taken and tapped for gasoline, no lakes or rivers to be used as sources of water. Everything Rommel needed to sustain his men and keep his tanks moving had to come by grotesquely stretched

supply lines—which ultimately reached across the Mediterranean to both Italy and Germany and were increasingly blasted by the British Royal Navy and Air Force. The defeat of Rommel's troops by Lt. Gen. Montgomery at the famous Battle of El Alamein came about in part because the German panzers had virtually run out of gasoline and the artillery out of ammunition while the British Eighth Army, with more secure supply lines, had at last been provided with plenty of both.

Fabled Indigo Warriors

Rommel's Afrika Korps troops were not, of course, the first or only warriors to sweep across the empty Saharan wilds and fall upon unwary victims. Among their predecessors were the notorious Tuareg, otherwise known as the "blue men of the veil." When billowy indigo-blue robes appeared on camelback at the crest of a sand dune, Saharan travelers knew they were doomed to decimation by the desert's most romanticized nomads. Even well into the

Tuareg men (*above*) stand
swathed in the heavy robes—one
dyed a traditional indigo blue—
that they wear as protection
against the Saharan sun. The
face veils are proof of adulthood.

Mantled by an early morning fog
after a chill night, the Oasis of
Douz in Tunisia (*left*) comes alive
as Tuareg traders prepare their
caravan for another leg of a
trans-Saharan journey.

20th century, the handsome, fiercely independent Tuareg would gallop their camels across the sands, wielding swords and brandishing lances, ready to plunder and kill anyone in their path.

Originally from Africa's Mediterranean coast and related to the warlike Berbers, the Tuareg migrated southward into the desert after camels were introduced to the North African region early in the first century A.D. There, for generation after generation, they controlled most of the central Sahara's north-south trade routes as both brigands and caravanners themselves. In ancient times they battled both Egyptian and Roman armies. Around the beginning of this century, they battled French colonists for control of their desert empire. In one of their final and largest encounters, in 1916, the Tuareg were subdued by the rapid-fire rifles of a French force near Oursi in present-day Burkina-Faso. Since then the Tuareg have lived primarily as traders and pastoralists, moving their camels, goats, and sheep from place to place throughout the year, transporting their tents, furniture, and other belongings on the backs of donkeys.

The "blue men" were named for the fact that the indigo dye in their voluminous robes rubs off on their light-complected, perspiring skin. Winter and summer, regardless of the Saharan temperature, they cloak themselves in their flowing garb and turbans. Many centuries ago they learned that the robes protect their skin from the sun's burning rays, slow evaporation, and minimize water loss by creating a layer of cool air around the body. Despite Muslim tradition—which directs women of the faith to keep their faces and bodies under wraps—Tuareg men are the ones who wear the veils in their society. Women, faces bared and at liberty to be assertive in public, are highly respected members of the Tuareg culture and, like men, can be property holders.

In addition to having a historic role as marauders, the Tuareg have long been important traders of salt, one of the desert's most precious resources. Salt is abundant in the Sahara; some mines are still worked, and scores of others have long been covered over by shifting sands. For centuries, Tuareg salt caravans have traveled during the winter to the salt pits at Bilma in present-day Niger.

DESERT DRIVERS ON THE EARTH AND THE MOON

For most of the 20th century, the boundless freedom and adventure of driving the desert's harsh expanses has lured countless motorists. Among the first to explore the desert by car was the American fossil hunter Roy Chapman Andrews, who was noted for discovering dinosaur eggs in Central Asia's Gobi in 1923. Using Dodge convertibles, Andrews and his team covered far more ground than a camel caravan could. The cars did not entirely replace camels, however; Andrews relied on 75 of the beasts to haul gasoline. That same decade, Ralph A. Bagnold, a young British army officer stationed in Cairo, was spending his off-hours exploring the Sahara in Model-T Fords. Bagnold always took a compass for navigation and enough passengers to push—often a necessity in soft sand. During World War II, Bagnold put his experience to work, commanding a fleet of customized Chevrolet trucks that tracked enemy movements in North Africa.

Each January, more than 100 hardy souls plow through similar territory in cars and trucks or on motorcycles for the 8,000-mile Paris–Dakar, a three-week rally into the heart of the Sahara. Drivers use satellite readings to navigate the often roadless course over dunes, through mountain passes, and along washboard-surfaced gullies. The race, which winds south through Algeria and west to Dakar, is one of Europe's biggest sporting events.

Dune busting is enjoyed by the hundreds of off-road enthusiasts who take their buggies, dirt bikes, and all-terrainers each week to the eastern Mojave in southern California. Off-road vehicles have become so advanced that the U.S. Navy specially ordered dozens of dune buggies from one California manufacturer for Operation Desert Storm.

By far the most specialized desert vehicles are the ones developed by NASA to explore unearthly arid lands—namely the Moon and Mars. The Lunar Rover served *Apollo 15* astronauts well for 17 miles of use on the Moon in 1971.

With the lunar Mount Hadley as a backdrop (left), Apollo 15 astronaut James B. Irwin prepares to drive the lunar rover over the Moon's waterless surface. First used on the Moon in 1971, the rover was tested extensively in the California desert.

California's eastern Mojave Desert attracts hundreds of off-roaders like the thrill seeker in the three-wheeler (above) who leaves a rooster tail of sand while circling a dune.

Wheels aloft, a truck struggles over an Algerian dune (left) as officials plan the 1988 route of the celebrated Paris–Dakar rally. Despite such reconnaissance runs and an official guidebook, many drivers lose their way during the 7,000-mile (11,290-km) Sahara portion of the course.

Months before the Tuareg arrive, local laborers dig pits in the ground to trap water from the late summer rains that fall on Niger's rock- and sand-strewn flatlands. As the water evaporates from the soil, it draws salt to the surface, leaving a thick salty residue that is then shaped into conical forms that resemble long-stemmed, flat-topped mushrooms. The Tuareg traders arrive on the scene after the cones have dried hard as rocks in the scorching sun.

One Tuareg caravan in the mid-1960's, for example, included 10 people and about 100 camels. At Bilma, the Tuareg traders bartered for salt cones at the equivalent of U.S. 15 cents apiece, wrapped them in straw matting, and then hoisted about six of the 40-pound (18-kg) packages onto the back of each camel. The Tuareg party then trekked southwestward for more than a month, across hundreds of miles of blazing sand in a desert region known as the Ténéré. Finally, at Agadès, an oasis in central Niger, the Tuareg turned directly south toward markets, like Maradi, in Niger, and perhaps Kano, in Nigeria. There

Shiny tentacles of salt splay into the desert to form a huge salt basin in northeastern Botswana (*left*). The salt remains when salt-bearing streams evaporate. Invaluable to animals as salt licks, such deposits yield a treasured trade item for numbers of desert peoples.

Men of the Assale tribe of northeastern Ethiopia (*above*) use huge wooden pincers to pry up salt from a dry lake in the Danakil Depression.

the Tuareg traded the salt cones at a profitable rate equivalent to U.S. $1.50 per cone for tea, millet, and sugar, all of which appear in their diet, and for the cotton used in their celebrated blue robes. Once the business was transacted, the trade route cycle began again as the blue men retraced their steps back to Bilma.

Arabian Harvest

For untold centuries, an isolated desert region in southern Arabia was the source of one of the world's most coveted commodities: frankincense, the aromatic gum resin known to the ancients as the "perfume of the gods." Worshipers in temples and churches from India to the Mediterranean basin have considered the aroma of burning frankincense a vital part of many religious ceremonies. During the heyday of the wealthy Mesopotamian city of Babylon, one temple alone burned more than two tons of it each year. Historians estimate that during the peak of the frankincense trade, in the second century A.D., 3,000 tons of it or more were exported annually from the desert lands of southern Arabia. Ancient records show that the best resin was almost literally worth its weight in gold.

Much of the international frankincense trade went through the long-vanished metropolis of Ubar—famed in legend for its lavish wealth and debauchery—in today's Arabian sultanate of Oman. Harvesters took the resin to markets there, where middlemen bought and sold it, and camel drivers prepared large caravans to carry the precious cargo northward to Babylon and other cities across Arabia's most forbidding desert, the Rub al-Khali, or "Empty Quarter"—the largest unbroken expanse of sand on Earth. It was doubtless, at least in part, the grueling trek over this 250,000-square-mile (650,000-sq-km) sea of sand in the peninsula's southern midsection that made frankincense such an expensive commodity in Rome, Constantinople, and points beyond.

The Rub al-Khali is a sweeping arid region that engulfs nearly one-fourth of the Arabian Peninsula. The choppy sea of cinnamon-orange dunes, some reaching 800 feet (240 m) high, and sandy salt plains are far too hostile to sustain more than a few species of hardy desert perennials. Plagued by scorching temperatures and hot, dusty winds that sweep in from every direction, the Rub al-Khali's uninterrupted desolation stretches more than 800 miles (1,290 km) at its widest point, in southern Saudi Arabia.

A few Bedouin tribes still roam the vast interior of the region they call simply ar-Ramlah, or "the Sand." But most people prefer to cluster along the seaside fringes of the peninsula, where water is more accessible and the climate more tolerable.

Now as then the source of the best frankincense, the Dhofar region of Oman lies at the point where the sandy southern reaches of the Empty Quarter give way to rocky highlands. Sitting halfway up the southeastern edge of the Arabian Peninsula, it is a land of hard limestone slopes on the flanks of the Qara Mountains. Here the prized frankincense trees, *Boswellia carteri,* cling in meager, scraggly stands. The oozing, white resin is also derived from related trees, such as *Boswellia sacra,* in the stark highlands of Oman, North and South Yemen, and in parts of Somalia and Ethiopia. But none was as fit for the world's kings and queens as a single droplet of the precious frankincense from Dhofar.

There in the rugged hills, frankincense is still harvested laboriously by hand as it was 40 centuries and more ago. Several times a year, beginning in winter and ending with the summer monsoon, men of the Bait Kathir and al-Mahra tribes, nomads who live in the arid desert highlands, slash or scrape the trees' bark using broad-bladed knives called *mingaf*s. Creamy-white droplets of resin, or *luban,* are quickly scraped from the wounds into baskets made of palm leaves. The collected sap is left for months to dry and crystallize into a translucent, brittle resin. When aged and well seasoned the resin is ready for use: it

Droplets of white sap—raw frankincense—ooze from a slash on a tree of the genus *Boswellia* (above) where the bark has been cut away. Frankincense has long been prized as the finest of all aromatic resins.

Low vegetation covers the foothills of the stark mountains of Oman (*right*), the sultanate on the eastern end of the Arabian Peninsula, where the best sources of aromatic frankincense are found.

is ignited, and then the flame is extinguished so that the smoking embers fill a room with a soothing, pungent aroma reminiscent of balsam pines.

Among all classes of society, frankincense has had many uses through the ages. It made an enticing perfume for the powerful and the well-to-do. It served as an insect repellent and masked the odors of unwashed bodies. Following a meal, Arab men held their beards over the fragrant smoke to remove food odors from the coarse hair. For those so inclined, frankincense was also used to inspire contemplation, religious fervor, and even ecstacy. The aromatic resin also served as a supremely valuable gift—as it

did, the New Testament says, when the Wise Men from the East followed a star to Bethlehem to pay homage to the infant Jesus.

The resin was highly valued for its medicinal properties as well. The Chinese prescribed it for respiratory disorders. Egyptians chewed it to fight bad breath, and the Romans used oil of frankincense as an ointment for skin infections and wounds. Many physicians today agree with the ancients that resin from the desert's gnarly frankincense tree does have medicinal value. It can be useful as an antiseptic, an anti-inflammatory, and an antifungal agent. What is more, the smoke, just as the ancient Chinese believed, can go a long way toward relieving the symptoms of asthma and lung ailments.

With so much known about frankincense, one tantalizing mystery remained: where was the long-ago trading center of Ubar, a city likened to Atlantis by T. E. Lawrence—Lawrence of Arabia—and one that was, for two millennia, the world's leading supply center for Arabia's most coveted commodity? To find out, archeologists turned to a space-age method of detection known as Space Imaging Radar. In 1984, while NASA's space shuttle *Challenger* orbited Earth, an ultrasophisticated camera on board focused on the southern region of

A nugget of pure frankincense (*above*), which turns an amber color when aged and ready for use, is dropped into the special kind of incense burner used in Oman.

the Arabian Peninsula. The resulting images, taken from hundreds of miles above the Earth, were combined with additional satellite data and then enhanced by computers to reveal details invisible to travelers on the ground. What appeared were traces of 100-mile-long (160-km) ancient caravan pathways, long buried beneath rock and shifting sands that, in places, had formed dunes 600 feet (183 m) high.

Armed with the evidence, a group of explorers and archeologists from the United States, Oman, and Great Britain began in 1990 to follow the tracks across the highlands of Oman. The trails finally led to a rock-strewn site atop a plateau 100 miles (160 km) inland from the ruins of Moscha, an ancient port on the Arabian Sea. There, buried in the sand at the edge of the Empty Quarter, the team discovered the ruined walls of the metropolis known not only as Ubar but also as Omanum Emporium, one of the great, opulent cities of Arabian antiquity that—quite fittingly—had long since succumbed to the irrepressible tides of the desert sands.

FROZEN FRONTIERS

One of nature's astonishing paradoxes is that deserts exist in places where sand is virtually unknown, where mammoth dunes are formed by blowing snowflakes, and where temperatures are bone-chilling more often than not. In some of these deserts, sharply defined shadows are a rarity, and the glow in winter's sky is the only hint of the presence of a sun far below the horizon. In others, solar radiation is more intense, and mountain peaks tower higher than anyplace else on the planet. These arid realms are the polar deserts—the snow- and ice-bound areas that surround the Poles in the Northern and Southern hemispheres—and the alpine deserts atop the world's tallest summits, where elevation, aridity, and bitter temperatures create conditions resembling those at the Poles. Like the sunbaked Sahara, these environments are true deserts in every sense of the word.

Most moisture in these barren regions is locked up in the form of ice, and therefore is largely unavailable to plants and animals. The interior reaches of Antarctica are some of the most arid places on Earth; the continent receives on average less than 2 inches (51 mm) of precipitation a year, and there are places on it where not a drop of rain has fallen for 2 million years. Two-thirds of the world's frozen water is contained in the sprawling ice sheet that covers all but 2 percent of Antarctica's rocky surface. However, since even midsummer temperatures seldom rise above freezing, the ice sheet—which in places is 3 miles (5 km) thick—never gets a chance to melt. No melting means scant moisture in the air and therefore only trace amounts of precipitation. The air above the continent of Antarctica is so cold and thin that it can barely hold any of what little moisture there is, much less turn that slight amount into clouds.

If one envisions the barren Antarctic Desert as a grandiose ice-covered rock surrounded by ocean, its polar counterpart in the Northern Hemisphere—the arid Arctic region—is quite the opposite. The interior region of this desert is like an exceptionally wide-brimmed bowl filled with the waters and ever-circulating ice floes of the Arctic Ocean. The North Pole floats, so to speak, in the middle. Smallest and shallowest of the planet's seven seas, the Arctic Ocean is covered year-round by masses of ice, although in summer the solid ice pack breaks up to some degree.

Encircling the Arctic Ocean bowl—southward from the sea's ice-encrusted perimeter—lie the northern-most reaches of Asia, Europe, and North America. This circumpolar zone encompasses parts of Russia, Scandinavia, Greenland, Canada, and Alaska. These rolling expanses of land are the Arctic tundra—regions of permanently frozen subsoil, or permafrost, which often reach 800 to 1,500 feet (244–457 m) in depth. Carpeted with low-lying, chill-resistant vegetation, the Arctic tundra zones lie north of the tree line, or tim-berline, the northernmost latitude where trees thrive.

Between the poles, on every continent except Australia, and along a wide spectrum of latitudes, Earth's surface is dotted with deserts on the peaks of mountains. These high-elevation arid regions are closely akin to the Arctic regions and Antarctica in their frigid climates, scant available moisture, fiercely drying winds, and even their physical appearance in many places. The highest of these alpine deserts are in the Himalaya, which on the border of China and Nepal rise to the highest point on Earth—29,028 feet (8,848 m)—on snow- and glacier-capped Mount Everest. A world away—above Africa's scorching Tanzanian plains less than 250 miles (403 km) from the Equator—the perpetually snow-topped desert peak of Mount Kilimanjaro towers at 19,590 feet (5,971 m) above sea level. Among others, alpine deserts exist in the European Alps, South America's Andes mountain range, the Rocky Mountains of North America, and places in the Atlas Mountains on the northwest coast of Africa. These high, dry peaks need not be topped with year-round snow; often, their slopes are covered with scantily vegetated permafrost or rocky soil.

Success in the hard task of polar or alpine desert living is limited to the few species that have evolved specialized means of coping with the lack of available moisture and food and the chilling temperatures in these windblown places. Although their homelands are similar climati-cally, the indigenous animals of the Arctic, Antarctic, and the world's highest elevations could scarcely be more unalike. The polar bear, the penguin, and the yak, for example, share little but their skill at survival.

Forbidding they may be, but the Arctic and alpine deserts are home to millions of people. Untold numbers have long existed along the slopes of desert-topped mountains, generally below the zones of perpetual snow cover. And more than 2 million people now live in the arid Arctic region; the first humans to migrate so far north were most probably Siberians, who moved into present-day Alaska some 12,000 years ago, after tra-versing the Ice Age land bridge across the Bering Strait.

But in Antarctica there have never been either indigenous peoples or permanent residents. Most who come to that icecapped desert continent do so in the name of science or for the thrill of adventure and explo-ration—as do most outsiders who journey to the Arctic or alpine deserts.

ON A BONE-CHILLING day in November 1992—a spring day in the Antarctic—a lone Norwegian set off on a record-setting mission that would take him across 814 miles (1,313 km) of the largest, coldest, windiest, and most desolate desert on Earth. Dragging a 276-pound (125-kg) supply sled, Erling Kagge left ice-bound Berkner Island on skis and forged into Antarctica, a land where shades of black, white, and gray dominate the landscape; where howling winds routinely blow at more than 40 miles an hour (65 kph); and where inland temperatures during summer's "heat wave" average only -40° F (-40° C). With nothing more than brief one-way contacts with the outside world by means of a portable satellite beacon, the 29-year-old Kagge completed his quest in 51 days and became the first person to trek solo to the South Pole.

During the last century and a half, others like Kagge have journeyed to the environs of the proverbial "bottom of the earth," in part because of the allure of the forbidden. Early navigators who sailed into Antarctic waters gazed in wonder at this most isolated of Earth's continents; today, cruise ship vacationers are undoubtedly as awestruck by the splendor of the icecapped land that juts up out of the polar sea—far from any other soil. Apart from a sprinkling of islands off its shores, Antarctica's closest neighboring point of land is South America's Tierra del Fuego at Cape Horn, about 600 miles (1,000 km) from the icy desert's Antarctic Peninsula. In between stretch the southern reaches of the Pacific, Atlantic, and Indian oceans—sometimes collectively called the Southern

Towering over the surrounding icy seas, the jagged, rocky spine of the Antarctic Peninsula (*left*) is an extension of the Andean mountain chain of South America. Chinstrap penguins (*above*) bask on the rocky coast of Elephant Island, just beyond the tip of the peninsula.

Ocean—whose cold waters are lashed by circumpolar westerly winds that are among the most ferocious in the world.

Unwittingly, the Australian geologist Douglas Mawson established his 1912 base camp in the midst of the most ferocious and unyielding wind corridor on the face of the Earth—at Antarctica's Cape Denison. Mawson and his party, who came to chart the wind-whipped desert coastlands 1,550 miles (2,550 km) south of Australia, found that nothing could be left lying about, lest it sail away on the fierce currents that averaged 50 miles per hour (80 kph) during the party's first full year. Supplies had to be lashed down and hut rooftops firmly secured to prevent them from being blown to smithereens— especially in the 60- to 90-mile-an-hour (100–145 kph) winds that blew almost continuously from March through May. If caught outside in the hurricane-force gusts— which now and then peaked above 200 miles an hour (320 kph)—Mawson and his party were hard-pressed to grapple their way to safety. In such blinding blizzards, far more snow may be churned up from the cold desert floor than falls in decades as precipitation. While stronger than gale-force winds can arise from the sea, they are also generated from within the Antarctic interior. Clocked at 110 miles an hour (177 kph), the katabatic—or down-flowing—winds plunge from atop high inland plateaus and sweep down ice-covered slopes to the glacier-gouged valleys of the eastern coast and the great Transantarctic Mountain chain, which arches across the continent for 1,370 miles (2,210 km).

Antarctic Desert

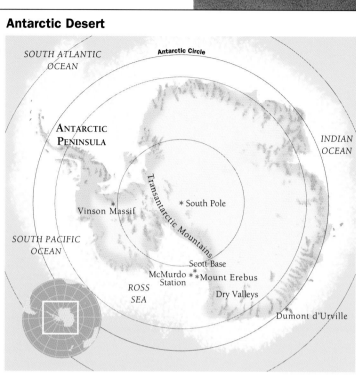

SOUTH ATLANTIC OCEAN

Antarctic Circle

ANTARCTIC PENINSULA

INDIAN OCEAN

Transantarctic Mountains

Vinson Massif

* South Pole

SOUTH PACIFIC OCEAN

Scott Base
McMurdo Station
* Mount Erebus
Dry Valleys

ROSS SEA

Dumont d'Urville

The Antarctic's enormous landmass, almost all of which is permanently covered with ice, is 1½ times the size of Canada. Mountains dominate the topography: the Transantarctic Mountains bisect the continent, and nearby is Mount Erebus, one of five active volcanoes.

On his way up the 16,067-foot (4,897-m) Vinson Massif, the highest peak on the bottom of the world, a climber (*left*) pauses to survey the vast Ronne Ice Shelf. Leaf fossils, such as these (*above*) found near the tip of the Antarctic Peninsula in the mid-1980's, supply evidence that a warmer climate existed as recently as 13 million years ago.

THE FRIGID ANTARCTIC

A place of unimaginable extremes, the Antarctic Desert and its ever-fluctuating canopy of clouds and clear sky have much to teach—not only about survival in the face of environmental adversity, but also about the world's weather patterns, its atmosphere, and activity in the solar system and beyond. The continent also holds in cold storage millions of years' worth of planetary secrets—clues, for example, to a long-gone Southern Hemisphere landmass called Gondwanaland—which understandably tantalize biologists, geologists, and other students of Earth.

The polar regions of both hemispheres were not always as icy and barren as they are today. Fossils of ferns, reptiles, and amphibians found early in this century seem to prove that Antarctica was once far warmer; fossils of trees dug up in the Arctic suggest that its climate was quite different also. To the untrained eye, all signs of a warmer, moister Antarctic Desert are gone. But paleobiologists are now examining rocky regions of Antarctica and using sophisticated drilling vessels to scour the depths of seabeds in the Antarctic Circle for limestone deposits of ancient foraminifera—shelled, single-celled marine invertebrates visible only under a microscope. These minuscule relics of the past—as well as other scientific discoveries in the vicinity of the South Pole—are providing exciting new clues to the dramatic geological and climatic changes that altered the deserts and other ecosystems of the Earth millions of years ago.

Geologists now believe that 200 million or more years ago Earth's continents were crushed into one super landmass, known as Pangaea. About 180 million years ago, as huge tectonic plates moved about on the surface of the globe, Pangaea began to split apart—at first by only centimeters each year. From its northern region would come a large continent, Laurasia, which would eventually split into present-day North America and Eurasia; from its southern portion arose Gondwanaland, which most likely had a subtropical climate, and gave rise to South America, Africa, India, Australia, and Antarctica. Over the course of millions of years, Africa and India moved away from South America, then from each other. The Himalayan mountains were formed when India collided with central Asia. The same sort of splitting occurred in the Northern Hemisphere: Europe and North America broke apart, leaving Iceland and Greenland in between.

Finally, Antarctica, Australia, and South America separated. In the process, tectonic collisions formed the crinkling that shaped South America's desert-topped Andes, as well as the mountains and volcanos of Antarctica. Only the tallest of these now poke above the surface of the ice cap; others are entombed beneath ice or coastal waters, under which lies evidence of an ancient land bridge that once connected the present polar desert to South America. After sliding to the southernmost region of the world and becoming surrounded by the sea, Antarctica began to cool off, perhaps by only 2 F degrees (a little more than 1 C degree) every million years. Great ice sheets began to build up about 3 million years ago, and most forms of life were eventually obliterated by the glaciation. Unlike the animals of the Arctic—which have long migrated across land to warmer, more southerly territory—most Antarctic reptiles, mammals, and plants were doomed to extinction on the isolated, frozen desert island.

Today Antarctica covers 5.4 million square miles (14 million sq km)—one-tenth of Earth's land surface. When vast areas of the surrounding sea water freeze in winter, the sea ice spreads to cover an additional 7.3 million square miles (19 million sq km)—all of which is icebound desert. During this season, Antarctica is larger than all the other continents except Asia and Africa.

The largest of Antarctica's 68 research sites, the sprawling U.S. facility at McMurdo Station (*above*) houses up to 1,200 scientists and technicians during the summer. After several mishaps, a nuclear power plant built near Mount Erebus was shut down.

Workers load construction materials (*left*) at Dumont d'Urville, a French base on the continent's Indian Ocean coast. Environmental groups opposed the building of a 5,600-foot-long (1,100-meter) airstrip, fearing long-term harm to wildlife.

A Polar Research Station

Today, Antarctica is the world's largest scientific laboratory. Eighteen nations operate 68 research stations on the desert continent, and 42 of them are occupied 12 months a year. Among those strung around Antarctica's fringe are the Italian base at Terra Nova Bay; France's Dumont D'Urville base; and Syowa, operated by Japan. Other bases—such as China's Chang Chen, or Great Wall; Britain's Signy; and Poland's Arctowski—lie on outlying islands. The U.S. Amundsen-Scott base at the South Pole and the Russian Vostok base, about 800 miles (1,290 km) away at the geomagnetic pole, are the continent's innermost facilities and are operated year-round. In all, about 1,500 people spend the winter in Antarctica; in summer the multinational population doubles that number.

The largest establishment in the Antarctic is McMurdo station, constructed on bare volcanic rock on the edge of Hut Point Peninsula. The U.S. research facility overlooks McMurdo Sound, named in 1841 for Archibald McMurdo, the navigator of an early British expedition headed by Sir James Clark Ross. Each spring, after icebreakers open the harbor, a navy container ship arrives loaded with tons of food and supplies, and a tanker brings millions of gallons of fuel. Then come the scientists and support personnel, by ship or aboard C-141 Hercules transport planes that land either on a strip located on the neighboring Ross Ice Shelf or on another strip smoothed on top of nearby sea ice. In the summer months, the station—which was established in 1955—is transformed into a humming, busy community isolated by more than 2,100 miles (3,400 km) of frigid sea and ice from the nearest town—Invercargill in New Zealand.

In the peak summer months, about 1,200 people arrive at McMurdo Station. Waiting for them is a polar metropolis of 90 buildings, including several dormitories and working laboratories, a water-distillation plant, radio shacks, a chapel, and a firehouse. Modern conveniences, such as electricity, telephone lines, up-to-date plumbing, stores, and a post office, are calculated to make life—and scientific investigation—possible in an ecosystem where humans are aliens.

Despite the best attempts to re-create the comforts of home, the fact remains that life is a struggle in the bitterly

Adélies (*left*), the most abundant species of penguin in Antarctica, are frequent visitors to Esperanza, an Argentinian base at Hope Bay.

cold Antarctic—as well as half a world away in the Arctic. In both places, bitter temperatures, weak sunlight, and sheer isolation can wreak havoc on both body and mind. The polar regions are ferociously cold because, being the farthest points from the Equator, they receive less of the Sun's energy overall than any place on Earth. Intense heat is out of the question—even during the short summers—because the Sun's rays strike the polar deserts at such an oblique angle that the solar energy received is greatly reduced. In its slanting path to the Poles, light must travel through much more of the atmosphere—the thick, filtering screen that cloaks the planet—than it does when it shines directly overhead at the Equator. Further, because of the Earth's tilt in relationship to the Sun, both the Arctic and the Antarctic receive very little sunlight during their long, predominantly dark winters.

The polar chill is exacerbated by the fact that these regions—and many of the deserts at the world's highest elevations—are largely covered with ice and snow. This frozen water—which keeps the available moisture down and aridity up—reflects 80 to 95 percent of the solar radiation received by Antarctica. By contrast, water, soil, and rocks absorb 80 to 90 percent of the energy in the sunlight that hits them. By radiating so much back into space, the ice-sheathed Antarctic actually loses more heat than it gains, except during its 3-month summer. Warm air from the temperate zone and from the surrounding ocean keeps the continent from getting progressively colder.

For those who overwinter at Antarctic bases, the stresses of cold, darkness, and separation from the rest of the world are compounded by the minimal sizes of work and living spaces. This is a result of the inaccessibility of building materials and the necessity for heat conservation. Tight quarters means little privacy; yet at the bottom of the Earth, loneliness can strike even in a cramped room. Some who stay through the Antarctic winters develop what is called "big eye," which has been defined as "a 12-foot stare in a 10-foot room." There are stories of men breaking under the stress: a worker who killed his chess opponent with an ax, and a staff doctor who burned down his clinic as winter approached so he would be sent home. Early expeditions carried straitjackets as part of their standard equipment.

The Robot Named Dante

In early 1993, the so-called "nerve cord" of one Antarctic explorer literally snapped—but a trip to a space agency repair shop, rather than hospitalization, was prescribed. Dante, an eight-legged robot that stands more than 8 feet (240 cm) tall and stretches nearly 10 feet (250 cm), from front to back, was paralyzed inside the rim of a belching volcano named Mount Erebus, while a -55° F (-48° C) wind chill enveloped the crest of the mountain. The robot was named for the medieval Italian poet Dante Alighieri, author of *The Divine Comedy*. This 14th-century masterpiece follows Dante's imaginary descent into the dark inferno of Erebus—the mythical hell named by the classical Greeks—and his journey into purgatory and heaven.

The star player in NASA's landmark U.S. $2 million research mission had just begun to creep down on all

Finding kinks in one of the fiberoptic cables of a robot named Dante (*above*), scientists were forced to scrap the arachnidal robot's probe of the volcanic cone of Mount Erebus in 1993.

A human explorer (*right*) plumbs a crater near the summit of 12,448-foot (3794-m) Mount Erebus, the world's southernmost active volcano.

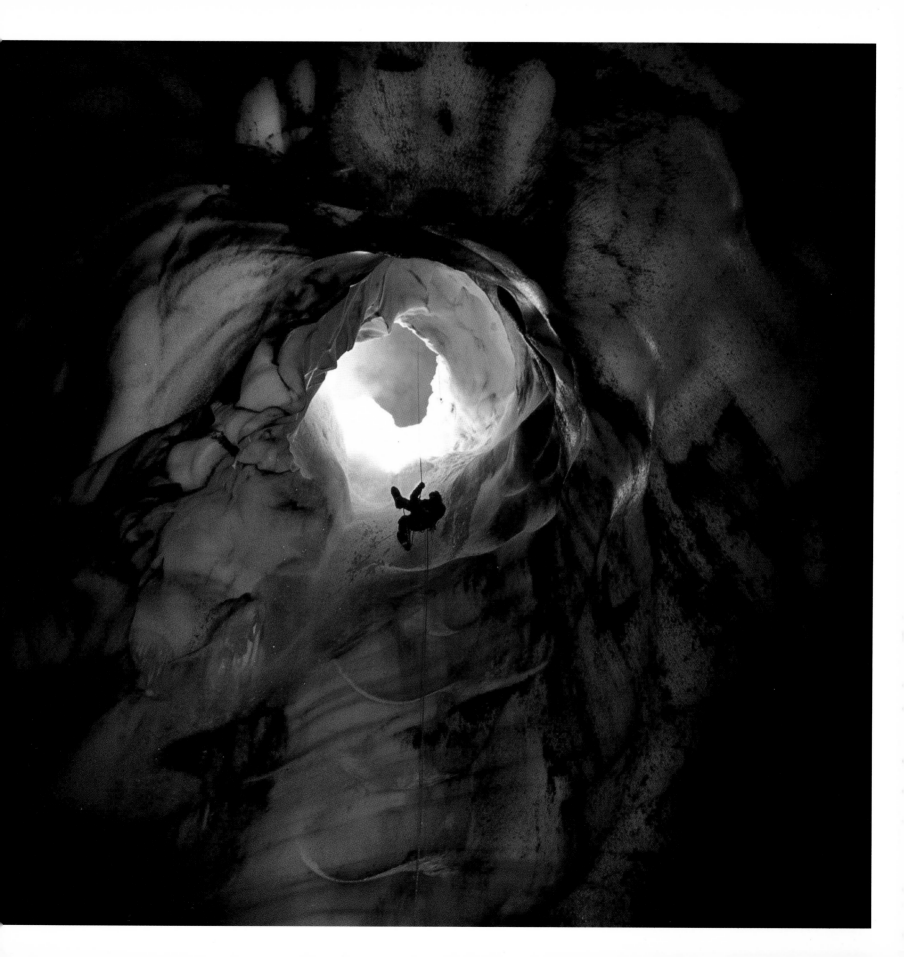

POLAR OZONE HOLE

In October 1992 the ozone hole over the South Pole reached as far north as the tip of South America. Many scientists believe a worldwide phaseout of ozone-depleting chlorofluorocarbons (CFC's)—chlorine-containing chemicals used in aerosols and coolants—by the year 2000 will lead to a steady replenishment in atmospheric ozone.

Ozone, harmful when breathed at the Earth's surface, at higher altitudes protects life by absorbing ultraviolet rays that otherwise would cause skin cancer in humans and kill sea plankton, one of the basic links in the food chain.

A weather balloon launched from McMurdo Station in Antarctica helps scientists understand natural causes of ozone fluctuation, including air currents, volcanic eruptions, and solar wind, as well as depletion wrought by CFC's.

Scientists first reported on the ozone hole—actually more a thin spot than a hole—over Antarctica in 1985, after measuring steady declines since the late 1970's. The depletion typically begins to appear in the stratosphere, some 12 miles (19 km) up, during late August, the end of winter in the Southern Hemisphere. It peaks in early October, and ozone begins to increase again in November.

Why does the ozone hole form over the South Pole? Scientists point to two combined phenomena of the dark, frigid Antarctic winters. One is the polar vortex, a strong, circular wind believed to trap CFC's. At the same time, icy crystals in stratospheric clouds trap and store chlorine molecules. When winter ends and sunlight starts approaching the Pole, its light frees the chlorine, which in turn breaks up ozone molecules.

eights into the 755-foot-deep (230-m) inner crater of Mount Erebus, which rises 12,434 feet (3,790 m) from the desert floor of Ross Island in McMurdo Sound. Suddenly, kink after kink developed in one of Dante's two lengthy fiberoptic cables, which acted as tethers in addition to linking it to its "brain," or computerized power and information base. One of the weakened kinks became severed, and the robot's mission was scrubbed.

Dante followed in the unsuccessful footsteps of geologists and volcanologists who had previously attempted to descend into the mountain's crater. A 1974 team of French, American, and New Zealand scientists were met by an eruption and canceled their plans. Some of them returned 4 years later and used a strong rope to lower a man into the crater. As he dangled just 98 feet (30 m) from the floor, a hail of rocks and gases erupted all around him and threw small volcanic bombs up near those on the rim of the crater. The scientist was swiftly hauled up on a rope that was only scorched, and his trousers were only slightly burned.

Frustrated twice, New Zealander Philip R. Kyle and his cohorts turned to NASA, which hopes someday to put robots on the Moon and Mars. The agency commissioned a team of robotics engineers to design and build a robot suitable for the job of trekking into the smoldering belly of Mount Erebus. Its task would be to do what no human had yet accomplished—collect rock specimens and take measurements of gases spewing from the fumaroles, or vents, of a smoldering lava lake in the crater, where temperatures can reach 1427° F (800° C).

Because there was not enough time to repair Dante's cable before winter arrived in Antarctica, the robot was shipped back to the United States and there awaited its next assignment: an exploratory trip into the crater of Alaska's 11,100-foot (3,383-m) Mount Spurr, a desert-topped volcano that erupted three times during 1992 and poses a threat to the city of Anchorage.

For millennia, people traveled to the southernmost continent in the comfort of their unbridled imaginations. Among the ancient Greeks, speculation abounded about a land called *Antichthones,* at the far end of the Earth; it was, some believed, guarded by ghoulish creatures and encircled by a boiling ocean. The native peoples of New Zealand, the Maori, tell of a legendary mariner named Ui-te-Rangiora, who sailed in a war canoe as far south as the frozen ocean. And for centuries European maps showed a mysterious place at the bottom of the Earth, *terra australis incognita* ("unknown southern land").

A Crop of Krill

The first documented crossing of the Antarctic Circle was on January 17, 1773, by British navigator Capt. James Cook, during his second voyage to the southern waters. Despite his proximity, Cook never sighted the edge of the desert continent, being kept at bay by masses of drifting ice. After circumnavigating the southern reaches of the world's oceans, Cook correctly surmised that there must be "a tract of land near the Pole, which is the source of all the ice spread over this vast Southern Ocean."

In the 1790's a wave of explorers descended upon coastal Antarctica. There, for the first time, people encountered the wealth of aquatic life along the edge of the desert continent and in its surrounding ocean desert environment. The surging, stormy oceans offer a more stable habitat than does the land, as well as far more sources of food for the birds and mammals of the region. Infinite quantities of plankton swirled about by the ever-

raging sea supply sustenance for krill, tiny 1.5-inch-long (38-mm) creatures resembling shrimp that proliferate so fast that they are the most abundant animal in the world. Swarms of krill covering 170 square miles (440 sq km) and containing an estimated 2 million tons of protein have been found off Antarctica's coast. Swimming among the plankton and the krill, and in some cases feeding on them, are 120 species of fish, many native only to Antarctic waters.

All of these species are inhabitants of an astonishing sort of desert. Like many parts of the world's oceans where precipitation is scant or is solidified as ice or snow, the oceans off most of the coast of Antarctica (and much of the Arctic Ocean as well) are technically arid. Thus, these regions are true deserts. Deserts at sea, like those on land, sometimes receive more precipitation than the 15-inch (381-mm) general rule of thumb for desert classification, but the rate of evaporation in these places exceeds precipitation.

The great age of Antarctic exploration began in the mid-1890's, after a 50-year hiatus during which Arctic expeditions were in vogue. The Sixth International Geographical Congress, which convened in London in 1895, decreed that "exploration of the Antarctic regions is the greatest piece of geographical exploration still to be undertaken before the end of the century." Leading off was an ill-fated expedition that sailed from Antwerp in 1897. The crew aboard the *Belgica* was a motley one, composed partly of Norwegians, including 25-year-old Roald Amundsen. Later he would head the first team to reach the South Pole, and go on to discover the Northwest Passage—a corridor through the Arctic Ocean that connects the Atlantic and the Pacific.

The *Belgica*'s trip was not easy. In the fall of 1898 the ship became hostage to the ice in the Bellingshausen Sea. Trapped as winter approached, it drifted about enshrouded in darkness throughout the coldest months of the year, and remained entangled in the bay on into the following fall. Scurvy was rampant, and the darkness and isolation drove a number of the sailors insane. A penguin- and seal-meat diet pulled the crew

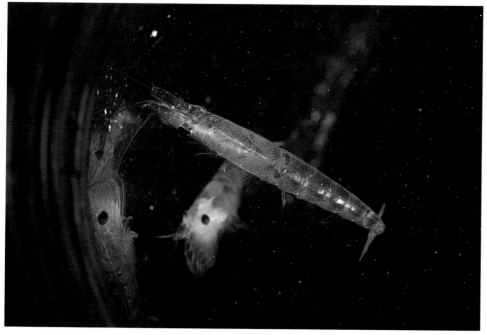

A crucial link in the food chain, eight-legged, thumb-length krill eat phytoplankton that grow in the sea ice around Antarctica. The crustaceans, numbering in the trillions, support other marine animals.

through the 12 terror-filled months, and they were actually able to make substantial climatic observations that assisted later expeditions.

Hardy Flora and Fauna

Expeditions, science, and the natural world are inextricably linked in the polar and alpine deserts. As teams of newcomers trekked ever onward toward the interior and around the perimeter of Antarctica, a new world of desert flora and fauna opened up to them.

Only two species of flowering plants live in this cold desert—one a homely bit of greenery that lives up to its plain name, bundle, or hair, grass; the other, the low-growing Antarctic pink, or pearlwort. Both survive in small clumps only on the relatively warm Antarctic peninsula that faces the sunnier north and is called the "banana belt." The earliest of these seeds were probably brought to the continent centuries ago, on the wings of birds flying in from South America's Patagonian Desert. Fertilized by birds and moistened by meltwater, bundle grass makes it through a yearly growth cycle partly because it can begin photosynthesis while still covered by snow.

A considerable variety of non-flowering plants thrive in Antarctica: 50 species of mosses, 350 species of lichens, and—along the coasts—350 species of algae. Lichens survive, growing mainly on rocks, because their snail-paced metabolism allows them to remain dormant during winter,

Clumps of hair grass (*right, above*) and a dense, cushionlike herb called *pink* (*center*) grow side by side on rocky King George Island off the coast of the Antarctic Peninsula. They are the only two flowering plants found below 60° South Latitude.

Hardy survivors, reddish lichens thrive on the stones of King George Island. A union of algae and fungi, Antarctic lichens face virtually no competition from other plants and can live thousands of years. They require little water and go dormant in winter.

the driest time of year. They reach their peak rates of photosynthesis and respiration in the late spring, when they pull trace amounts of water vapor out of the air and store it. In addition, being mostly black enables them to absorb the maximum amount of heat. And they save energy by being very slow growers, increasing in size less than 0.02 inch (0.5 mm) a year. At that rate, a lichen measuring 10 inches (25 cm) could be 500 years old. Biologists think that there are individual plants on Antarctica dating back 4,000 years. Lichens called cryptoendoliths—a name that means "hidden in rock"—insert themselves just under the surface of sandstone rocks, where they form black, white, and green stripes. There, frigid desert life is more tolerable, as temperatures can be 20 and more F degrees (11 C degrees) warmer within a rock than on its surface—and more humid as well.

Mosses also adapt well to Antarctica's coldness and aridity. One form produces more energy at low light levels just above freezing than at warmer temperatures. Because of the brutal polar climate, moss beds are seldom more than 4 inches (10 cm) deep. They grow in dense clumps, which not only helps them collect moisture but also reduces evaporation. As an aid to survival, some mosses produce a chemical, much like an antibiotic, that prevents lichens from colonizing on top of the beds and smothering the mosses.

Like its plants, Antarctica's land animals are limited to a few tiny creatures. The largest is a midge, *Belgica antarctica,* that can grow as long as 0.5 inch (13 mm). The rest are even smaller—a collection of lesser midges, nematodes, rotifers, and other invertebrates that live in the soil or huddled in plants, or in crevices that turn into tiny streams of meltwater in the summer. Like the plants, they have adapted to survive. Freezing of their structures is the great enemy. Some midges are engineered so that ice crystals form between the cells rather than inside them, and the cells are thus kept from exploding when frozen. Most of the tiny arthropods produce an antifreeze, called glycerol, so their body fluids remain liquid even when the temperature drops to -30° F (-34° C).

Few people venture to Antarctica who do not marvel at its animal population. Although several species of seabirds breed on the continent, including the graceful, swooping Antarctic skua and the Antarctic petrel, the trademark of the world's southernmost animal kingdom is

Petrels fly past an ice cliff in Bransfield Strait (*top*). The densely feathered, web-footed scavengers of the coast are called "stinkers" because of a foul oil they emit when disturbed.

Penguin breeding season means good eating for skuas (*above*) near a rookery on Ross Island. Skuas prey on penguin chicks at hatching time and switch to fish and krill the rest of the year.

the penguin. Waddling and flightless, these birds lost their ability to use their wings millions of years ago when the continent was on the move and heading for its polar isolation. Of the few penguin species that live and produce their young on Antarctica, the most numerous are the smaller Adélies. They congregate by the thousands on the ice near the shore, wobbling about and chattering, then toboggan toward the shore on their chest feathers, splashing into the water to feed. Paddling furiously, they can quickly pop back up onto the shore as if by levitation.

Larger and more stately are the emperors, penguins that stand 4 feet (120 cm) tall and weigh about 65 pounds (30 kg). Their size allows them to follow one of nature's strangest breeding and egg-incubation cycles. The females lay their large eggs in early winter, then go off to sea to feed while the males are left to incubate the eggs. As winter's ferocious windstorms and blizzards whirl past, the caretakers balance the eggs on their feet to protect them from the chill of the ice cap. During this grueling ordeal the males lose a substantial portion of their body weight, but most survive by living off a rich layer of fat stored under their skin. So do the chicks, which molt and then reach independence in spring and summer, when some of the great sheet of winter sea ice has broken up. Then, the edge of the sea is nearer and its waters are teeming with food. Were the chicks born later, they would never be mature enough to survive the next winter.

Rich layers of fat—similar to those that allow the male emperors to make it through the winter while cradling eggs—are also the key to the survival of seals and ten species of whales that live on or migrate to the bitterly cold desert shores of Antarctica. The region is the permanent home of four species of Antarctic seals: the Weddell, the leopard, the Ross, and the crabeater. All have cushions of fat under their skin to ward off the cold, as do two other species—elephant seals and fur seals—that periodically wander south into Antarctic waters. So effective is this insulation that Weddell seals can live under sea ice all winter—eating fish, squid, and crustacea—all the while chewing at the ice to keep open the blowholes needed for breathing. After birth, their pups go from the warmth of their mothers' bodies—about 99° F (37° C)—into air temperatures hovering around 0° F (-18° C), and begin to swim in about a month.

Fatal Race to the Pole

To this day, Antarctica remains the object of affection and obsession for many, scientists and explorers alike. Two of the most tenacious and immortalized South Pole devotees were Robert Falcon Scott—who, in 1901, stood at the helm of the Antarctic-bound ship *Discovery*—and his colleague Ernest Henry Shackleton. After overwintering at

Emperor penguins (*left*) on Ross Island display the charming behavior that makes them favorites of humans. They can grow up to 4 feet (120 cm) tall.

A female fur seal (*above*) takes a pup under her flipper. Thick, two-layered coats that help conserve heat also explain why they were hunted to near extinction.

McMurdo Bay, the two men and a naturalist named Wilson made the first attempt to reach the South Pole. They failed, and staggered back to the ship half dead from exhaustion and scurvy.

Enamored like Scott of Antarctica and the Pole, Shackleton returned in 1907 to try again and once more failed, then mounted yet another expedition in 1914. This time his ship, the *Endurance,* had hardly entered the Weddell Sea, where a first base was to be established, when it became locked in the ice. So began one of the great sagas of Antarctic exploration. Slowly but inexorably the ice crushed the ship, reducing it to a mass of splinters. Shackleton and his men were forced to camp for months on the dangerous, shifting pack ice. At last the pack shifted northward toward open water. Shackleton and his men had saved the lifeboats, which they now launched into the sea, and managed to reach barren Elephant Island. From there, Shackleton sailed one of the boats 900 miles (1,451 km) through raging storms to South Georgia Island, the site of a Norwegian whaling station, to get help. It took some months for a ship to get through the ice to Elephant Island and rescue the rest of Shackleton's

The inside of Scott's hut (*above*) on Ross Island is much the way he left it 8 decades ago during his fatal polar expedition. The original dining table, saddles, and pantry—now a British historical monument—have been used by later explorers.

A blizzard on Cape Evans (*below*) engulfs the wooden hut that was the base for British explorer Robert F. Scott's ill-fated 1911 race to the South Pole. Scott made the pole, but not before Roald Amundsen of Norway. Demoralized, Scott and his four-man crew died on the return trip.

party. Throughout the entire 2-year ordeal, however, not one of the men died.

Meanwhile the competitive Scott had mounted another campaign, sailing back to McMurdo and trying again to reach the Pole. Setting out on November 1, 1911, he and his team of four men marched inland with ponies and dogs carrying supplies. Reach the South Pole they did—only to find there a Norwegian flag and a shelter tent left by Amundsen about a month before, on December 14, 1911. "The worst has happened," Scott wrote in his diary, "the Norwegians are first at the Pole." The rest, of course, is tragedy. One of Scott's men soon died in a fall. Another, his frozen feet turning gangrenous, intentionally allowed himself to freeze to death. On March 19 the remaining three men were trapped by a blizzard only 11 miles (18 km) from a cache of supplies. Their bodies were recovered the following November along with Scott's diary.

Peaceable Kingdom

Even before the heroic age of Antarctic exploration and discovery, the continent had been literally divided up like a pie, with a host of nations making often conflicting territorial claims; among them were Argentina, Australia, Chile, France, Great Britain, Norway, and New Zealand. Instead of vying with one another, however, these countries and others have for the most part cooperated, coordinating their scientific studies. The history-making first multi-nation International Polar Year (IPY) was held as early as 1882–83, during which time 12 countries established 14 bases to study climate and Earth's magnetism. A second IPY was held 50 years later, in 1932–33. It was so successful that an international council of scientists decided to hold another and to do it in a more timely manner. This turned into the celebrated International Geophysical Year of 1957–58, during which 40 stations were set up on the continent and 20 more on the Antarctic islands, staffed by scientists from no less than 67 different nations. The United States established a permanent base at the Pole; the Russians, one at the most remote spot on the continent, the Pole of Inaccessibility; and a British and New Zealand team made the first land crossing of Antarctica via the Pole.

Further cooperation led to the conception of an Antarctic Treaty, which was ratified in 1961. The main points of the agreement state that "Antarctica shall be used for peaceful purposes only" and that scientific coordination would continue. It was followed in 1991 with an appended protocol in which the 26 countries active in the area committed themselves to doing everything possible to protect the delicate Antarctic ecosystem—and to clean up the waste dumps that had accumulated after decades of exploration and study in this unparalleled desert.

Arctic's Surprising Variety

Past rain forests and sizzling hot deserts, 12,000 miles (19,350 km) from the South Pole, lies Ellesmere Island, the tenth largest island on Earth and a land frosted in most spots with a 0.5-mile-thick (805-m) mantle of ice. This chunk of Canada rising from the frigid Arctic Ocean is also the site of 8,500-foot (2,600-m) mountains, the southerly exposed rocky faces of which radiate the Sun's heat to the tundra plains beneath towering glaciers. Alongside Lake Hazen, in the north, a virtual thermal oasis is formed as warmth from the mountains joins forces with heat reflected from the predominantly ice-covered lake. Less than 4 inches (102 mm) of precipitation falls yearly, so Ellesmere is truly a desert island; and here, as in every arid corner of the globe, one can always expect the unexpected.

A team of dogs pulls a sled across the frozen flats of Baffin Island in the Northwest Territories of Canada. A well-trained sled pack can run at 20 miles per hour (32 kph).

On this northernmost extension of the North American continent, for example, air temperatures can span a full 140-F-degree (78-C-degree) range between winter and summer—from -70° F (-57° C) to an occasional balmy 70° F (21° C)—because of relatively warm water currents that flow north from the Atlantic alongside the west coast of Greenland and to points beyond. There is not a tree in sight for more than 1,000 miles (1,600 km)—southward past the Arctic Circle—but while the late

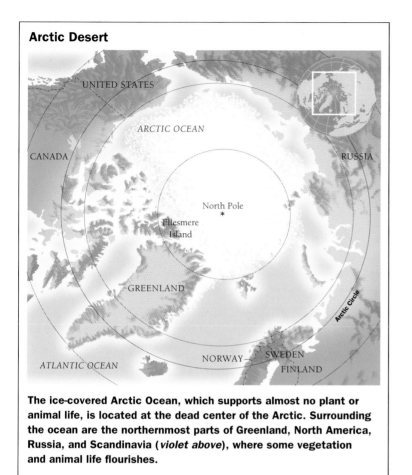

Arctic Desert

The ice-covered Arctic Ocean, which supports almost no plant or animal life, is located at the dead center of the Arctic. Surrounding the ocean are the northernmost parts of Greenland, North America, Russia, and Scandinavia (*violet above*), where some vegetation and animal life flourishes.

spring thaw is still underway, the emerging ground begins to blossom, as does the ground in most of the world's tundra lands. First to burst forth on Ellesmere are the tiny but flamboyant petals of the seemingly fragile purple saxifrage. Shortly after, silver catkins on the creeping Arctic willow emerge; eventually, they metamorphose into yellow and orange, enlivening with color the muted backdrop of lichens and spongy brown and green tundra.

Ellesmore once teemed with alligators, snakes, lizards, and flying lemurs—but that was millions of years ago, when Earth's warm climate made this a land of forests and swamps. Now, as in other tundra lands, it is the chilly desert home of seven species of mammals: musk oxen; Arctic hares, foxes, and wolves; caribou; collared lemmings; and ermine. Many of these animals are plagued by the vast clouds of bloodthirsty mosquitoes and flies that swarm over the island in summer, as they do throughout much of the polar region. But one of the least bothersome insects on Ellesmere is one of the most curious bumblebees in the world—the Arctic's own *Bombus polaris.*

Warm Belly of the Bumblebee Queen

About midnight, just 2 days after the summer solstice, University of Vermont biologist Bernd Heinrich grabbed a hand-held insect thermometer and set out into the desert on a hunt for the Arctic bumblebees. His mission, in the season's perpetual daylight, was to take the body temperatures of the queen bees. Fuzzy and striped with yellow and

Lake Hazen (*left*), on Ellesmere Island northwest of Greenland, is mostly frozen. Along its coast, warmer conditions allow the blooming of 100 flower species.

Sporting its grayish summer coat, an Arctic fox (*right*) patiently stalks its prey. Foxes, often trapped for their fur, feed on lemmings and scraps left by polar bears. The collared lemming (*far right*) population rises and falls with regularity every 3 or 4 years, as do those of its predators.

black bands, the females—collecting pollen from the purple saxifrage flowers—flew erratically above the snow, and hovered now and then with their short wings flapping more than 150 times a second. It is their way not only of staying aloft but also of warming themselves while exercising their flight muscles.

Heinrich, who studies thermoregulation in insects, believes that since mated *Bombus polaris* females are the only members of their species to survive Arctic winters, they have a built-in mechanism for accelerating egg production after they emerge from their dormant state in spring. *Bombus polaris* queens have adapted to the Polar climate and can shunt the heat generated by wing-flapping and shivering to their abdomens. On other bee safaris, Heinrich had checked the body temperatures of bumblebees in warmer climates; there, the insects have much lower abdominal temperatures than do the females in the Arctic. Hot bellies give these polar desert insects a jump start on egg production, enabling them to squeeze the life cycles of their offspring into the short Arctic summers.

Polar bumblebees, like this drone collecting nectar from a dandelion, fight the cold by rapidly beating their wings to produce heat. The warmth is then transferred to their abdomens, which have higher temperatures than those of bumblebees in hotter climates.

Seasons of the Tundra

Arid tundra lands, like Ellesmere Island, fringe the northernmost parts of Asia, Europe, and North America. Wrapping around the edges of the icy Arctic Ocean basin and lining most of the coast of ice-capped Greenland, tundra covers 5 million square miles (13 million sq km) throughout the Arctic lands. In the semidarkness of winter, most of these lands are blanketed in ice or snow and lashed by fierce winds that have nothing but unencumbered expanses standing in their way. During the spring thaw, three-fifths of the Arctic Desert land surface becomes ice-free. Much of the tundra is transformed into a marshy, waterlogged region dotted with boggy lakes and ponds of standing water formed from meltwater. Because the ground below the permafrost is permanently frozen, this water has little opportunity to drain.

Although birds like snowy owls and snow buntings stay in arid tundra territory all winter, migratory waterfowl and other birds—bramblings, redpolls, and siskins—fill the skies as temperatures rise and the spring vegetation and insects emerge. Animals on foot, like wolverines, mink, coyotes, moose, caribou or reindeer, and elk, return north from their respective winter residences in the taiga, the grand—and more humid—coniferous forests that encircle the globe south of the tundra.

Because of the harsh Arctic climate, the diversity of species in the Arctic tundra and the more icy regions toward the North Pole is limited, and the biological food chain is a fragile one. If a harsh winter claims the lives of an extraordinary number of small, plant-eating mammals, for example, it will drastically reduce the food supply for larger, carnivorous predators.

Winter chill is not the only cause of large-scale die-offs. In periods of abundant vegetation, for example, the furry-footed, short-tailed rodents called lemmings may produce 4 or 5 litters—often more than 25 offspring—in a year. When their numbers soar and starvation threatens

Like most polar plants, yellow Arctic poppies (*above*) mature and produce seeds twice as fast as their temperate counterparts.

Hilly upheavals called pingos (*left*) occur in the tundra when underground water freezes and expands, forcing terrain upward. Quilted patterns, or polygons, are formed when frost causes a patch of ground to swell laterally, pushing large stones outward.

Short-legged Arctic musk-oxen (*above*) are kept warm by their shaggy manes, which sometimes freeze to the ground. When threatened by wolves, the adults encircle their calves, displaying bony horns that fan ominously across their foreheads.

Both male and female walruses, shown here on a shore rock (*right*), have tusks that they use to root clams and other shellfish from the ocean floor. The Inuit have long depended on the flesh and hides of the animals, which can grow to 2 tons (1,800 kg).

local populations, lemmings instinctively begin huge migrations across the frozen lands. Contrary to legend, they do not commit mass suicide by flinging themselves off cliffs into the sea. They do, however, travel en masse in search of food, stopping at nothing. Thousands die crossing lakes or bogs, and often there are few survivors. In turn, the populations of lemming predators—Arctic foxes, wolves, weasels, and snowy owls—are affected. They face death, too, unless they move on to other hunting grounds when their tiny food sources drown or freeze to death.

The largest tundra-dwelling animals—the shaggy, horned musk oxen—live there all year. During the last ice age these animals evolved a protective, dual-layer coat of fur, but members of the herd—about 30 animals—also warm up by standing in a circle, side by side with their heads pointing outward. Encircling their young in the same formation, the adults protect their calves from predaceous Arctic wolves, but human hunters have come upon circles of musk oxen and gunned down entire herds in a matter of minutes. By the early 20th century, these 440- to 880-pound (200- to 400-kg) animals were hunted to extinction in Alaska and nearly so in northern Canada, around Hudson Bay. Conservation measures have enabled them to proliferate again, however, and a quarter million are now estimated to exist throughout the Arctic regions.

Living on Thick Ice

Unlike the uninhabited Antarctic, the band of arid lands that encircles the globe above the tree line has long been home to peoples of diverse ethnic groups. Some 100,000 Inuit, descendents of the Asians who migrated across the Bering Strait during the last ice age, today inhabit the tundra and parts of the perpetually ice-covered lands of the northernmost desert reaches of the Western Hemisphere. Inuit communities are scattered from the coastlands of Greenland, across northern Canada, and into the north and west regions of Alaska. From there, directly across the Bering Strait, is the Chukchi Peninsula, home of some 1,500 Inuit who live on the continent of their ancestors, in northeastern Siberia.

In the Arctic desert lands—where year-round plants are scarce—sea and land mammals, birds, and fish are critical components of indigenous peoples' lives. In age-old Inuit tradition, whales were hunted from long boats called umiaks, which held crews of eight. Such risk on the open seas was worth it: one 60-ton whale could feed more than

Polar bears prowl the pack ice along the west coast of Hudson Bay, seeking seal, a favorite food. Streamlined, with a small head and long neck, the agile polar bear is an excellent swimmer and can jump from the water to an ice shelf with a 100-pound (45-kg) seal in its mouth.

DESERT DISGUISES

Many desert creatures are endowed with camouflaging techniques to make themselves less obvious to predators. The coloration patterns of some animals and insects are different from those of other members of the same species. These color shifts can occur when identical creatures live within a few miles of each other. Tiger beetles living on black-pebbled streambeds, for example, are black, while the same species when found on mottled sands are splotched with brown, bluish-black, and tan.

Disruptive coloration is designed more to confuse predators than to conceal prey. The distinctive patterns of the giraffe and the zebra perform this function, helping them to elude lions. When hunting, a lion focuses on the spots of a giraffe or the stripes of a zebra rather than on the animal's outline. Stripes and spots are particularly hard to see in the fading light of dusk, when lions are most likely to attack.

A few creatures are able to change color to match their backgrounds. Horned lizards take on lighter or darker tones when moving in and out of sunlight. The willow ptarmigan (*opposite page, bottom right*), an Arctic bird, molts three times a year, switching feather colors from brown or black to white to match the season.

Camouflage can help predators as well as prey. The sidewinding adder of the Namib Desert hunts by burrowing into a soft dune, leaving only its pebbly eyes above the surface as it waits for an unsuspecting lizard. Polar bears' white coats make them hard to see against the Arctic ice pack.

Geometric spots on the western diamondback rattlesnake (above) mimic the stony ground of its dry North American habitat, helping to compensate for its conspicuous length of up to 7 feet (2 m). Heat-sensing pits on their heads let rattlers detect warm-blooded prey.

Part of the background, a group of lions (left) hides in a stand of dry grass, eyeing quarry in the Kalahari Desert. Slow, deliberate stalkers, lions approach, then freeze, choosing the ideal moment to spring; one in six attacks usually succeeds.

If threatened, the pichi (top), a South American member of the armadillo family, retracts its feet and pulls its earth-toned shell tight against the ground.

A willow ptarmigan (above), barely visible in the Arctic snow, changes plumage—from brown to white—to fit the season.

Fillets dry on a line at a fishing camp in Nachvak Fiord in Labrador. For generations, the Inuit people have relied on the sea's abundant cod, salmon, trout, and Arctic char. Many Inuit are now commercial fishers.

Caribou, known as reindeer in Europe and Asia, ford a river in Alaska. Buoyed by hollow hair, which also affords insulation, and using broad, flexible hooves as paddles, caribou are marathon swimmers.

a dozen hunters and their families for a year. Caribou were also pursued by groups of hunters: one team would drive a herd into a lake, where another waited in kayaks to spear them. Meat was shared with other villagers, and all parts of the carcasses were used. Hides were used as blankets, or cut and laced into clothing or coverings for sleds or kayaks. Knives were made from walrus tusks, harpoon tips either from walrus tusks or caribou antlers. Walrus stomachs were used as air-filled buoys to keep harpoons afloat and to mark the position of speared seals. The Inuit used nets to snag birds as well as to catch fish, mainly salmon. The bravest of Inuit hunters went after the dangerous and highly prized polar bear.

Twentieth century technology, education, and instant communication with peoples to their south have added a new twist on life for modern Inuit, who were formerly known as Eskimos, as they have for other desert peoples in the Eurasian Arctic. Some Inuit still hunt, but now skimobiles and outboard motors are often favored over kayaks and dogsleds. As prefabricated government housing has replaced the traditional sod homes and igloos, so

Inuit women pass a quiet time in Uelen, a fishing village on the Siberian side of the Bering Strait. One of a very few Inuit settlements in the Siberian Arctic, the hamlet features an ivory carving factory, where walrus tusks are crafted.

store-bought clothes have replaced skins and furs, and television satellite dishes are becoming a part of the Arctic landscape as well.

The sprawling Arctic lands of northernmost Siberia are inhabited by more than 300,000 people, representing at least a dozen ethnic groups. The lives of the last Siberians to succumb to Russian rule, the Chukchis, focus on the sea. Hunters of whales, walruses, and other marine animals, they inhabit the frigid Arctic lands on the far eastern peninsula of the same name. They call themselves the "people of the long spring," for springtime is their "long day." For them, a new year commences on the day when their winter of darkness is interrupted by sunlight over the southern horizon.

Today, many indigenous peoples across the far northern reaches of Siberia—the Yukaghir, Dolgan, and Nenets, for example—as well as the Lapps, or Saami, of Scandinavia, lead lives that revolve around domesticated reindeer herding. In the winter, children are often sent to boarding schools in the towns and cities of the tundra, while adults remain in the rural areas.

HIGH AND DRY

People and animals who live in or travel through the world's highest deserts—on snow- and ice-covered mountaintops or along slopes of alpine tundra—are up against the brutalizing effects of a natural hostile environment. The yak is the highest-dwelling mammal in the world and will rarely descend below 14,000 feet (4,300 m) in its wild state. Like most alpine animals, yaks have dark-colored fur that absorbs heat and blocks harmful ultraviolet rays.

With increasing elevation there is a significant rise in the amount of solar radiation present. There, the sun's rays have less atmosphere to pass through and become blinding, desiccating, and dangerous. At high altitudes the air thins dramatically, and oxygen levels are severely reduced. People often have difficulty breathing at 10,000 feet (3,048 m), and at 18,000 feet (5,486 m) physical exertion can be excruciatingly uncomfortable to those who are not aerobically fit. At 24,000 feet (7,315 m) people may hallucinate and pass out quickly if not rigorously trained to withstand oxygen deprivation; most will die of

anoxia, or excessively low oxygen levels in the body. Some people who live at high elevations have adapted to the severe conditions by producing a greater number of red blood cells, which allows them to use a higher percentage of what oxygen there is in the air; some even have larger hearts and greater lung capacity.

Approximately 90,000 Sherpas, people of Tibetan descent, live in the high mountain deserts of Nepal and India. Carrying gear and supplies on their backs, these exceedingly fit mountain dwellers have long worked as porters and guides for the climbers and commercial traders who ascend the rugged mountains. The most highly paid are those who climb the most dangerous routes at the highest elevation; they can receive up to U.S. $2,000 in 3 months, more than 11 times the average annual income in Nepal. Tenzing Norgay, a Sherpa who had worked as a guide for early expeditions of Sir Edmund Hillary, was asked to be a party member in his own right during the New Zealand mountain climber's history-making 1953 ascent of Mount Everest. On May 29 of that year, armed with oxygen and minimally loaded back-packs, Norgay and Hillary became the first to reach the 29,028-foot (8,848-m) summit, the highest desert point on the planet.

Bearing a snow crown that never melts, Mount Everest is the highest-altitude arid zone on Earth, similar to the polar desert. The tallest peak's southwest face is shown, its summit in the clouds.

LONESOME THOROUGHFARES

Each season brings a new face to the dry plateaus, sandy plains, and far-reaching inland basins that lie midway between the Equator and the Poles. Temperatures in these lands, the cold-winter deserts, span a range so great that summertime climates often mimic those of arid places in the subtropics, though half a year later snow may cover the ground and the mercury plunge below zero. The temperature disparity from one season to the next is the common bond among these deserts and sets them apart from all others.

The continent of Asia contains nearly all of the cold-winter deserts of the world because it has more land area within the 35° to 50° latitude bands than any other continent north or south of the Equator. In its southwestern region lie the arid Iranian Plateau and the Turkestan Desert, where, like other deserts along the same climatic band, summers are warm and winters bitterly cold. One of the world's largest sandy deserts, the Taklamakan of northwest China, has some of the most dramatic temperature fluctuations: summer temperatures can rise to 100° F (38° C), but those in the winter average 16° F (-9° C). Northeast of the Taklamakan, the grasslands and barren gravel fields of the 500,000-square-mile (1,300,000-sq-km) Gobi stretch from northern China into Mongolia. It is the coolest of the Asian deserts, averaging 70° F (21° C) in July and 10° F (-12° C) in January.

The cold-winter deserts of North America—the Colorado Plateau and the Great Basin—cover more than 340,000 square miles (880,600 sq km) of sagebrush-dotted land in Nevada, western Utah, and parts of New Mexico, Arizona, California, Oregon, and Idaho. Travelers crossing these vast expanses—like those in other cold-winter deserts—have perished in the blistering heat of summer, and others have frozen to death in winter's chill. Far to their south, below the steamy Equator, the Patagonian Desert of southern Argentina receives most of its sparse precipitation in the form of snow during the winter months of June, July, and August, when cold winds blow continuously across the arid plateaus. In summer, however, temperatures may climb above 100° F (38° C).

Another feature that many cold-winter deserts share is geographical barriers, which play a major role in their formation and perpetual aridity. The rain-shadow effect occurs where mountain ranges act as barriers to keep rain clouds from going from one side to the other. The Andes mountains, for example, lie west of the Patagonian Desert in South America, and the Sierra Nevada and Cascade ranges border the Great Basin Desert. In both of these Western Hemisphere regions, moisture-laden air masses from the Pacific Ocean have no place to go but up as they encounter increasing elevations along the western coasts of the two continents. The air cools as it climbs the windward sides of the mountains, drops rain or snow before rounding the crests, then carries little, if any, moisture to the interior desert lowlands on the other side. On this, and on the leeward sides of other mountain ranges, expansive desiccated lands in the rain shadow hold out hope for only the hardiest of plants and animals.

Many lands are so isolated from oceans, the primary water sources of the planet, that they are destined to be deserts. In Asia, the landlocked Gobi, Taklamakan, and Turkestan deserts are at least a thousand miles (1,600 km) from the nearest ocean; their innermost reaches lie several thousand miles inland. By the time ocean winds reach these deserts, any moisture is long gone.

High elevation is another common characteristic of most cold-winter deserts. The Gobi, for example, ranges from 3,000 to 5,000 feet (900–1,500 m) above sea level, and the Iranian Desert, on the eastern half of the vast Iranian Plateau, has an average elevation of nearly 3,000 feet (900 m). Many cold-winter deserts—like the Great Basin, whose floor ranges from 1,000 to 6,000 feet (300–1,800 m) above sea level—have large interior catchments into which water flows from the surrounding highlands or mountains. Often these are the sites of permanent or seasonal lakes, which may have no effluent arteries. As evaporation occurs, salt is leached from the soil, and the water left behind either is highly saline or dries up completely, leaving a lake bed encrusted with salty residue. Tens of thousands of years ago the Great Basin was home to several enormous lakes. The largest, Lake Bonneville, covered more than 20,000 square miles (51,800 sq km). Since then, evaporation and repeated droughts have reduced the once-massive lake to several far smaller lakes, the largest of which is the 2,400-square-mile (6,200-sq-km) Great Salt Lake in Utah. A phenomenon unchanged by time, the world's cold-winter deserts are often regarded as places to be crossed as quickly as possible—be it by a 5th-century camel caravan hauling skeins of silk from one Chinese oasis to the next, or a steam locomotive chugging across the windy plains of the Patagonian Desert. The harsh and massive expanses are, to many, something to be crossed between here and there.

Each September, the beginning of spring in the southernmost reaches of South America, hundreds of thousands of Magellanic penguins amble awkwardly ashore onto the edge of the Patagonian Desert to embark upon their annual procreative ritual. Like an off-key chorus of foghorns, the birds' nasal chatter fills the desert air with a hee-haw braying sound—making sense of their other name, jackass penguins. They have overwintered more than 1,500 miles (2,419 km) to the north, in the warmer waters off Brazil, following the schools of squid and small fish on which they feed. But as the seasons begin to change, they return to the semiarid, windswept coastline of Argentina's Cabo Virgenes, where the Atlantic Ocean meets the Strait of Magellan.

In October, the females begin to lay their eggs in the pebbly underground burrows that have been carved by the male penguins, or beneath the desert's scraggly bushes. Through the next month of spring heat, both members of each monogamous couple take turns incubating and guarding the eggs until they hatch in November. Afterward, both parents are responsible for catching extra fish, which they regurgitate into the mouths of their hungry young. The juvenile penguins do not venture from their nests until February—late summer—when, for the first time, they take to the ocean and begin their long northward journey, getting a head start on the adults, who return to the warmer Brazilian waters in mid-autumn. The jackass penguins are in their element when they hit the frigid ocean surf. A layer of blubber beneath their black-and-white skin insulates them from the cold, and their fins and tails propel them effortlessly through the water.

Mount Fitz Roy (*left*) towers 11,286 feet (3,440 m) above Argentina's Patagonian steppe. Snow persists all year on the peak, named for the captain of the H.M.S. *Beagle,* on which Charles Darwin sailed.

A Magellanic penguin chick (*above*) brays in the breaking dawn on Argentina's Valdés Peninsula. For two to three months after they hatch, chicks remain in their nests, where both parents feed them.

The penguin population was once viewed as inexhaustible. Some early European explorers slaughtered the birds by the tens of thousands to provision their ships; tons of salted penguin meat was stored onboard for later consumption, and oil from the blubber was used to fuel lamps. Since the mid-1980's, hundreds of thousands of Magellanic penguins have died, victims of residue from oil tankers that serve the expanding petroleum industry of Argentina and Chile. Some scientists are concerned that increased tapping of Patagonian oil reserves could further reduce the region's penguin population.

Other desert animals native to Patagonia are also dwindling in number. Large herds of guanacos, relatives of the camel, once grazed vast regions of the arid inland plains. They traveled in groups of 4 to 10 females led by a single male; during fights with rivals, the high-pitched screams and growls of the leader could be heard echoing across the wide expanses.

On his voyage around the world in the 1830's, the young Charles Darwin came across the bones of several guanacos in a ravine. He speculated that the animals intentionally traveled to common sites to die. But scientists now believe that such remains are those of groups of guanacos in search of scarce wintertime forage; as they huddle together for warmth, the heat from their bodies melts the snow, which later freezes into a fatal "ice corral."

Today, cold winters are not the gunacos' biggest enemy. Mile after mile of fencing on Patagonia's immense cattle and sheep ranches keep guanacos from traversing the desert during annual migrations. And although hunting the animals is illegal, thousands of guanacos fall victim to illegal poachers every year.

South American Wilds

For centuries, the sweeping expanses of Argentina's Patagonian Desert have conjured limitless images in the human imagination. Bigger than Spain and Portugal combined, but sparsely populated, the vast Patagonian is the largest desert of any kind in the Americas. The 260,000-square-mile (673,400-sq-km) arid region meets the Atlantic Ocean head-on to the east and is bounded by the Andes Mountains to the west, the waters of the Río Colorado to the north, and the Strait of Magellan to the south.

From the sharp bluffs along Patagonia's desolate Atlantic coast, the land begins a gentle, terraced ascent west to the foothills. This tableland, or steppe, is almost devoid of trees; instead, there are mainly scrub and dry grass, and the occasional stunted beech tree. To the south, the plateau is higher and rockier. The southern reaches of the high Andean range form a spectacular 1,000-mile (1,610-km) western border to the Patagonian Desert. Home to some of the only permanent ice caps outside the polar regions, the mountains contain ice fields and glaciers, which in past millennia carved out grand lakes that now lie amid verdant alpine forests.

Like the land itself, Patagonia's climate is also one of extremes. Spring and autumn quickly give way to the long spans of summer and winter, when the thermometer cannot be ignored. Most of the desert's scant precipitation comes as winter snow, and temperatures can be bitter—plunging sometimes in the south to less than -20° F (-29° C). Yet in summer, the mercury can top 100° F (37° C).

In the shady desert ravines, some flowers—such as evening primroses and hoary-leaved mullein—actually thrive, as do small animals like the mara, a short-eared, long-legged rodent that resembles a rabbit, and the tuco-tuco, a cousin of the North American gopher. At night this gray-furred animal leaves its burrow to seek out grasses and roots, which it eats with its bright orange-colored teeth. Once common Patagonian prairie animals, tuco-tucos have been driven to near extinction by extensive sheep farming. Reduced too, are the flocks of rheas, 4-foot-tall (120-cm), flightless birds native to South America that are similar to ostriches.

Legends abound concerning the origin of the name *Patagonia,* but most tales go back to the first encounter between Europeans and Tehuelches, a group of South American Indians. In one version, Antonio Pigafetta, the chronicler of Magellan's expedition of 1520, saw huge footprints in the snow and called the people Patagones, from a Spanish root word said to mean "big feet." Another story maintains that Pigafetta, after seeing the hide clothing and battle headdresses worn by the Tehuelches, was reminded of a dog-headed monster, the Patagon, featured in a contemporary Spanish story.

The indigenous Tehuelches once roamed the southern half of the continent, hunting and depending on huge herds of guanacos—humpless relatives of the camel—much as Indians of the North American plains depended

The ice cliffs of Moreno Glacier (*above left*) stretch for 2 miles (3 km) along Lake Argentino in the southern Andes.

An ostrichlike rhea (*above*) ignores a band of penguins nesting at Punta Tombo, Argentina, for the summer breeding season. Both of these Patagonian birds escape their predators by means other than flight: rheas are swift runners, penguins champion swimmers.

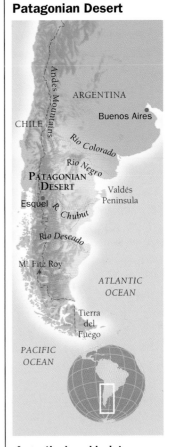

Patagonian Desert

Argentina's cold-winter desert is formed as rain clouds drop precipitation west of the Andes (*orange above*), so only moisture-depleted air gets inland.

Sheer cliffs along Argentina's Valdés Peninsula (*left*) are typical of Patagonia's abrupt coastline.

on bison. Along with other peoples native to this arid area, like the Onas and ·the Haushes, the Tehuelches were wiped out by disease and slaughter as European settlers turned Patagonia's grasslands into sheep and cattle ranches. In his 1879–93 campaign, dubbed the Conquest of the Desert, General Julio Argentino Roca—who later became president of Argentina—led a 5,000-man army into Patagonia and oversaw the massacre of most of the remaining Tehuelche population.

This conquest paved the way for massive migration into the virgin plains of Patagonia. Welsh, Slavic, German, Polish, Arab, and English settlers came in successive waves, enticed by the Argentine government's offer of cheap or free land. Among the first to arrive, in 1865, was an unlikely band of 150 immigrants from Wales, fleeing hard labor in the coal mines and British suppression of Welsh language and culture. They arrived on a ship called the *Mimosa* to carve out a new life for themselves in Patagonia. Despite hardships— extreme isolation and alternating periods of drought and flood— their proficiency at raising sheep and their knowledge of irrigation

helped them make the desert's Chubut River valley a pleasant, if solitary, place to live. Although their mother tongue is Spanish, the present-day physical features—as well as the culture—of many of these people betray their Celtic heritage.

By Rail Through Patagonia

In deserts where temperatures fluctuate dramatically between summer and winter, population centers are generally few and far between, and people are frequently intent on getting from one corner of the barren landscape to the other as quickly as possible. Overland journeys through Argentina's stark Patagonian Desert require much patience. The main train line serving the northern part of Patagonia, named *General Roca*, runs from Buenos Aires to Bariloche, more than 1,000 miles (1,600 km) to the south and west, in the Andean lake district. To venture south into the desert's interior, passengers must change trains at a small junction called Ingeniero Jacobacci, where a narrow-gauge spur of track continues for 260 miles

A steam locomotive pulls people and goods through mile after mile of Patagonian desolation (*left*). Persistent winds disperse the dark smoke billowing from an oil-burning engine.

Horseback is a common way to tend flocks on Patagonia's semiarid steppe (*above*). Sheep, introduced by Welsh settlers in the 19th century, flourish in the desert's grasslands.

(420 km) southwest to the city of Esquel in the Andean foothills. Depending on wind conditions—or snowstorms—a one-way trip takes about 14 hours across rolling hills and windswept plains, which are sprinkled with shrubs, hardy grasses, and a few squatty trees.

Most of this wilderness is ranch country, the main obstacles to speed being horses, cows, and flocks of sheep that wander onto the tracks. It was here in Argentina's remote Chubut province that Robert Leroy Parker—better known as notorious bank and train robber Butch

Cassidy—holed up for several years. The United States, wrote the outlaw from his Patagonian refuge, had become "too small" for his illegal shenanigans. From this "unsettled and comparatively unknown" country he sent word to a friend in Utah: "I am a long way from civilization."

Still in operation is the 1922 Baldwin steam engine that pulled the first string of train cars across the desert to the region's isolated ranching settlements and on into Esquel when the track was completed in the 1940's. Laying the narrow-gauge track required 10 years and thousands of workers. The first cross-ties and track were laid by a crew composed mainly of Yugoslavians. Within days, they confronted the first mountain that needed chiseling out with dynamite to make way for the rail line. All told, 60 such mountain passages were carved, 10 bridges were constructed, and 1 tunnel was dug.

It was a locomotive on this line that writer Paul Theroux immortalized in his 1979 travelogue, *The Old Patagonian Express:* "The laboring engine chugged," he wrote, "always seeming on the verge of spewing its guts out." Locals, who for half a century have depended on the train for transportation across the wilds, call it, simply,

El Trochita—"the little narrow gauge." The rail line runs across rocky hills and dry gullies, which to Theroux gave the windblown desert "a prehistoric look." Every 30 miles (50 km) or so, the train stops to take on water—a steam locomotive requirement. It is not unusual for passengers to disembark and scrounge among the endless stands of scrub bushes for twigs to stoke the stoves that heat the passenger cars.

The desert towns that prospered around El Trochita's 12 stations are today largely in decline, but in the train's heyday 25,000 tons of freight were hauled between the towns each year. Three times a week, wool, flour, cement, and oil made the trip alongside the passengers on El Trochita. Now, however, inexpensive and frequent airline flights from Buenos Aires come to Esquel, and new Argentine highways make paved overland travel possible for automobiles crossing the desert. Many wonder whether the narrow-gauge railroad, one of the few of its kind in the world, will still be running in the 21st century.

ALONG EURASIA'S SILK ROAD

In China, when the Beijing government began its push to settle and modernize the arid, untamed western provinces in the 1950's, a major goal was to link the existing eastern and western train lines, which were separated by a 25-mile (40-km) gap near Lanzhou. Because most of the solid ground in the region is prone to earthquakes, the tracks had to be laid across the shifting dunes of the Tengger, a 25,600-square-mile (42,700-sq-km) sandy waste at the southern edge of the Gobi Desert. But first, the dunes had to be stabilized. Like other desert peoples who live where blowing sand needs to be checked, the Chinese came up with an innovative solution to anchor the dunes. Thousands of workers laid yard-wide squares of straw, in grid fashion, over a 1,600-foot-wide (480-m) railroad bed. For more than three decades, this latticework, which drapes up and over the dunes, has largely prevented the hills of sand from creeping with the wind toward the train tracks.

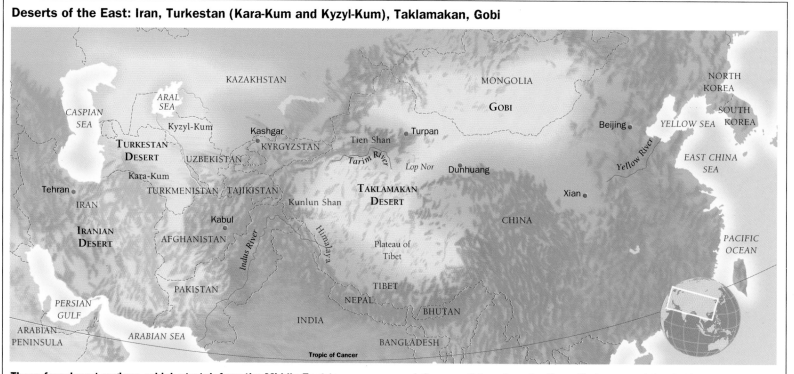

Deserts of the East: Iran, Turkestan (Kara-Kum and Kyzyl-Kum), Taklamakan, Gobi

These four desert regions, which stretch from the Middle East to Beijing, are the cold eastern portion of a continuous band of arid land that starts in the west with the superheated Sahara. Mountain ranges influence all four deserts: those that surround the Gobi, Taklamakan, and Turkestan remove moisture from the air that reaches them; in Iran, mountainous terrain keeps the region high and dry.

Spanning the "roof of the world"—the Pamir Plateau of northwest China—the Karakoram Highway leads from China's remote Xinjiang Province through mountain passes once crossed exclusively by camel caravans.

A nomadic Tajik family (*inset*) moves to higher ground, seeking greener summer pastures in the Pamir Plateau. One of several Islamic ethnic groups in northwest China, the Tajiks were among the Pamir's earliest inhabitants.

Since the fall of the Iron Curtain in 1989, the international business world has been in a state of dramatic upheaval. Long-restricted Central Asian republics are opening themselves to free trade, and modern Western companies are eyeing their first chance to enter untapped markets in places like China, Mongolia, and the Turkic republics of the former Soviet Union. Across these vast regions, where vast deserts dominate much of the often-frigid land, the seemingly novel flurry of commercial activity is actually anything but new. It is, remarkably, just another ripple in the centuries-old cyclical ebb and flow of trade for those who live along the ancient silk roads, the main arteries of exchange between East and West for thousands of years.

What is often referred to in singular as the Silk Road actually encompassed numerous routes that shifted over the centuries to suit changing markets and to avoid warring kingdoms and bands of robbers. Traders and their caravans trudged across rugged desert and mountain regions that now lie in parts of Turkey, Iran, Afghanistan, Uzbekistan, and Pakistan—with feeder routes leading into Arabia and India. All together, the network of silk roads stretched some 6,000 miles (9,700 km)—westward from the ancient Chinese capital of Xian and across the desolate

Taklamakan to Kashgar, Samarkand, and Bukhara. From there, the routes headed around the Caspian Sea, either north or south, depending on the vicissitudes of the day. Traders would then continue west into Byzantium—now Istanbul—or veer south to the Mediterranean port cities of the Levant. Goods at the harbors would be loaded upon ships sailing to Rome and Alexandria.

One of the most feared and dangerous stretches of the silk roads took traders over the Pamirs, mountains whose peaks soar to 20,000 feet (6,000 m) and higher, and into one of the world's most treacherous deserts, the Taklamakan of northwestern China. The Taklamakan is situated 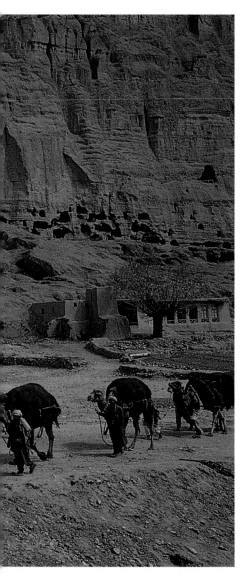 in the middle of a large basin virtually surrounded by mountains—the Pamirs on the west, the Kunlun on the south, and the Tian Shan, or Heavenly Mountains, on the north. Flowing from west to east along the northern edge of this vast bowl is the landlocked Tarim River, whose seasonal tributaries are fed by melting snow and springs from the mountains. From the south, dozens of seasonal streams carry new deposits of alluvial sand down from the mountains, but most die long before reaching the Tarim. The basin drains into Lop Nor, a once-large, marshy lake that is now a series of smaller sinks whose waters rise after a thaw, only to evaporate in the hot months of summer. At 210,000 square miles (543,900 sq km), the Tarim River basin is slightly larger than France.

Within the heart of the basin lie the shifting desert dunes of the Taklamakan, the name of which derives from a Turkic word that means "labyrinth"—or, more literally, "once you enter, you never return." In summer, the heat on the shadeless dunes is excruciating, with temperatures reaching 100° F (38° C). Winters are frigid; air temperatures average in the mid-teens Fahrenheit and the negative single digits Celsius. Two prevailing currents of wind, one from the north, the other from the northwest, converge near the center of the Taklamakan, creating a variety of dune formations that are commonly several hundred feet tall and sometimes rise to 1,000 feet (300 m). Howling sandstorms, known as the *kara-buran*, reduce visibility to a few feet and can easily choke a person to death.

Over the centuries this mighty Asian desert has swallowed entire towns; buildings eroded by the wind now lie half-buried in the sand. Niya, for instance, a once-thriving settlement of 3,000 people some 75 miles (121 km) into the heart of the Taklamakan, was abandoned sometime in the 4th century A.D. The river that supplied the town had gradually receded, its mountain-born waters drying up farther away from the settlement with each passing year. People living upstream most likely contributed to the

A caravan passes cave dwellings and a giant Buddha (*far left*) in the Bamian Valley of northern Afghanistan. This statue dates from at least the 7th century A.D., when it was noted by a Chinese traveler. Genghis Khan destroyed the settlement here in 1221.

Sturdy, cargo-laden Bactrian camels (*left*) plod across the gravel floor of the Pamir Plateau in the Taklamakan Desert in northwest China. The two-humped Bactrian is the most dependable form of desert transportation.

death of Niya and other desert towns by diverting water for crops. Some scientists fear that today's latest influx of human habitation into the Tarim Basin is placing a heavy burden on an already taxed water supply.

Supporting Life in the Taklamakan

Although the Taklamakan can test the limits of human endurance, a surprising array of life manages to thrive there, particularly along the Tarim River and its seasonally flowing tributaries. In the green swath provided by the Hetian, or Khotan, River, for instance, grow some 40 species of vegetation, including poplar, tamarisk, cattails, and reeds. This corridor of life, which trails alongside the desert's largest river aside from the Tarim, is home to about 50 species of animals including Bactrian camels, wild boars, gazelles, meridian sand rats, red deer, and a variety of hares. Occasionally, in the hush of the wilderness, the rat-a-tat-tat of woodpeckers or the hoot of owls can also be heard.

For centuries people, too, have managed to survive the desert's extremes. Most of the 50 or so settlements ring the region's vast, sandy interior. To the north, cities and towns thrive along the 580-mile-long (970-km) Tarim River. To the south, where a flat, 30-mile-wide (50-km) piedmont of gravel separates the mountains and the sands, snow-fed streams gurgle past irrigated fields before disappearing into the sandy wastes. An abrupt demarcation line separates the stark, barren desert from the green farmland. In this, one of China's coldest wintertime regions, inhabitants raise apricots, wheat, grapes, melons, and other crops in the summer warmth.

The Taklamakan Desert is situated in China's northwesternmost province, Xinjiang. Although the desert is within the boundaries of the People's Republic, the region is nevertheless considered a hinterland by Chinese who live elsewhere. Xinjiang is beyond the Great Wall, and China's citizens still refer to the area as "outside the mouth," meaning that it lies beyond the settled, civilized confines of their country's familiar eastern half.

Despite a heavy influx of Chinese since the revolution in 1949, the principal

Uighur farming villages cluster around oases formed on lower slopes of the mountains ringing the Taklamakan. Here, farmers in south Xinjiang Province clear gravel away in preparation for planting.

ethnic group of Xinjiang is the Uighurs. They are a Turkic-speaking, Islamic people who were once nomadic herders but had settled into oasis farming communities by the 12th century, largely thanks to the living that could be made serving the thriving silk trade. Over the years, caravans would use different routes to skirt the Taklamakan. The more-settled and better-watered northern road along the foot of the Tian Shan range was the path of choice in times of political stability. But when petty nomadic kingdoms clashed, caravans would stick to the drier southern road along the Kunlun foothills; it was less civilized but not as easy for bands of raiders to hide in.

Perhaps the most important caravan stop at the edge of the desert was Kashgar, or Kashi, on the far western end of the Taklamakan. At that thriving intersection, merchants heading east could choose either the northern or the southern route around the desert. Today the bustling oasis city of Kashgar is home to millions of people and remains one of Central Asia's largest markets.

Kashgar and other oasis cities and towns of the Taklamakan retain a traditional flavor, despite burgeoning populations, modern buildings, factories, and electricity. Most homes are made from mud bricks. In many towns, Uighur women gather once a week to bake a supply of flat, round bread in outdoor ovens; the pitalike bread does not spoil in the arid land because the humidity seldom exceeds 4 percent.

Irrigation is the key to civilization in the desert, and the city of Turpan—which is nestled in the foothills of the Tian

A Uighur woman carries produce along a poplar-lined path near Kashgar (*top left*), a commercial trading center at the edge of the Taklamakan Desert. Planting these quick-growing trees next to roads is a common means of breaking the ever-present wind.

Spices, like these at a market in Qinghai Province, China (*top right*), are some of the goods traded along the Silk Road.

Bakers sell loaves (*below*), a common sight in Taklamakan towns, at the market in Kashgar.

Mud-brick ruins near the Taklamakan city of Turpan (*above*) show how climatic fluctuations can render the desert uninhabitable. Cities and towns that thrived during a wet period about A.D. 300 were abandoned by the 15th century after a prolonged dry spell.

Modern Turpan (*right*) gets water from springs and melting glaciers high in the Tian Shan range in northwestern China. The water flows through a network of tunnels, called *karaz,* to homes and irrigated fields.

Shan northeast of the Taklamakan, within the world's second-lowest depression after the Dead Sea—has one of the oldest and most intricate water-bearing systems in the world. A series of underground tunnels and wells, called *karaz,* bring water from the mountaintop glaciers as they melt. Turpan's irrigation network consists of more than 1,500 miles (2,400 km) of channels, some portions of which are centuries old and were most likely copied from the *qanat*s in the arid plateaus of ancient Persia. Thousands of human-sized holes speckle the region's desert landscape and provide subterranean entry for laborers who descend in baskets tied to donkeys. Once the workers are below the surface, they begin the agonizing job of cleaning silt and rubble from the watercourses or repairing the ancient lines.

Today, local oasis dwellers along the old silk trade routes depend primarily upon buses that travel the long hops from village to village. The 700-mile (1,130-km) stretch from Turpan to Kashgar, for example—which took ancient merchants 2 months to travel—can now be completed in 4 days.

Intrepid Desert Travelers

For Asia's silk traders of yesteryear, such oases were islands of safety in arid seas of danger. Great caution had to be used in trekking across the vast expanses that lie between one watering hole and the next. Water could be found between towns but was far from plentiful; merchants had to gauge, before setting out, how many animals and people the sparse supplies of water could support. "It is necessary to cross in a small company no greater than fifty at once," wrote Marco Polo, who braved the Taklamakan with his father and uncle on his trip from Italy to China during the 13th century. A mistake as simple as straying from one's caravan could mean almost certain death on the dunes. Merchants, particularly when riding at night to avoid the heat, commonly tied bells around their animals' necks to stay within earshot of their comrades and to keep themselves from dozing off.

Desert travelers also had to be on the watch for hot winds that would rise out of nowhere, bringing choking sandstorms. Most common in spring, the hurricane-force storms are created when updrafts of air from the warm desert surface alter prevailing wind patterns by bringing in fierce northeasterlies. A first-century Chinese chronicler wrote that camels always sensed these thermal winds approaching—they would groan, huddle together, and bury their noses in the sand. Alert merchants would quickly cover their own faces with blankets. "The wind is sudden, and only lasts a short while," the writer warned, "but if you take no protection you can expect death."

In the Gobi and the Taklamakan, winter crossings were no less danger filled. Friar John of Plano Carpini, a papal emissary to Mongolian Kuyuk Khan—a successor of Ghengis Khan—complained of waking most mornings to find his body dusted with snow, a common wintertime phenomenon. Friar John's effort to convert the Mongolian leader to Christianity was not met with open arms, especially after the khan realized that the emissary had come from Rome with no tributary offering. The great

A SEA TURNS DRY

Boats are left among dunes once part of Turkestan's Aral Sea.

At the end of the last ice age, about 10,000 years ago, the arid salt flats of northwestern Utah were the floor of a 20,000-square-mile (51,800-sq-km) lake. In this century, parts of the American West were turned from fertile grasslands to overgrazed Dust Bowl. And today in Central Asia an inland sea is becoming a desert. Sometimes climate causes these changes, sometimes it is human activity.

A dramatic example of human-induced desertification is taking place at the Aral Sea in Central Asia's Turkestan Desert. The Aral basin, fed by two great rivers—the Amu Darya and Syr Darya—began filling 140,000 years ago. In 1960 the Aral was the world's fourth largest inland body of water. About that time, leaders of the former Soviet Union, seeking to boost cotton production, began to irrigate vast stretches of arid land along the Amu Darya and Syr Darya, diverting water that would have flowed into the Aral. Cotton blossomed, but by 1989 the Aral's shoreline had receded by 40 percent.

The Aral's fishing industry has virtually disappeared. The sea once supported 20 species of fish and yielded 160-ton catches each day. Now, virtually nothing survives in its saline water, and Muynak, a once-bustling fish-packing town, is 20 miles (32 km) from shore. Reduced flow along the rivers has harmed vegetation and made drinking water scarce. Food is harder to grow, and disease is common. Experts say that only if irrigation is sharply curtailed can the Aral Sea be saved.

khan insisted, in response, that the pope himself come to his capital, not to preach but to serve him.

Many travelers sought divine protection before embarking across the arid steppes and sand-covered plains of the Asian interior. According to legend, a 4th-century merchant stopped at a group of cliffside caves, home to a small colony of Buddhist monks outside Dunhuang—the last outpost of civilization before entering the vast no-man's land. There he commissioned an artist to decorate one of the caves as a temple, then paid the monks to pray in it regularly for his overland safety. For another thousand years, within the so-called Caves of the Thousand Buddhas, artists continued the tradition, adorning the walls of nearly 500 caverns with murals, frescoes, carvings, and statues of Buddha. For centuries, hundreds of thousands of devout Buddhists made pilgrimages to the caves, which honeycomb a mile-long (1.6-km) side of a 200-foot-tall (60-m) desert cliff. In the 20th century, much of the sacred art was vandalized, and blowing sands continued to ravage the caves' exteriors; to preserve them, the Chinese government began construction in 1963 of protective concrete walls along the cliffside. Today the world's greatest collection of medieval Buddhist art—which reveals much about the history of the desert region and silk road commerce—continues to draw visitors, who come by land and air to its remote site.

Silk was not the only product that made its way through Asia's cold deserts on the backs of camels. Although these dreaded lands served to isolate China from the West, the silk trade enabled a host of products and ideas to trickle in and out. Cotton, wool, grapevines, alfalfa, peaches, and pears came through the desert from the West, as did Buddhism, Islam, and to a lesser degree, Christianity. Tea, porcelain, lacquerware, and the art of papermaking accompanied silk on the westward journey to the Middle East and Europe. Ironically, the Mongols' iron-fisted control over most of Central Asia's wilds resulted in a stability that made travel on the silk roads safer than ever. According to one saying, a girl could walk from one end to the other with a gold dish upon her head without being molested. By the 16th century, the silk roads had diminished in importance, largely because of improvements in sea navigation and the fact that the once-mysterious art of silk making had been discovered and mastered in the West.

The 67 caves at Bezeklik (*above*), in the sandstone hills north of the Taklamakan city of Turpan, contain frescoes with Hellenic, Persian, Chinese, and Indian features and clothing, affording evidence of the rich exchange of cultures along the Silk Road.

An ancient Buddhist monastery (*left*) holds its own against encroaching sand. The structure is part of the Thousand Buddha Caves complex in central China, where travelers and traders pray before embarking into the desert.

The Nomad's Ubiquitous Tent

Ever in search of fresh water and pastureland for the herds on which they depend, nomads of the world's deserts have devised ingenious mobile homes that provide effective shelter. Among many nomadic groups, the traditions of the tent—including the ritual placement of important objects and the division of living space by gender or status—are strictly observed.

Among the oldest styles of desert tent still in wide use is the Bedouin black tent (*opposite page, upper right*), which dates at least to biblical times. The Arabic word for this tent, *beit sha'r,* means "house of hair," owing to the fact that the tent cloth is typically made of goat's, sheep's, or camel's wool. The cloth, despite its heat-absorbing dark color, provides shade, and its loose weave allows enough ventilation to keep the inside as much as 30 F degrees (17 C degrees) cooler than the outside.

Lapps, who inhabit the tundra of northern Scandinavia and survive by following reindeer herds, use *katas,* tents similar to the Native American tipi. A canvas covering is supported by three forked birch poles and a series of smaller rods. For the floor, blankets and reindeer skins cover a layer of twigs. In the middle of the *kata* is the hearth, over which cooking pots are suspended from hooked chains.

Another tried-and-true movable abode is the Mongolian *ger,* more widely known by its Turkic name, *yurt.* The key feature of this circular tent is its lattice frame, which is unfolded like an accordion to form a chest-high base. A series of poles connects the top of the lattice with a wheel-shaped crown, which is held by upright posts to form a smoke hole. Over this sturdy frame are placed layers of canvas and felt. The cloth—supplemented by a yak-dung stove or, increasingly, electric heaters—keeps inhabitants warm on winter nights. Family-size yurts can be erected in roughly 30 minutes and are common sights in Mongolia, from the remote steppes to Ulaanbaatar, the capital city.

A sea of aqals, traditional one-family tents (above), fills a camp of nomadic Somalis near a disputed area on the Ethiopian border. The portable domed frames, made from pliable branches, are covered with rags, cardboard, flattened cans, or other suitable material.

A sealskin tent affords shelter during an Inuit hunting expedition in Canada's Northwest Territories (left). Many Inuit have settled in towns and are nomadic only in warm months.

Black tents, pitched at a Bedouin camp in the western Sahara (above), are seen throughout North Africa and the Near East in a number of variations. The tents—made from the hair of goats, camels, or sheep—are simple in design, yet withstand high winds even on soft sand.

Inside her warm yak-hair tent, a Himalayan woman (above) prepares tea for a guest. For most nomads, hospitality is paramount.

Palm mats laid over a frame of branches (left) make up the huts in a Tuareg campsite in the Sahel region of Mali.

THE DRY CHINA SEA

In the Mongolian language the word *gobi* means "waterless place"; in Chinese it means "gravelly, pebbly plain." Westerners, somewhat inaccurately, have used the term *gobi* to refer to the 500,000 square miles (1.3 million sq km) of rambling wilderness that stretch across southern Mongolia and northern China. Within its loosely defined boundaries lie diverse landscapes that give new breadth to the term *desiccation:* windswept gravel plains, dry steppes cloaked only in grasses, tabletop mesas covered with scrub, monolithic buttes carved out of sandstone, a few dune-studded sandscapes, bone-dry basins, and gullies. Across these often frigid lands roam wild horses, dzeren gazelles, reptiles, sheep, a variety of rodents, Bactrian camels, and wild asses, which can go waterless for longer periods than any other equine species.

Fossil Hunting in the Gobi

This grand swath of desert is one of the world's most fertile grounds for hunting fossils; thousands of prehistoric finds have been unearthed there. For the past half century,

the Gobi was inaccessible to Western scientists, but that began to change in the 1980's, as relations with China started to thaw. With the collapse of the Soviet Union, paleontologists have been streaming into the Mongolian regions of the Gobi as well.

Tens of millions of years ago, when the dinosaurs thrived, the Central Asian plateau—where the arid Gobi now lies—was somewhat wetter than it is today. Although not lush and teeming with plants, the land was capable of supporting more abundant vegetation than do the dry lands today. Landlocked basins held shallow alkaline lakes, probably similar to Great Salt Lake in North America's Great Basin Desert. Scrub bushes at lower elevations and coniferous forests at higher ones afforded food for plant-eating reptilian species. Some scientists believe that sporadic heavy flooding in the days when dinosaurs roamed may have been what killed—and entombed for posterity—many of the animals whose fossilized bones are now being unearthed by wind erosion and paleontologists' brushes.

One of the most significant and revolutionary fossil discoveries to date occurred during the summer of 1992, on the arid steppes of the northern Gobi, when a team of American paleontologists discovered the remains of a 65-million-year-old skeleton. Those fragile bones found in the desert sent ripples of excitement around the globe and supported the theory that today's birds are actually modern-day dinosaurs.

Mononykus was no bigger than a wild turkey. The predatory but wingless proto-bird had sharp teeth, a long tail, and feathers. Its skeleton, which has both reptilian- and birdlike characteristics, bears evidence that *Mononykus,* meaning "one claw," evolved from an earlier flying animal, just as the land-bound ostrich is believed to have descended from an airborne species. The discovery of *Mononykus* could mean that, in a sense, some dinosaurs

A sand dune rises incongruously behind an irrigated cornfield (*left*) in the southern Gobi outside Dunhuang. Despite the extreme aridity, China's desert areas support a burgeoning population.

Workers gather sand from dunes near Dunhuang (*above*) to use in making bricks. Dunes are rare in the Gobi, covering only about 5 percent of its 0.5 million square miles (1.3 million sq km).

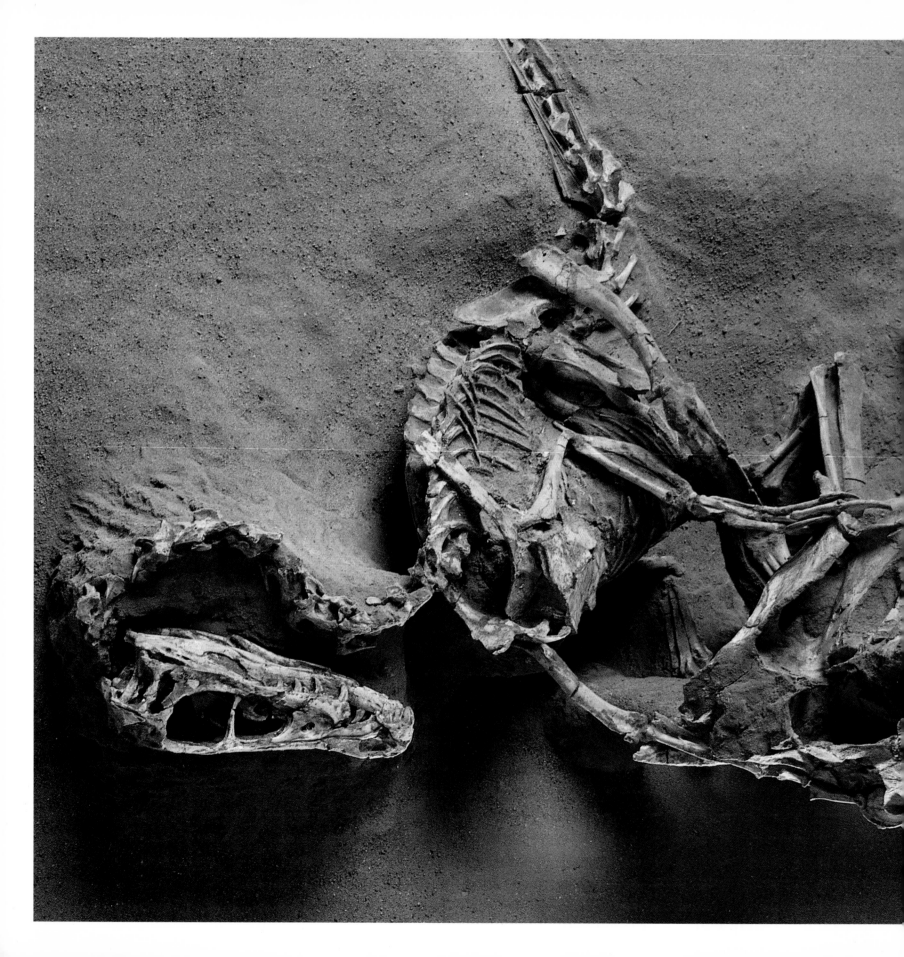

The fossilized bones of prehistoric predator and prey—a herbivorous *Protoceratops* and a meat-eating *Velociraptor* (*its head is at the bottom of the picture at far left*)—lie commingled in the soft sandstone of the Gobi floor where they died fighting. This region of Mongolia was less dry some 80 million years ago, when dinosaurs roamed its reedy salt marshes.

A paleontologist (*left*) scrambles over rocks near the Flaming Cliffs area of Mongolia while searching for dinosaur eggs. Since relations with China have improved, joint Western and Mongolian fossil expeditions have proliferated.

never became extinct—they merely became birds. A growing number of scientists now believe that just as humans and baboons are both primates and mammals, so chickens and eagles are both birds and dinosaurs. According to this theory, the first birds were theropods, members of a meat-eating branch of the dinosaur family tree that also included the infamous *Tyrannosaurus rex.*

Numerous other prehistoric riches have lured 20th-century paleontologists to the Gobi. From the sandy, red-orange soil of the southern Gobi, a 1988 team of Canadian and Chinese scientists unearthed the skeletons of five baby specimens of *Pinacosaurus*—a plant-eating dinosaur from the late Cretaceous period that lived roughly 80 million years ago. Each the size of a sheep and all buried within feet of each other, the skeletons were the first brood of young dinosaurs ever found together. The discovery adds significantly to a growing body of evidence that certain types of dinosaurs lived in groups and that adults fed and nurtured their young, much like nesting birds or even mammals.

The *Pinacosaurus* skeletons are significant for other reasons, as well. Although found only in the deserts of Asia, the ancient reptilian species was similar to the *Ankylosaurus,* a type of dinosaur that lived in North America. The discovery of these and other similar prehistoric species has led to speculation that dinosaurs may have migrated between the two continents across an early occurrence of the Bering Strait land bridge, over which humans are believed to have crossed from Siberia into the Western Hemisphere tens of millions of years later.

Equally significant finds have been made elsewhere in the world, and it is unlikely that more dinosaurs lived in the Gobi region than in Europe or North America. However, since most of the Gobi receives only about 8 inches (205 mm) of annual rainfall, the aridity serves to preserve prehistoric animal bones—and more recent human remains—in a way that happens in few other regions. Another probable reason for such a cache of fossils is that the vast desert is in the middle of the Asian continent and is therefore sheltered from the grinding boundaries of tectonic plates. Even the grass-covered sections of the Gobi feature rock outcroppings that are often ideal places for paleontologists to find fossils.

The Real Indiana Jones

All of these scientists are following the desert footsteps of Roy Chapman Andrews, a determined, gun-toting adventurer from the American Museum of Natural History who set out into the Gobi in 1922 with the intention of finding evidence that the first humans emerged from Central Asia rather than Africa. He deflected the scoffs of many colleagues, never found his sought-after "missing link," and, according to the latest scientific consensus, chose the wrong side of the Africa-Asia debate. But Andrews did prove that the Gobi—known at the time only to the nomads and traders who traversed its lonely expanses on camelback—was a treasure trove of the remains of dinosaurs and prehistoric mammals such as mastodons.

Andrews's most celebrated find came on a July afternoon in 1923, during the second of his five Gobi expeditions. Within a small sandstone ledge, his colleague George Olsen discovered what appeared to be three large,

partly broken eggs. Because the sediment was clearly from the late Cretaceous period, Andrews and Olsen reasoned that the fossilized eggs would have predated any birds. After brushing away more of the soft desert stone, the scientists found the bones of a small, toothless dinosaur, an apparent predator caught in the act of snatching the eggs. Andrews concluded that the 13 oblong objects could only be dinosaur eggs—the first ever discovered. When word of the eggs hit the press back home, it touched a chord in the public, and Andrews was an overnight celebrity. William Randolph Hearst offered Andrews U.S. $250,000 for exclusive rights to the story of the eggs and later finds.

Although none of Andrews's successive discoveries were as well publicized, some were arguably more important. At about the same time that the eggs were unearthed, another of Andrews's assistants found a tiny skull embedded in a piece of sandstone. Although the field team in the scorching Gobi recorded the find as

From a rocky vantage, American adventurer and explorer Roy Chapman Andrews (*above*) surveys the remote Gobi during one of his five expeditions to the Mongolian Desert in the 1920's.

A fleet of Dodge convertibles (*right*) embarks from Andrews's base camp at Zhangjiakow, China, for the Mongolian badlands. Andrews was one of the first to explore the Gobi by car.

"unidentified reptile," scientists studying it back at the museum found it to be mammalian—proof that mammals had evolved prior to the time dinosaurs died out. Some scientists theorized that mammals contributed to the dinosaurs' downfall by eating their eggs.

The desert held another fascination for Andrews: He pioneered the use of cars—Dodge convertibles—in the Gobi. Although the expedition depended on a team of 75 camels to supply the auto fleet with gasoline, the cars could cover in a few days the same distance it would take a caravan months to traverse. After Andrews and his party burst onto the Gobi scene, some Gobi nomads—long dependent on their Bactrian camels—were driving cars obtained from Andrews's party.

As much adventurer as scientist, Andrews always carried a revolver and a loaded cartridge belt, which were handy in encounters with snakes, feral dogs, and bandits. He also enjoyed hunting quail, wild sheep, and antelope. Some suppose that Andrews, who sported a single pheasant feather in his battered hat and was known as a quintessential "man's man," was the inspiration for movie character Indiana Jones. He knew well how to embellish a story: "Water that was up to our ankles was always up to Roy's neck," a colleague once quipped.

As the 1920's came to an end, civil wars in China and the Soviet incursion into Mongolia made Andrews's work in the desert nearly impossible. He was stopped by Chinese soldiers, who accused him of smuggling opium or ferreting out oil reserves. At one point Andrews was tailed across the Gobi by Soviet spies, some suspicious that he was helping the U.S. and British governments annex Mongolia. In 1930 Andrews left the Gobi for good. His original theory, that mammalian life—including human—originated where deserts now cover Central Asia, is doubted by most contemporary scientists. Yet Andrews's contribution to science remains significant.

CAMELS AND CARAVANS

Despite the allure of modern four-wheel-drive vehicles, many people who traverse arid lands still opt for four-legged dependability and choose the tried-and-true "ship of the desert"—the camel. Highly adapted to harsh environments and rugged terrain, the animal has long been a prized means of transportation for humans and heavy cargo alike. Like its smaller yet robust South American relative, the llama, the two-humped Bactrian camel of Asia and the one-humped dromedary of Africa and the Middle East can endure the most torturous overland journeys. Camel caravans in the desert may plod along at only 2 miles per hour (3 kph), but they can easily outlast trucks and automobiles—which may overheat in the sun, run out of fuel, or get stuck in sand or snow. When speed is needed, a galloping camel is comparable to a horse; some have been clocked at 40 miles per hour (65 kph).

To thrive in both hot and cold arid lands, where water sources are few and far between, camels have evolved extraordinary means of holding large quantities of water within their bodies. Depending on climate and workload, they can go for 10 days or longer without taking a drop, but when they do drink there seems to be no end to their thirst. Much of the water is stored in the animal's red blood cells, each of which can expand to more than 200 times its original size. The camel's hump plays a vital role in water conservation, although it does not act as a simple holding tank, as legend has it. Unlike most mammals, which have a heat-insulating layer of fat evenly distributed under the skin, a camel stores virtually all of its fat in its hump or humps. When a camel fills up on water, much of it is chemically incorporated into the hump's fat.

The one-humped camel, or dromedary, remains a valued possession to Saudi Arabia's Bedouins (*left*). Domesticated 5,000 years ago, the camel made possible extensive settlement of the Middle East.

Then, with activity, fat is oxidized and converted into energy and water, which is released for use within the body. Each ounce of fat converted can produce just more than a fluid ounce of water (1 g fat, 1 ml water); a 100-pound (45-kg) hump, therefore, could provide the body with more than 12 gallons (45 L) of water.

During prolonged absence from water, camels' humps shrink noticeably, often sagging to one side. But when a caravan reaches an oasis, each animal can gulp down more than 25 gallons (95 L) of water in a matter of minutes; afterward, their humps slowly expand to full shape. A human can withstand the loss of only about 12 percent of body weight from dehydration, but a camel can lose more than three times that much and replenish itself with little, if any, physiological damage.

The camel has developed ways to cope with other desert extremes such as intense sun, frigid winters, blowing sand, and limited vegetation. The camel's long legs keep the rest of its body above the hottest layer of air, which hugs the desert floor. Thick hair insulates the body from both hot and cold temperatures. On those rare occasions when a camel sweats, its pelt slows evaporation. The protruding oval shape of the camel's midsection keeps most of its body surface shaded and out of direct sunlight. Large eyebrows act as visors; long lashes and sealable nostrils keep out sand. Because the camel can gather food with its rubbery lips without exposing its tongue, little moisture is lost from the mouth during grazing. Camels have learned to be content eating whatever oasis vegetation is available, including plants most other animals would refuse: saltbush, acacia leaves, and the prickly, water-holding shoots of the camel thorn. Famished camels are so easy to please that they will consume leather bridles,

Camels crowd a watering trough in Saharan Somalia. Although they can go 10 days or longer without drinking, camels waste no opportunity to tank up; water is stored in the fat of their humps, which sag after long dry periods.

bones, fish, and even tents. When American humorist Mark Twain visited the Middle East he remarked, "I expect it would be a real treat to a camel to have a keg of nails for dinner."

North American Ancestors

For roughly 5,000 years the highly adapted camel has been a lifeline for human migration and commerce across the broad geographical sweep of arid lands that stretches from the cold deserts of Asia to the heat-stricken sand seas of the Sahara. The animal's evolutionary forerunner, however, emerged 30 to 40 million years ago, halfway around the world, in what is now North America. These short-legged camelids, about the size of a pig or a large dog, evolved over the next 15 million years to more closely resemble long-necked versions of today's llamas.

During the Ice Age of the Pleistocene epoch, some 2.5 million years ago, herds of the early animals migrated northward and crossed over into Asia by the land bridge that traversed the Bering Strait. Other early camels migrated into South America, where their hoofed descendants still roam the steppes and Andean foothills of Argentina, Chile, Peru, Bolivia, and Ecuador.

Today, herds of guanacos can be found as far north as southern Ecuador and as far south as Tierra del Fuego, and they are common in the arid Patagonian desert of Argentina. A full-grown guanaco stands roughly 5 feet (150 cm) tall, weighs 250 pounds (113 kg), and looks like a smaller version of its cousin the llama, which was domesticated as a work animal by the Incas. Other South American relatives of the guanaco include the domesticated alpaca, bred for its long wool, and the wild vicuña, which scientists say is rebounding after being hunted almost to extinction for its wool.

Like the camel, a guanaco can go for long periods without water, drawing moisture from the shrubs and grasses it eats. It can cope with elevations of up to 13,000 feet (3,900 m), and its padded feet help it walk through sand and snow.

Mated guanacos travel in family groups, while unmated mature males congregate in herds of 50 or more. In a cruel-seeming ritual, full-grown males have been known to scare off a yearling in order to mate with its mother and make way for another offspring. During this rite, the adults square off, rear up on their hind legs, and smack chests, much as rams butt horns.

At one time, tens of millions of guanacos roamed much of the South American continent. Because of their numbers and their importance to the Patagonian Indians as a source of meat, hides, and sinew, some scientists refer to them as the bison of South America. Like the bison, or buffalo, they were hunted wholesale by European settlers in the cold desert region, mainly for their hides. Ranching further reduced the guanaco population: sheep and cattle infringed on their grasslands, and fences across vast stretches of the countryside inhibited their natural migrations. Today, an estimated 50,000 to 150,000 guanacos remain in the wild. Although

Probably closer in appearance to their common evolutionary ancestors than to camels, South American guanacos are smaller and have no humps. Related to llamas and alpacas, guanacos thrive in the semiarid region.

Bactrians—perhaps 1,000 in all—still wander some areas of the Gobi, seeking out the shrubs and water of oases. Their massive size and thick, shaggy coats help them withstand the frigid desert winters. Domesticated Bactrians are strong enough to carry 400 pounds (181 kg) or more through the intense heat of the desert summers.

Scientists believe that the sleeker, one-humped, camels—called dromedaries—evolved from the two-humped animals. As recently as 2,000 years ago, large wild camel herds roamed the deserts of the Middle East. Although today thousands of the one-humped camels are bred annually—primarily in the Middle East and North Africa—wild dromedaries are now extinct in those regions. The world's only feral, or free-roaming, herds—numbering between 40,000 and 60,000—roam the arid interior of Australia, where they have descended from the thousands of camels imported to the continent in the 19th century.

In his 1861 painting *Pilgrims Going to Mecca* (*above*), French painter Léon Belly depicted a cross section of Islamic society braving the desert by caravan to visit their holy city.

Traditional designs are shaved into the hair and tail of this camel (*left*) at the annual livestock fair in Pushkar, near the Thar Desert in India.

Human Cargo

For millennia, camels have been essential for human survival in the deserts. Until about 1000 B.C., when camels became available to the commoner, the Middle East was "like an ocean atoll," wrote two Arab scholars, "nothing more than a thin rim of cultivated land." Domesticated in Mesopotamia some 5,000 years ago, the dromedary enabled inhabitants of the region to leave their sand-locked Fertile Crescent for extended voyages of discovery, trade, and colonization throughout the Middle East. Caravans of camels, sometimes a thousand strong, crossed the wilderness lands of such disparate locales as India, Ethiopia, China, and the eastern shores of the Mediterranean Sea, and worked their way deep into the sandy heart of the Sahara. Desert warriors on camels had the advantages of height, speed, and endurance over those on horses. And on camelback, fierce Bedouins burst out of the Arabian Peninsula to spread the word of their new prophet, Muhammad, in the seventh century A.D.

In the desert, the use of the caravan has changed little over thousands of years. Even recently, when a Japanese film crew documented the interior of China's Taklamakan Desert, a caravan of about 5 dozen camels was the only

protected, they are still hunted for their hides. Besides poachers, the animals are stalked by their natural predatory enemy, the 150-pound (68-kg) Patagonia puma, which prefers young guanacos, known as *chulengos*.

For reasons unknown, the early camelids that remained in North America failed to adapt, and they died off. Only bones and fossilized hoofprints offer evidence of their presence on the continent. On central Asia's Gobi plateau, however, those that migrated across the land bridge adapted to the soft soil and extreme dryness of their new home. They evolved into thick-necked, two-humped camels, which were later named Bactrian after an ancient valley in Afghanistan called Bactria. Herds of wild practical way to move the 30 people and 4 tons of gear. As the novices soon learned, it can take several people, a sturdy rope, and a lot of pulling to get the most stubborn of the beasts to kneel long enough for 400 pounds (181 kg) of supplies to be lashed onto its back. Balancing the load and tying the ancient knots requires an experienced hand; the ability to tolerate a camel's brays and dodge its occasional nips also helps.

Besides transportation, the camel supplies meat and milk. Its hides and fur are used for clothes and tents, its dried dung for fuel. Some Bedouin women wash their hair in camel urine, claiming it adds sheen, kills lice, and prevents itching; men sometimes warm their hands in it on cold mornings. Cairo's main camel market sells as many as 1,000 head a week, but nowadays most of them go to the butcher rather than to Bedouin tribes. Yet, as nomads from the cold deserts of Mongolia to the hot Arabian Peninsula increasingly settle into towns and adopt modern lifestyles, camels have begun to take on different roles.

Today, scientists are taking a second look at the resilience of camels; some believe that with advances in breeding, camels could become the dairy cows of the desert. The humped animals can survive long periods without water and can get by for more than a week at a time on just the moisture gleaned from desert vegetation. With such advantages, camels—unlike cows—can continue to produce milk in drought conditions. In parts of Africa, for instance, 1 camel may be able to yield as much milk as 10 cows. Moreover, camel milk is nutritious. On long trips across the sands, some Saharan nomads have been able to live on vitamin C-rich camel's milk for days on end.

One obstacle to the widespread use of camels for milk is that camels have a low reproductive rate. Females do not become sexually mature until 5 or 6 years of age, and even then they breed only in the spring and have a 13-month gestation period. Hormone injections, now under experimentation, may one day enable two-year-old females to conceive. Also being tested with camels is embryo transfer—a method often used with other farm animals in which several eggs are taken from a prize beast, artificially inseminated, and then placed into host bodies of other females.

A group of camels is led to the annual livestock fair in Pushkar, on the edge of India's Thar Desert. During the fair, buyers, sellers, and camel breeders temporarily swell the village's tiny population to over 100,000.

AMERICA'S LAST CATTLE CROSSING

From Nevada, its heartland, the vast Great Basin Desert sprawls out across a vast area including the southeastern portion of Oregon, southern Idaho, and western Utah. Sometimes called the Sagebrush Desert, the Great Basin is carpeted with boundless tracts of that gray-green desert shrub, which supplies shelter or food for many wildlife species including sparrows, sage grouse, rattlesnakes, lizards, mule deer, and the Western Hemisphere's fastest animal, the pronghorn. Paiute Indians lived for centuries primarily on a diet of the abundant jackrabbits, ground squirrels, and grasshoppers they found in the sagebrush, and they supplemented these staples with the seeds of wild rye and ricegrass.

Among the dozen or so species of sagebrush native to the Great Basin, the largest and most common is *Artemisia tridentata,* or big sage. It usually measures 6 feet (2 m) tall and can tower up to 15 feet (4.5 m) in especially fertile soil. In the never-ending competition for the cold desert's scant water resources, sagebrush often wins out over other plants because of its deep taproot and unusually wide outstretching network of other roots just beneath the soil. The soft, silvery hue of the shrubs' wedge-shaped, toothed leaves is caused by a coating of minuscule, downy-soft hairs that reflect sunlight and trap moisture from the air. For generations, Great Basin travelers and indigenous peoples alike have prepared campfires from the highly burnable woody trunk of the sagebrush, and Native Americans have long believed in the healing properties of the plant's aromatic leaves, which are frequently used in tribal ceremonies.

In essence, the rugged landscape of the Great Basin, like much of the western United States, resulted from the convergence of two huge tectonic plates—the North American Plate and the Pacific Plate—which meet under the Pacific Ocean. About 17 million years ago, when the land that is now the Great Basin was a gentle plain, the two plates jammed against each other, and enormous tectonic stress was created. Scientists believe this stress, which created California's earthquake-prone San Andreas fault, over time also caused geological upheaval far inland. The once-flat land between eastern California's Sierra Nevada and Utah's Wasatch Range—which are the general boundaries of the Great Basin Desert—broke apart. Some

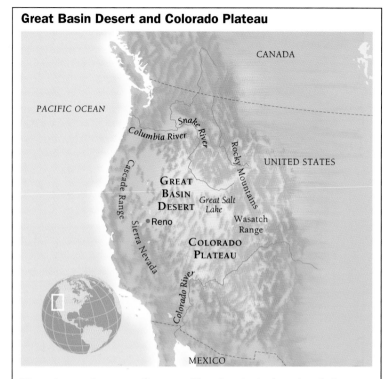

Great Basin Desert and Colorado Plateau

These two regions are often considered a single desert and share many plants and animals. However, the northernmost of the two, the Great Basin, is distinguished by rivers that have no outlet to the sea. The Colorado Plateau is drained, and shaped, by the river system of the same name.

Pronghorns (*above*), native to North America's desert grasslands, are named for their curved horns. Built for speed, they easily outdistance animal predators.

Yellow-flowered rabbitbrush (*right*) thrives on the alkaline floor of Lava Beds National Monument in California. Animals of the Great Basin browse on these low shrubs.

HOW RAIN SHADOW DESERTS ARE FORMED

Mountain ranges influence and sustain desert conditions around the world. As massive barriers, they prevent moisture-laden air from reaching inland areas, which become arid because they lie within the mountains' "rain shadow." When warm, moist air encounters a mountain, the air is forced up the slope, and with increasing elevation, the rising air cools. As a result, the moisture it holds is released as rain or snow on the windward side of the mountain range. Dry air rides over the crest of the mountain and drops down the leeward side. There is scant moisture left for the interior land.

The lands where mountains and rain-shadow deserts formed were once flat and fertile. As illustrated in the drawing at top right, moisture from oceans was carried inland as rain. Over millions of years, however, mountain ranges were built by the unyielding and continuous shifting of Earth's tectonic plates. Tectonic plates are made of the crust and the outermost part of the planet's mantle and ride on a layer of heated rock. The continents and ocean floors are embedded in the crust.

The mountains in the drawing at bottom right were formed when an oceanic plate (*light brown*) was forced under the continental plate (*dark brown*). There, the rock beneath the ocean floor melted. This molten rock, or magma (*orange*), was forced upward and burst through its surface creating massive volcanoes. Subsequent folding and faulting produced mountain ranges. Once-fertile regions were now walled off from sources of moisture, and over millions of years became increasingly arid landscapes (*yellow*).

This type of tectonic activity gave birth to the Cascades, the Sierra Nevada, the Sierra Madre, and the Andes mountain ranges, which run along the western coasts of North and South America. They are all striking examples of mountains that cause pronounced rain shadows. The deserts most affected are the Great Basin, the Colorado Plateau, and the Chihuahuan deserts in North America, and in South America the Patagonian and Atacama deserts.

Before mountain-building occurs, warm, moist ocean air rises and is carried inland by winds. Where it falls as rain, regions remain green and fertile.

When tectonic plates that compose the Earth's shell (light and dark brown layers), collide, the collision forces molten rock upward (orange) to form volcanoes and mountain ranges. These barriers keep moisture from inland regions, forming deserts.

chunks fell, others rose; in some of the fractures, lava bled upward from beneath the crust and then cooled. The result is the so-called "basin and range" structure of the Great Basin Desert: vast, flat expanses broken by long, narrow mountain ranges that generally run north to south. These ranges typically have a tilt, with one side sloping gently, the other jutting sharply from the level desert floor. Over millennia, weathering and erosion have carved spectacular canyons and otherworldly topographical formations out of the rock.

One of the results of these tectonic forces is that water in the Great Basin drains internally. Like those of the cold-winter Taklamakan, its rivers flow inward rather than reaching the sea. Utah's Great Salt Lake is the largest catchment in the Great Basin, with countless smaller lakes scattered throughout the region; their water levels rise and fall depending on the whims of rainfall and evaporation.

The climatic conditions of the Great Basin change in cycles of several thousand years each. At present, the desert is in the midst of a long hot, dry spell, but some 12,000 years ago the climate was cooler and wetter, and much of the flat ground was under water.

The asphalt pavement of Interstate 80, which stretches across the Great Basin Desert, was not begun until the middle of the 20th century, but the path of Nevada's major interstate highway was well trodden more than 10 decades before by California-bound gold prospectors and settlers. Joseph Walker was not the first to cross the vast expanse that encompasses nearly all of Nevada, but he

was the one who, in 1833, discovered the route that tens of thousands would take across the rain-shadow desert to the Sierra Nevada and the promised land beyond. His path left the Bear River in southern Idaho, cut briefly into Utah, and then entered the northeast corner of what is now Nevada. There, the trail followed the fickle waters of the Humboldt River in a winding diagonal and continued westward to present-day Reno. Within a decade, Walker—who, one companion said, "could find water quicker than any man I ever met"—was leading wagon trains along the riverside on what would be known as the California Trail.

For a settler in the 1840's, following the trail that Walker pioneered was a hit-or-miss proposition. Maps were to be had, but as often as not the rivers and lakes marked on them proved dry upon arrival. On other occasions, a presumably dry lake bed would be a marsh, its water bitter but drinkable. Unpredictable water holes and sparse vegetation became more precious with each passing wagon; in 1849 alone, some 22,500 settlers, accompanied by 60,000 beasts, followed the fickle river many would call the Humbug.

Today, Interstate 80 follows the same arched path across the Great Basin of northern Nevada, through Elko and Winnemucca, along the Humboldt River. Each day, more than 25,000 vehicles travel between the California state line and the gambling hub of Reno—a distance of less

A rising sun reflects on the surface of Great Salt Lake in Utah, the only significant body of water in the Great Basin Desert that is full all year. Because of evaporation, the lake is seven times as salty as the ocean.

In full gallop, wild horses cross the snow-dusted surface of the Black Rock region of northern Nevada's Great Basin Desert. Horses, mountain lions, elk, and deer flourish in the higher regions of the Great Basin, where frosty mornings like this one can occur as late as May or June.

than 20 miles (32 km). Only about one-fifth of those vehicles ventures along any given desolated stretch of the interstate's remaining 380 miles (612 km) east of Reno to the Utah border. Farther south, Nevada's other transstate highway, Route 50, has been dubbed the "loneliest road in America." Crisscrossed by old Pony Express trails, the highway is sparsely dotted with tiny towns: Ely, Eureka, and Austin. In between are mile after mile of salt and shrub flats—broken only by dry streambeds—and jagged mountain ranges. The paved ribbon winds gently, then seems to disappear as it descends to another flat. Along the way, signs boast: "Next Services 113 Miles" and "Cattle Crossing Next 83 Miles."

Monotonous though it may seem to the weary driver, the heart of the Great Basin is, during all seasons, a bustling ecosystem thriving with well-adapted forms of life. In fact, the arid state of Nevada, which encompasses portions of both the Great Basin and the Mojave deserts, has been called the "poor man's Alaska" because of its remote, untrampled beauty. A growing number of outdoor enthusiasts are getting to know its 150-plus mountain ranges, the narrow, north-south bands of diverse life that are separated by an equal number of vast

Bighorn sheep peer from a rocky perch (*center*) in southern Utah. Sharp-eyed, sure-footed desert travelers, bighorns can also swim if necessary. Males with the largest horns typically dominate peers and mate with more females.

Fastest bird of prey, the peregrine falcon (*left*) uses razor-sharp talons to attack other birds in midair. Perfectly adapted to its environment, the peregrine is threatened by hunters, egg collectors, and chemical pesticides.

desert basins. Although they lie within a cold-winter desert, the peaks of the ranges are home to alpine forests, lakes, flower-covered meadows, breathtaking views, and a host of wildlife including bighorn sheep, coyotes, bald eagles, and mountain lions.

Since the early 1980's, conservation groups have been pushing the U.S. Congress to declare about 1.4 million acres (560,000 ha) of U.S. Forest Service land—making up roughly 2 percent of Nevada's total area—as wilderness, a designation that would protect it from development. This activism resulted in the dedication in 1986 of the 77,109-acre (30,844-ha) Great Basin National Park, Nevada's first, in the eastern part of the state. It features the state's second highest mountain, 13,063-foot (3,919-m) Wheeler Peak, as well as decorated limestone caverns and stands of bristlecone pines. Some of the bristlecones are dated at 4,000 years of age and are believed to be the world's oldest living things, more ancient even than California's redwoods. Since the park was established, about 700,000 additional acres of forest have been declared wilderness, and proposals that would place even more of Nevada's vast wilderness acreage on the protected list are extant.

SCULPTING THE DESERT

Wind, water, and sand are the tools with which nature continually chisels the contours of desert lands. This process of erosion—the physical wearing away of soil, then the rock beneath—happens easily in arid lands, where there is scant vegetation to stand in the way of the abrasive forces. Deserts, as shown here, are the grand showcases for the most awe-inspiring and bizarrely shaped geological formations on Earth.

Like many other desert peoples, the ancient Nabateans—who lived in present-day Jordan—sought shelter among natural rock formations. They built their well-hidden city of Petra, shown at right, in the natural indentations and caves of the reddish sandstone cliffsides, which have been pummeled and polished by winds for thousands of years. Wind can blow sand so powerfully across the desert floor that upright surfaces, such as sedimentary rock cliffs, can be pelted with the erosive force of a jackhammer. After taking such a beating for millions of years, land can be so whittled away that all that remains of a once expansive mesa, or steep-sided small plateau, is a butte, whose tabletop silhouette stands out unmistakably on the flat horizon. Thousands of years later, wind and sand can further disintegrate it into a mere top-heavy pinnacle of rock, called a pedestal, whose bulbous top will someday topple off its thin stalk and crash to the desert floor below.

Water is the mightiest of all erosive forces—especially in deserts. In one afternoon of flooding, as rainwater runoff carves deep ravines into the face of barren land, a storm-swollen, rushing river can break past its banks and change its course forever. And over millennia rivers have etched huge gorges—sometimes thousands of feet deep—into the surfaces of rocky plains, turning them into sheer-cliffed canyonlands. The largest of these is the Grand Canyon in Arizona, carved out of the arid Colorado Plateau by the Colorado River.

Eroded by wind and water for thousands of years, pale gray sandstone spires jut hundreds of feet above an arid Himalayan plateau near Ladakh in northern India.

At Petra, in present-day Jordan, ancient Nabateans built temples and dwellings in the multicolored sandstone cliffsides (above), where desert winds still create swirls and hollow pockets in the rocky facades.

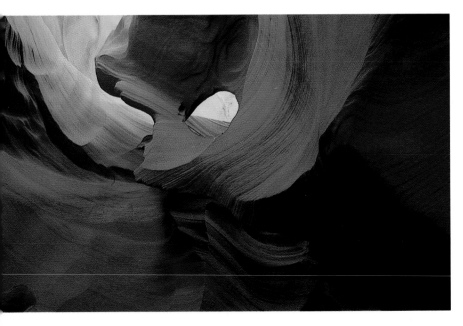

Antelope Canyon (left) is one of many slot canyons found in the Colorado Plateau. Its smooth sandstone walls are carved by flashflood waters that swiftly carry abrasive gravel and sand through the narrow chasm and down to the Colorado River.

About the same size and shape as beach balls, sandstone spheres dot the Mojave Desert floor (above). A small particle—sand or an insect—is the nucleus around which sedimentary material collects and gradually forms these distinctive rock formations.

Shiprock, in the Four Corners region of New Mexico (left), towers 1,700 feet (518 m) above the dry Colorado Plateau. This sacred Navajo site is all that remains of an ancient volcano, one of many that once dotted this landscape.

Tragedy at Stillwater

During World War II and after, deserts in countries all over the world have seemed ideal places for testing bombs and disposing of nuclear and other toxic wastes. One such site is Fallon Naval Air Station's top-secret training grounds in the Great Basin Desert.

During the winter of 1983–84, this desolate region about 60 miles (96 km) east of Reno, Nevada, received unusually high rain- and snowfall—more than twice its usual 8 inches (205 mm) of seasonal precipitation. After the melt, the marshy Stillwater National Wildlife Refuge flooded, turning into a temporary lake. When those waters finally receded in the summer of 1986, there was a ghastly surprise: 7 million dead fish. Simultaneously, birds native to the refuge began dying, and scientists counted hundreds of deformed hatchlings. These finds were especially alarming because the Stillwater marsh is also an important stopover on the Pacific flyway.

The Navy had used the 64-square-mile (166-sq-km) expanse for 20 years to test new kinds of conventional bombs. The testing range is abutted by the marshy wilderness of the Stillwater area, where despite the occasional misaimed bomb or errant piece of shrapnel, many forms of wildlife—including jackrabbits, coyotes, waterfowl, and

Activists gather at Mercury, Nevada, near the Nevada Test Site (*above*) for this 1987 protest against nuclear testing. Conducted deep beneath the ground, bomb tests have continued, albeit less frequently, since the end of the Cold War.

Dozens of detonations have cratered Frenchman Flat (*right*), a dry lake bed northwest of Las Vegas, Nevada. Scientists once built a railroad bridge and a motel on the site to observe the effect on them of an atomic blast. Neither survived.

The snowy gypsum dunes of White Sands National Monument in southern New Mexico's Tularosa Valley result from eons of rain erosion, which carries gypsum down from nearby mountains. When the runoff evaporates, the gypsum's white crystals are blown into dunes.

Navy's own Environmental Protection Department disagreed. A 1988 toxicity report said Fallon Naval Air Station's training grounds in the Great Basin Desert contained 27 "potentially contaminated sites," 21 of which posed "a potential threat to human health or the environment." The desert lands in west-central Nevada were contaminated with chromium and other elements and had been saturated with several varieties of napalm. The report warned that contaminants carried downstream by surface water could threaten habitats used by bald eagles and peregrine falcons—both endangered species—as well as waterfowl and wildlife in the Stillwater refuge, and possibly livestock on nearby ranches.

As a result of the 1988 report the Navy launched a seven-week effort in 1989, which they called Operation Ugly Baby, to clean up the test ranges. It found 1,389 live bombs, 2,230 dummy bombs, 28,136 rounds of ammunition, and 123,375 pounds (55,519 kg) of shrapnel.

The Nuclear Wastebasket

The world's first atomic bomb was detonated as part of the Manhattan Project in 1945 in New Mexico's White Sands region, part of the subtropical Chihuahuan Desert. Since 1951, more than 700 nuclear devices have been exploded in the Great Basin's Nevada Test Site, about 65 miles (105 km) northwest of Las Vegas. The test site is larger than the state of Rhode Island.

In 1963, concern over the spread of radioactive fallout in the atmosphere led the U.S. military to begin conducting all its tests underground. Such detonations are generally carried out at the bottom of 12-foot-wide (360-cm) shafts drilled straight into the ground to about a mile (1,580 m) below the surface. Other tests are conducted deep within the Great Basin Desert's mountains, where miles of tunnels have been mined over the past 30 years. With the end of the cold war, tests have been scaled back but not halted entirely. Eight devices were tested by the United States in 1991, about half the number conducted in 1985. Each test costs anywhere from U.S. $20 million to U.S. $150 million.

Some obvious qualities seem to make deserts ideal locations for such hazardous activities as weapon testing and toxic waste disposal. Few people live in deserts. Although about 35 percent of the earth's landmass is considered arid, it contains only about 15 percent of the

lizards—have flourished, and people have fished, hunted, and camped. Few people regarded the test range as a threat. "It's a desert out there," said one naval official. "Nothing grows on it."

Navy officials maintained that the creatures at Stillwater had died of natural causes. High concentrations of salt—the result of evaporation—in the waters had killed the fish, they contended, and the birds may have drunk water contaminated by mercury that seeped from nearby gold mines or by naturally occurring selenium. But the

federal government would bury radioactive waste.

A big argument against using Yucca Mountain for a nuclear dump is tectonic. Lathrop Wells volcano is 12 miles (19 km) from Yucca Mountain. The volcano was formerly thought not to have been active for 300,000 years. But a 1988 study conducted by a University of New Mexico geomorphologist produced evidence that it may have been active in the past 10,000 years. Moreover, there is concern that years of underground nuclear explosions at the test site have increased stresses along the faults in the region, boosting the chances of earthquake or volcanic eruption.

Chances are good, some scientists fear, that sometime in the next 10,000 years an eruption or earthquake will snap the bedrock in the region and create new fissures for groundwater seepage. The water table may be thrust even higher. And because such water has a large salt concentration it could eat away at metal waste containers, allowing the radioactive particles to seep out into the rock.

Other scientists say that water is not the only potential drawback to using Yucca Mountain as a dump site for nuclear waste. High winds, which can erode rock rapidly, create another problem in storing any kind of waste in a desert. Any exposed nuclear waste could easily be spread by the mini-tornadoes common to hot sites; called dust

population. Barren, empty land is easier to clear for construction. The fact that groundwater in the region is usually low and often moves as slowly as 130 feet (40m) annually decreases the chance that it will seep into containers of nuclear or toxic waste.

These are among the arguments that the U.S. Department of Energy is using to support its plan to use Yucca Mountain, in a corner of the Nevada Test Site, for the underground disposal of high-level nuclear waste from around the United States. While debate continues, highly radioactive spent nuclear fuel rods continue to pile up at reactors. By the year 2000, some 48,000 tons of high-level nuclear waste are expected to have accumulated.

Only about 6 inches (152 mm) of rain falls annually in that portion of the Great Basin Desert. As little as 1/50 inch (0.5 mm) is absorbed by the soil, while the rest evaporates. The water table is more than 1,760 feet (530 m) beneath the surface, far below the level to which the devils, these winds are powerful enough to lift cars and uproot mobile homes.

There has been one ironic advantage to using deserts in either war games or actual combat: since being pelted with millions of bombs during the U.N.–Iraqi war of 1991, the desert of Kuwait has been left alone. Hunters and shepherds who previously made their living in the sandy, arid expanses are afraid to risk being blown to bits by remaining land mines. Surprisingly, when the desert surface was churned up by the military activity, it became more receptive to moisture and plant growth—much like a newly tilled garden. Quickly roughed up, then left alone, the aerated land encouraged seeds to sprout. Where people and sheep refuse to venture out, ducks and coots are reappearing as the war-ravaged desert begins to bloom again for the first time in decades.

One Chinese desert town not located on tourist maps is Malan, in the Tian Shan foothills on the road from Turpan to Korla. Malan is not an ancient desert outpost buried in the sands; it was built in the 1960's as headquarters of the 38,600-square-mile (100,000-sq-km) Lop Nor Nuclear Weapons Test Base, where about 90 miles (150 km) southwest of the town, China detonated its first atomic bomb on October 16, 1964.

Life in the fierce, arid region was far from easy for the facility's construction workers. At one point, the tens of thousands of laborers, about two-thirds of whom were

Preparing for lift-off, the Chinese carrier rocket Long March 2 is positioned in the 180-foot-high (55-m) launch pad of the Jiuquan Satellite Launching Center in a remote Gobi Desert site in Gansu Province. The center launched China's first human-made satellite in 1970.

prisoners, ran out of vegetables and resorted to eating elm leaves and other wild desert plants. Today, the town's airport, hospital, bank, and several restaurants are open to area residents. But access to the area where much of the country's nuclear research takes place, about 80 miles (129 km) north in the desolate foothills, is restricted.

Like those in other countries, China's early nuclear tests were not without their health and environmental costs. By 1967 it was clear that many scientists and technicians had been exposed to high levels of radioactive fallout; some of them were losing their hair. This could have been due to the fact that some workers were assigned to drive vehicles into the test area to measure shock waves and radiation, while others drove armored units to ground zero to test the combat readiness of the vehicles in a nuclear blast.

Today, the huge nuclear missile test site is littered with debris, and the ground is strewn with explosion craters. A pair of journalists on a recent visit described the vista across the once-pristine wilderness: broken cars, blown-up armored personnel carriers, and dilapidated concrete buildings covered with melted glass. Despite the worldwide surge in environmental consciousness, the concept of deserts as wastelands still seems ingrained in the minds of many.

This finned hunk of metal was once used at Nevada's Nellis Air Force Base for military target practice before it was abandoned on the desert floor.

DIAMONDS IN THE SAND

Waves from the largest oceans of the world pound relentlessly upon the shores of some of the most untamed and desiccated places of all, coastal deserts. These strips of seaside wilderness owe their existence to a particularly rare, yet finely tuned, interplay between wind, water, and land that creates ecosystems unlike any others on the Earth.

Coastal deserts lie along portions of the western edges of the continents of Africa and North and South America. On these shores prevailing winds—caused by the rotation of the Earth—blow inland from the sea almost continuously. South America's Atacama Desert, for example, is actually the driest, most forbidding section of a much larger arid coastal region that stretches 2,500 miles (4,032 km) along the continent's western shoreline through southern Ecuador, the length of Peru, and southward into Chile, heart of the Atacama. Similarly, the Namib Desert runs along the western coast of Namibia, in southern Africa. And north of the Equator, Baja California—a narrow peninsula wedged between the Pacific Ocean and the Gulf of California—is one of the most arid regions in Mexico, albeit not a separate desert per se.

The extreme aridity of the world's few coastal deserts is greatly influenced by frigid offshore ocean currents that flow from the North and South poles. South of the Equator, the Benguela Current, which originates in the icy waters off Antarctica, flows north along the western edge of Africa; likewise, the Humboldt, or Peru, Current follows the west coast of South America. These currents supply the cold waters that crash upon the coastal cliffs and sand- or pebble-strewn shores of the Namib and Atacama deserts.

These currents—as well as chilly upwellings from the depths of the Atlantic and Pacific oceans—also cool the layer of air that absorbs moisture just above the surface of the water. Because these coastal deserts are situated at low latitudes, a blanket of air heated by the subtropical sun hovers above this cool, saturated layer. This phenomenon, in which cold air stays beneath warmer air, is called a temperature inversion because it is contrary to normal atmospheric conditions. Usually, air temperatures decrease as elevation increases. These particular inversions off desert coasts cause air saturation, thick fog, and low-altitude stratus clouds—but virtually no measurable precipitation.

In the quintessential coastal deserts—the Atacama and Namib—fog formed above the ocean is frequently blown inland 50 miles (80 km) or more before evaporating. Rarely does the moisture condense to fall as rain. Locked in the grip of fog-shrouded aridity, these deserts actually receive more moisture from the frothy saltwater spray of ocean breakers and from fog—which is ingeniously used by plants and animals—than they ever do from raindrops. Parts of the Atacama, for example, are so dry that virtually nothing survives there. One town in the Chilean highlands received rain only five times between 1972 and 1982, for a total of 1.5 inches (38 mm). Half of that fell during one abnormally wet year.

Since coastal deserts lie within roughly the same latitudinal bands as the subtropical deserts, they are influenced by the same atmospheric high pressure cells. In coastal deserts, the frequent blanket of morning fog prevents the skies from being as clear—or the temperatures as hot—as in other dry lands along the Tropics of Cancer and Capricorn. But the combined evaporative powers of the sun and the high pressure systems' dry air, which dives down from above, generally do the trick of burning off the fog as the day wears on. Temperatures in the Atacama Desert are moderate, averaging in the low 70's F (20°–24° C) during the summer, and about 50° F (10° C) in the winter. Air temperatures in the Namib are relatively mild, typically no more than the upper 80's F (29°–32° C) inland, and cooler—between 50° and 60° F (10°–16° C)—along the coast.

Deprived of moisture, in part by the desiccating effects of wind and ocean waters working in tandem, the sweeping coastal deserts are also sculpted time and again by these same forces, which act as nature's perennial chisels. The relentless offshore breezes blow sand upon the shores, then carry it far inland to create ever-changing seas of dunes. In other places, rocky cliffs are eternally buffeted by the breakers at the water's edge. Much of the Atacama's desert floor is a mixture of hard-packed gravel and sand brought down millennia ago by runoff water flowing through deep channels along the slopes of inland mountains. Near the shores, these massive deposits fan out, settle, and are called, appropriately, alluvial fans.

Most people and animals that thrive in the Atacama do so where the sea touches the desert and in the scattered oases perched along rivers that flow down mountain channels. But deep in this desert's interior—as in that of the Namib—highly adapted plants and animals manage to survive, primarily because of moisture gathered from the reliable banks of fog.

The majority of people who live in these coastal deserts congregate in port towns along the shorelines, where life revolves, for the most part, around exporting minerals gleaned from the interior of each desert. Although wanting for water and vegetation, these two arid coastal regions are abundant with riches beneath their desolate surfaces. Copper is chief among the natural resources that support those living in the dry Atacama; and in the sparsely populated Namib, raw diamonds are far more abundant than either watering holes or people.

ONE OF THE EERIEST PLACES ON EARTH is the Valley of the Moon in the Atacama Desert, where the lunarlike terrain and the rarity of living things are unavoidable realities. Razor-sharp cliffsides and eccentric rock formations poke holes through the frequent blanket of fog; in return, the solemn greyness penetrates down onto the barren land, creating an otherworldly bleakness in every eroded crevice below. On a clear evening, salt crystals in the crusty red soil reflect light, and the desert floor shimmers and glows. Here, in this valley, the Atacama masquerades as the moon; elsewhere, this coastal desert's guises are no less unearthly.

Wedged between the Pacific Ocean on the west and the Andes mountain range on the east, the Atacama Desert encompasses the northernmost 600 miles (968 km) of the South American nation of Chile. By most accounts, it is the most arid spot on Earth, receiving less than 0.5 inch (13 mm) of rain per year on average. In some places there is little evidence that it has ever rained. Although the Atacama's frequent fog is a natural blanket of moisture, it rarely provides rain; the humidity it brings inland, however, can reach 80 percent in the barren environment. This coastal desert is so dry that snow on peaks above 18,000 feet (5,486 m) often evaporates before it

melts, forming pointed, stalagmitelike columns. Local inhabitants call this phenomenon "penitent snow" because it looks like nuns in prayer.

Temperatures are comfortably moderate throughout most of the Atacama—from its shoreside alluvial fans and dunes to its high plateaus with their sprawling salt flats, or *salars*, which were lakes before they evaporated. Although this might seem ideal for plant growth, the desert's limited moisture means that the vast majority of the Atacama is devoid of plants and animals—except alongside the ocean, along the few mountain-fed rivers and sporadic oases, and upon certain parts of the inland plateaus.

Intersected by the Tropic of Capricorn, the Atacama is influenced by more than just wind, seawater, fog, and the powerful high-pressure cells at that latitude. Oddly enough, it also affected by what could be called a *reversed* rain-shadow effect. Normally, mountains near coasts prevent ocean-born moisture from reaching interior lands.

A dirt road (*far left*) snakes between ancient rocky outcrops covered with salt crystals in the Valley of the Moon, an unearthly segment of Chile's parched and forbidding Atacama Desert.

Llamas (*below*), native to the Andes, drink at a rare waterhole on the Altiplano, a high plateau region where the Atacama Desert rises toward the Andean cordillera.

The Andes, however, keep rain from moving eastward from inland tropical rain forests to the coastal region; though saturated air can drop more than 120 inches (3,077 mm) of rain each year on some slopes in the lush jungles of tropical South America, the lofty Andes, which in places rise to 20,000 feet (6,096 m), prevent the moisture from crossing over the peaks to the Atacama, which receives none of the wet bounty.

CHILE'S FOGGY COAST

In the fog-shrouded Atacama—where not a trace of rain may fall for years at a time—50 gigantic plastic nets stretched across a barren mountain are harvesting water from the clouds and infusing new life into the desert village below. The few hundred residents of the impoverished Chilean fishing village of Chungungo are taking advantage of the most untapped resource in coastal deserts—the thick fog that tumbles in from the ocean nearly every day. In the first project of its kind in the world's arid lands, inaugurated in May of 1992, 40-foot-long (12-m) mesh fog catchers are strung along the mountaintop. As the cold, dense clouds from the Pacific Ocean—a few miles to the west—brush up over the 2,600-foot (792-m) crest of El Tofo, moisture condenses on the double-layered nets. One by one, drops form and run down the 13-foot-high (4-m) nets, then into troughs and a series of pipes that wind down the mountainside to Chungungo.

Each net harnesses about 45 gallons (170 L) of water a day—a staggering feat considering that 10 million droplets of fog are needed to form one drop of

Carefully angled panels of netting collect moisture from seaborne fog at a research station established on the Pacific coast of Chile to trap water for the dry Atacama.

Atacama Desert

A frigid ocean current, the Humboldt, and cold air trapped above the Tropic of Capricorn turn a strip of South American coast into Earth's driest spot.

High, eroded cliffs plunge into the Pacific at the western edge of the Atacama. Tall bluffs have made it impossible to establish settlements along much of the desert coast.

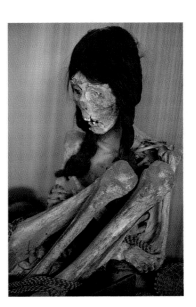

Her body mummified by the parched air of the Atacama, a prehistoric Indian woman still sits in repose with legs drawn up. Hundreds of mummies, along with a wealth of ancient artifacts, have been found near the oasis town of San Pedro de Atacama, proving that early Indian peoples lived in the Atacama as long as 7,000 years ago.

water. The 50 nets, which cost about U.S. $17 each, collect enough water to provide more than 6 gallons (23 L) a day for each of the village's 350 inhabitants, who were used to getting by on about half that amount, which was hauled in twice weekly by truck. The fog water is cleaner, more palatable, and cheaper than the sometimes contaminated supplies brought in from elsewhere. There are prospects of adapting and using the Chungungo fog-catching project—which is funded by the International Development Research Center of Canada—in other arid and semiarid regions of the world where fog is abundant. For the time being, it has dramatically boosted the quality of life, as well as the possibility for sustainable small-scale farming, for the poor, isolated desert community in the barren Atacama.

In spite of its aridity, the Atacama has been home to scattered groups of people for centuries. According to archeological evidence, some Indians may have lived along the coast as early as 7,000 years ago. Further inland, at oases such as San Pedro de Atacama, hundreds of mummies and intricate artifacts, perfectly preserved by the dry climate, have been discovered. Freeze-dried bodies of young children have been found in the volcanic peaks further up; they are believed to be Incan sacrifices. Even today, in the slightly less arid Altiplano region that stretches into southern Bolivia, Chipaya Indians live in thatched-roof sod huts and grow *quinua*—a pigweed—in the flat, sandy ground.

Today most of the Atacama's people live in coastal cities, the largest of which is Antofagasta, midway along the desert's shoreline. Water, piped in from mountain springs 100 miles (161 km) away, must be filtered because of its high arsenic content. Although the city of 200,000 is a bustling export center for the desert's mineral wealth, virtually everything its residents need for day-to-day living must be imported. Water is too precious to permit the large-scale irrigation needed for agriculture. Despite the Atacama's size and the importance of its mines to the nation, only 8 percent of Chile's population lives in the coastal desert.

Mining Interests

In 1535, after the Spanish explorer Pizarro conquered the Incas in what is now Peru, he sent his partner Diego de Almagro and 570 men south into the harsh, uncharted Atacama Desert to find gold. There was none to be found, and the soldiers were left disgruntled. Upon their return north, they engaged in a long struggle in which Pizarro, Almagro, and Almagro's son were killed in turn. To European colonists who came later, the desert seemed just about as worthless—so much so, in fact, that Chile, Bolivia, and Peru cared little about whose borders it fell into.

But in the early 19th century it was discovered that the Atacama holds the world's largest natural deposits of caliche, a raw form of sodium nitrate, which is used to make gunpowder and fertilizer. By the late 1870's, the desert was a prize worth fighting over. In the War of the Pacific 1879–83, Chile, which controlled most of the mining and was backed by European interests, seized control of portions of the Atacama that had belonged to Bolivia, a country that lost its coastal access entirely.

After Chile took the Atacama in 1883, prospectors (known as *cateadores*) began crisscrossing the gritty plains with their pack mules, horses, and llamas, seeking new caliche deposits. Their paths from the coast to the caliche beds were not always the shortest distances between the two points. Instead, they zigzagged between scarce water sources a day's ride apart. Over the next 40 years, sodium

A rusted basketball backboard (*above*) arches toward the ruins of an abandoned nitrate mining town in the Atacama. The German discovery of synthetic sodium nitrate doomed much of Chile's nitrate industry.

Bartolo Confre (*left*) makes his living as a miner at one of the few sodium nitrate mines still functioning in the Atacama.

nitrate mines would provide Chile with two-thirds of its income. Boomtowns sprang up in the desert, and roads and railroads were built to transport the mineral.

But in the 1920's, a cheap synthetic form of sodium nitrate came into widespread use. By the decade's end, the Chilean nitrate industry had bottomed out, and the jobs of tens of thousands of laborers were lost. Only two caliche plants, called *oficinas,* are still in business; the rest are decaying ghost towns—some of which are now national monuments to the early desert heyday.

Fortunately for Chile, the Atacama is a cornucopia of other valuable minerals including some of the world's richest copper reserves. One can often pluck mica, copper, and sulfur right off the bare ground. These and other minerals keep the nation afloat; were the desert truly barren beneath its gravelly surface, it would most likely be inhabited today by only the few Indians who have lived for centuries as subsistence farmers along widely scattered rivers and oases.

A Varied Topography

Although Antofagasta is the principal port today, serving the huge inland copper mine at Chuquicamata—about 150 miles (242 km) away—ports like Tocopilla and Iquique to the north remain bustling centers where the desert joins the sea. In general, the coastline rises sharply from the sea. There are few beaches, and sheer cliffs can rise to 3,000 feet (914 m). To the extreme north is Arica, which is both a port and a popular resort, with its sunny weather and warmer-than-usual beachfront.

Most people of the Atacama live on the coast, as does the vast majority of the desert's wildlife. Seals and a host of seabirds including gulls, pelicans, penguins, and petrels thrive on the abundant fish in the cool Pacific waters.

Leaving the busy, palm-lined coastal cities, today's travelers can still see the wagon-wheel ruts that crease the dusty, grey-brown desert floor. But where those early *cateadores* would cover 30 miles (48 km) in a day, one can now drive the width of the Atacama Desert in a matter of hours. The width of the Atacama, like that of the rest of the country from the ocean to the Andes, seldom exceeds 100 miles (161 km). As one goes inland, the rolling, treeless plain rises thousands of feet almost imperceptibly; one can reach more than a mile (1.6 km) above sea level without ever sensing the change in elevation. The ground surface is a bleak mixture of sand, pebble, and salt residue in which nothing grows. Dust, picked up by the westerly breeze, seems to get into everything.

Occasionally, the road will pass a nitrate ghost town, like Chacabuco, where 3,000 miners once lived and worked in spartan conditions. Buildings of wood and corrugated steel sit frozen in time, and the debris-strewn ground is powdered with the white caliche residue.

The bleak expanse of the central Atacama plains is broken occasionally by a patchwork quilt of green irrigated fields in the valley oases, either at springs or along rivers. One such town is Calama, with a population of 92,000. It is situated on the banks of the Río Loa, a curving, 275-mile (444-km) river that flows from the Andes to the coast. The Loa is not the Atacama's only river, but it is the only one that makes it all the way to the ocean. Along the

Sandwiched on a low shelf of land between the Pacific and the rocky wastes of the Atacama, the sprawling city of Antofagasta—which sits exactly on the Tropic of Capricorn—is the principal export center in northern Chile for the country's copper and other minerals.

Lush green fields outside the city of Calama (*left*), irrigated by water from the Río Loa, stretch along a valley floor beneath a row of looming, arid cliffs.

way, waters are siphoned off for irrigation and drinking, so that by the time it reaches the Pacific it is nothing more than a trickle.

Heading further into the interior, the road rises to nearly 8,000 feet (2,438 m) before reaching the oasis village of San Pedro de Atacama. The town's mud and stone buildings, which house its 1,600 residents, lie at the northern edge of Chile's largest salt flat, the Salar de Atacama. Further east of the flat expanse, volcanic peaks, some letting off steam, jut into the sky.

Salars, or dead lakes, abound in the high basins of the eastern Atacama, particularly in the 12,000-foot (3,658-m) puna, or Altiplano, region that stretches into Bolivia. Typically flatlands surrounded by volcanic mountains, they are the remains—like the salt flats of the Great Basin Desert in the United States—of lakes whose tributaries petered out and whose water evaporated. Some are still wet, with grassy marshes; others are covered with salt-rich mud. Here, waterfowl, such as ducks and flamingos, make occasional stopovers, and vicuñas sometimes drink from the freshwater springs that, in places, feed into the salars. At one of the dried-up lakes, Salar de Pujsa, legend has it that a village is buried in the salt sediments, punished like the biblical Sodom for its wickedness.

Copper Town

One of the world's largest human-made holes, a 1,400-foot-deep (427-m), 2-mile-long (3-km) terraced gash in the Atacama highlands, provides Chile

with at least 25 percent of its annual export income. Chuquicamata, or Chuqui for short, is the largest open-pit copper mine on Earth. A small city has sprung up around the mine and includes a hospital, stores, homes, and recreational facilities.

The hole continues to grow every day as workers dynamite more of the rock and load it into trucks or rail cars. The copper ore is then hauled to the mine's crushing plant, where it is ground down and the rough copper melted into 350-pound (159-kg) slabs for export.

Copper burial ornaments found near Chuqui suggest that desert-dwelling Indians were smelting the metal there even before the time of the Incas. Modern opportunists did not discover Chuqui's value until the early 1900's; the U.S.-owned Anaconda Company bought the mine in

A gaudy flight of flamingos (*above*) takes wing from a salty lagoon near the Atacama coast. The birds' pink color comes from a chemical in the algae and other foods they strain from the water with their beaks.

Superheated gases and steam (*left*) blow from a geyser on Mount Tocorpuri, an Atacama volcano near the Bolivian border. One of many Andean volcanoes, the mountain is mined for its high-grade sulfur.

Almost pure copper gleams from rock (*left*) found in the mountains of the Atacama Desert. An aerial photograph (*below*) shows smoke rising from a processing plant at the Chuquicamata copper mine in Chile, the largest such open-pit operation in the world.

1916. By then, nitrate deposits were dwindling and prices plummeting because of competition from synthetics. By the late 1960's, Chile was in the process of gaining part ownership of Chuqui and other U.S.-owned mines. But the mines were nationalized in 1971 under President Salvador Allende's Marxist administration. Although Augusto Pinochet's government later compensated Anaconda, Chile's three largest mines are still state owned.

San Pedro and other once-sleepy oasis villages nearby have prospered from their proximity to Chuquicamata. Chuqui's workers are some of the country's best paid. The desert mine also gives village farmers a market for the vegetables and fruits they grow: pomegranates, grapes, and apples, to name a few.

CLEAR DESERT SKIES

Perched in the Andean foothills southwest of the Atacama Desert in Chile, Cerro Tololo Observatory has the largest telescope in the Southern Hemisphere.

Late one night in February 1987, on an arid 8,000-foot (2,400-m) peak in northern Chile, a young university dropout used a small, jury-rigged telescope to record the first supernova, or exploding star, observable by the naked eye since the 17th century. As the first person to report the sudden flash on the southern horizon, Ian Shelton, a Canadian, joined the likes of the Renaissance astronomers Tycho Brahe and Johannes Kepler, who were the first to report supernovas that occurred in their lifetimes.

Astronomical discoveries as exciting as Shelton's, which was made at Las Campanas near the Atacama Desert, are rare. Yet data gleaned day to day at observatories around the world—many in arid regions—are changing the way scientists view the universe. Deserts, with their isolation from smog and light and lack of view-obscuring precipitation, are ideal locations for observatories.

For centuries, desert inhabitants have charted the skies. The Mesopotamians, surrounded by desert, were the first to record celestial movements, some 5,000 years ago. The domed Mayan observatory at Chichén Itzá in the Yucatán and a ceremonial Anasazi kiva in New Mexico's Chaco Canyon, pierced by a shaft of sunlight at each summer solstice, are but a few of the ruins that attest to the sophistication that desert-dwelling Native Americans brought to their observations of the heavens.

Today, New Mexico's desert is home to one of the most advanced observatories in history, a cluster of 27 radio telescopes called the Very Large Array (VLA), that can be moved back and forth over nearly 40 miles (65 km) of railroad tracks. Unlike conventional telescopes, the VLA's dishes pick up faint, invisible radio waves emitted by galaxies, quasars, and black holes millions of light years away. A similar, if smaller, radio telescope array in Australia monitors the skies of the Southern Hemisphere. In 1992, scientists from California to Australia began aiming radio telescopes into outer space to listen for signs of extraterrestrial life that might be detected from encoded radio waves.

For observations aimed at space a little closer to Earth, an ideal desert is Antarctica, where clear skies and perpetual daytime during the southern summer make it possible to watch the Sun for weeks at a stretch. Using solar cameras, spectrometers, and other astronomical instruments, scientists at the Amundsen-Scott Station at the South Pole have discovered, among other things, that the surface of the Sun rotates at a much different rate from that at which the lower layers do. Dark polar winters mean excellent star gazing for the few who can brave temperatures of -100° F (-38° C).

Antarctica is useful to astronomers for more than observation. Its extreme cold, dryness, and isolation make it the closest thing on Earth to the surface of the Moon and Mars. Recently, scientists have used the icy continent as a testing ground for high-tech gear—everything from space suits to waste-recycling systems to robotic rovers—destined for extraterrestrial use.

The Very Large Array (VLA), a group of 27 radio telescopes that fan across the Plains of San Augustin near Socorro, New Mexico, monitors invisible electromagnetic waves to chart distant galaxies.

SOUTHWEST AFRICAN DUNES

Like frothy swirls of pumpkin-colored meringue, the majestic dunes of the Namib Desert bask in the evening's lingering rays of sunlight. A gibbous moon peers over the African horizon, awaiting its turn to drench these desert sands in softer, cooler hues of yellow and gray. At any given moment, somewhere in these dunes—which stretch as far as the eye can see—the unfailing wind is whipping sand up a slope and over its crest, from which a gritty tongue of sand is cascading down. Billions of sand grains are in motion on the surface of this windswept land, piling high into newly formed peaks and realigning the contours of dune-studded valleys below. Tonight the mountains of sand still radiate warmth from the sun, but a westerly breeze cools the air; by morning, a thick fog will most likely have rolled in as well. At this lonely spot in the coastal desert, the waters of the South Atlantic Ocean are out of view, but the stirring salty air is a constant reminder that the shoreline is but a few miles away.

From this panoramic vantage point, the ever-undulating sandscape appears like an ocean itself; it lends credibility to the name *Namib,* which in the language of southern Africa's indigenous Nama peoples means "area of nothingness."

Their hair braided in traditional fashion, women of the Himba tribe (*above*)—a cattle-raising people native to Africa's Namib Desert—care for their infants.

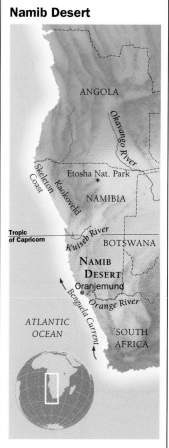

Extending 1,200 miles
(1,935 km) from Angola to
South Africa, where it merges
with the Kalahari, the Namib
is influenced by air currents
above the Tropic of Capricorn
and the Benguela Current,
which carries icy water
from Antarctica.

Atlantic mist drifts over coastal
dunes (*left*) to provide the
virtually rainless Namib with
moisture vital to plants and
animals. Flamingos soar over
a lichen-covered reef.

Yet these desert sands are far from barren, as a moment of silence will prove. A mysterious clicking, not unlike that of amplified crickets, pierces the early night. From their intermittent beginnings, the chirps soon mount to an a cappella chorus, emanating from all directions. These are the mating cries of the sand-dwelling lizards known as barking geckos. Males, perched atop the dunes on their webbed feet, call out to lure females and keep other males at bay. Their noisemaking continues for hours. Geckos are but one of hundreds of species of reptiles, insects, and other creatures that live inside the dune sea, as much as 12 feet 8 inches (389 cm) below the surface. Scores of other animals, including elephants, giraffes, jackals, and several species of antelope roam the dunes or rocky flats, making an improbable living from what seems an impenetrable wasteland.

Ancient Formations

At 55 million years old, the Namib is one of Earth's oldest and most arid deserts. It is a long, narrow band—1,200 miles (1,935 km) long, but only between 50 and 100 miles (81–161 km) wide—wedged between the Atlantic and Namibia's inland hills. Although about half a dozen river beds cut through the desert from the interior highlands, only the Orange, at the southernmost boundary of the desert, and the Cunene, on the Angolan border, carry water for more than a few days at a time. Most are more like drainage basins that flow only when fed by occasional thunderstorms hundreds of miles from the coast—storms that can sometimes occur a year or more apart. Yet water remains in these riverbeds, in small pools or under the ground, for months, nourishing plants and animals. Some scientists call the rivers linear oases. They support several kinds of trees, including acacias. Even during long dry spells, elephants and baboons somehow know where to dig to find rare underground supplies of water. In some cases, other species use these animal versions of wells once the diggers have moved on.

Millennia ago, the Namib Desert was formed on southern Africa's west coast by a chain of events that still continues to link the waters of the Orange River, offshore ocean currents, and prevailing southwesterly winds.

Leaving behind a curious horseshoe track, a sidewinding adder (*left*) hitches itself across the loose red sands that cover parts of the Namib.

A desert chameleon (*above*), native of the more fertile edges of the Namib, swivels a large round eye in search of insect prey, which it snags with its long sticky tongue. The cold-blooded reptiles turn black during the cool morning hours to absorb warmth from the sun's rays, then later turn white to reflect the desert heat.

Meerkats (*below*), a sociable species of mongoose, emerge from their Namibian burrow for sentry duty, warning their den mates of predators.

Geographically speaking, the age-old process is a partially counterclockwise one, which continues without fail, century after century. Sandy sediment is washed down the mighty, 1,300-mile-long (2,097-km) river from Africa's interior, then dumped into the Atlantic Ocean at the river's mouth beside the Namibian city of Oranjemund. There in the Southern Atlantic, the ice-cold Benguela Current carries the sand north. The ocean breakers pound

A wind-carved wall of orange-brown dunes encroaches on a section of two-toned sand in the Inner Namib. Despite their desolate appearance, these dunes can support a variety of bushes and tall grasses.

it onto the shore, and prevailing winds whip it up and ever inland.

One of the Namib's main rivers, the Kuiseb, exerts another kind of influence on the desert by preventing the dunes south of its meandering course from migrating north, where an expanse of gravel plains predominates. South of the Kuiseb, whose mouth is about midway along the coastal desert, the dunes drift inland for 100 miles (160 km). On the opposite side of the river, however, dunes become more sporadic and give way to gravelly expanses, resuming along the northern coast of the Namib. Although the Kuiseb floods only occasionally, its rushing waters still cut away the sandbanks. Yet there is an ongoing tug of war

as the advancing sands continue to push parts of the riverbed northward.

Throughout most of the Namib's sand sea, the multicolored dunes range from a few feet to more than 400 feet (122 m); they reach their highest point—about 1,000 feet (305 m)—at Sossusvlei, roughly 70 miles (113 km) south of the Kuiseb and about 40 miles (65 km) from the Atlantic Ocean. Despite the relatively mild air temperatures, the blazing subtropical sun often warms the sand surface to 150° F (66° C) at midday. The dunes are constantly being recharged by the ocean waves that relentlessly crash into the shore. So much sand is jostled about by wind and wave action along the Namib that the map-line margin of this southwest African coast has actually changed shape in a matter of only centuries, according to cartographers.

The Door with Silk Hinges

In the dune-studded regions of the Namib wilderness, where the floor is sand and the ceiling often a 1,000-foot-thick (305-m) fog bank, a staggering variety of insects, lizards, and mammals have adaptive ways of coping with their hostile, nearly rainless environment. Average precipitation in the Namib Desert is scant, at best; years can pass between showers. But when the drops fall, they are not wasted. Within a few days, hardy grasses carpet the troughs between dunes, and small creatures that have not been seen since the previous rain spring to life. The eggs of a brightly colored beetle called the blue weevil, for example, hatch overnight. Within days of emerging from the sands, the small insects will feed on the new grass, mate, and die—but not before laying their own eggs, which will lie dormant until the next rain months or even years later.

Although most creatures of the Namibian sands have found ways to exist between the rains, many are dependent on grasses to tide them over. Almost as soon as the plants emerge, they wither and are blown into fragments by the wind. In this detritus ecosystem, dried seeds and well-worn grass particles are the keys to life: they collect in the swirling breezes on the leeward sides of the dunes, where they will be eaten in the coming months or years by scavenging insects and lizards collectively known as detritivores because of their diet. These tiny sand dwellers are at the mercy of the wind, which not only brings in life-giving

Phymateus morbillosus, a specially adapted grasshopper common in the Namib, gorges on euphorbia, a cactuslike succulent that is poisonous to most other creatures. The plant makes the grasshopper poisonous to birds and other predators.

seeds and crumbled vegetation but can also squash out life by burying that same food beneath the sand in a sudden gusty storm.

Breezes also bring in sea-born fog, the primary source of moisture for the plants and animals of the Namib dunes. Many insects and cold-blooded reptiles gather moisture directly from the fog, which condenses in drops on their cool bodies. Of the hundreds of indigenous beetle species in the desert, many are experts at fog catching. Industrious button beetles, for example, construct sand ridges and furrows perpendicular to the direction of the desert's inland-blowing winds; later, the insects suck moisture trapped by the minuscule embankments of sand. Head-stander beetles, on the other hand, are more direct in their water-collecting approach: they practically tilt upside down with their long hind legs so that droplets of early-morning fog water will dribble down their backs and into their mouths.

Several species of spider have adapted to dune life. The trapdoor spider gets its name from the fact that after digging a burrow into a dune, it spins a web, then quickly covers it with a thin layer of sand grains to make a false wall—or door with silk hinges—through which it can easily spring to capture a beetle or other prey. In a variation of that process, white lady and back-flip spiders hide beneath sand-coated webs that blend in with the desert floor, then wait until insects—such as dune crickets—are caught in the grip of their camouflaged silken traps.

Performing its patented flip, a head-stander beetle coaxes drops of dew to flow down its body to its mouth. Droplets condense most readily in the morning when the beetle's shell is cool from a chill Namibian night.

The golden wheel spider, whose quarter-sized body is covered with shiny yellow hair, is one of several species that has evolved a handy method of escaping from predators. When threatened by its number-one enemy—a quick-digging female pompilid wasp—the spider jumps from its den, pulls in its five-jointed legs, and rolls, in wheel-like fashion, down the dune face at speeds of up to 5 feet (more than 1 m) per second. At a rate of about 44 spins per second, scientists say, the golden wheel spider is revolving nearly as fast as the wheels on a car traveling 200 miles per hour (323 kph). If the spider lucks into a building site for its burrow at the top of a dune, it has a good chance of escaping the wasp by rolling sometimes hundreds of feet at a time. Otherwise, the wasp would paralyze the spider with its sting, take its catch to its own foot-long (31-cm) den, and lay an egg in the arachnid's live body—food for a soon-to-hatch larval wasp.

The searing desert sands invite all sorts of body contortions and movements. One desert lizard, the *Aporosaura archietae,* has learned to cool its heels on the hot grains by lifting two legs at a time—first its right front and left rear, then its left front and right rear—in a kind of dance. Yet in the cool mornings, the lizard uses the sand to warm itself by lying on its belly. The sidewinding adder slithers sideways over the dunes, much like its distant North American relative, the sidewinding rattlesnake. When it is ready to hunt, the adder buries itself in the sand, leaving only its small, golden-brown eyes protruding like two pebbles from among the tiny grains. When an unlucky lizard happens along, the adder springs from the sand for the kill, then swallows its prey in one piece.

The sands harbor another unique predator, the golden mole. Eyeless, this sand-burrowing animal uses its small, pink nose and highly developed sense of smell to seek out the bugs and lizards on which it feeds. The mole virtually swims through the dunes, breathing the air trapped between the fine grains of sand.

Land of Tall Elephants

Farther north in the Namib, past the Kuiseb River where a troop of the largest baboon species—called *chacmas*—survive in an isolated gorge, the dunes give way to an area of vast gravel plains, often pinkish in color, and steep, rocky outcroppings. This is the Kaokoveld, home to large creatures like elephants, zebras, rhinoceroses, giraffes, and antelopes such as springboks and gemsboks. For most of these animals, life is spent on the move in an ongoing search for water and food. The highly adapted elephants of the Namib, believed to be the tallest elephants in the world, can go without water for several days and travel up

Quiver trees, so called because native Bushmen use the hollow branches to store arrows, are tree versions of the aloe lily. The trees grow in rocky parts of the Namib.

Unique to the Namib, a *Welwitschia mirabilis* (*above*)—some specimens of which live to be hundreds of years old—trails its leathery frayed leaves across the desert sands. A giraffe (*right*) steps gingerly toward a water hole in a wildlife sanctuary.

to 45 miles (73 km) a day from isolated springs to riverbeds, where underground water nourishes plants on which they feed. Giraffes also inhabit the riverbed oases, such as that of the Hoanib. Here they get their food and water simultaneously by eating the leaves of the acacia trees, which provide surfaces for condensation of moisture from fog and dew. Another source of water—as well as of nutritious pulp and seeds—is the naras plant, whose roots plunge deep beneath the surface to locate untapped water. Eaten by the desert's human and animal populations alike, the pulpy, softball-sized, green naras fruit grows on the desert surface, among the plant's sand-hugging, thorny branches.

One of the desert world's oldest plant species, the *Welwitschia mirabilis,* is found only in the Namib desert. Looking tattered and disheveled, the plant produces only two leatherlike leaves during its entire lifetime, which for some of the oldest specimens may be nearly 2,000 years. Over time, the slow-growing leaves split and fray into many strands, which sprawl over the ground, gnarled and intertwined among each other. While much of its moisture is obtained from fog, the *Welwitschia*'s roots can grow laterally to collect water just below the ground surface; in the driest of times, however, a taproot reaches straight downward to seek out deep moisture under gravel plains or dry riverbeds.

The Diamond Coast
Mixed in with the Namib's wealth of sand are riches of a more dazzling and lucrative sort: this coastal desert is the world's single largest source of diamonds. Nearly one-fifth of the world's supply of gem-quality diamonds comes

A bulldozer (*above*) scoops up diamond-laden gravel in a huge hole only yards from the shore. In 1992, digging operations in the region recovered 1.5 million carats of diamonds.

Fog blankets the Atlantic shore (*left*) where the Namib's gem-laden Diamond Coast meets the ocean.

from the Namib's southern dunes, most of them from a narrow strip of beach only a few dozen miles long that is often called the Diamond Coast.

Working around the clock, bulldozers and underwater scrapers plow through thousands of tons of sand every day to expose the diamond-yielding gravel near the bedrock. The sand and gravel are sent to processing plants, where U.S. $1 million worth of diamonds are filtered out every day. Hundreds of workers, most of them contract miners from nearby native tribes, pick through the bedrock exposed by the dozers for any remaining gems.

These diamond-studded sands are the exclusive quarry of Consolidated Diamond Mining (CDM), a subsidiary of DeBeers, the South African multinational company that controls some 80 percent of the world's diamond trade. Since 1920, the company has held an exclusive concession, lasting until the year 2010, to a guarded *Sperrgebiet,* or restricted zone, in the coastal desert. Today, this 21,235-square-mile (55,000-sq-km) area includes much of the southern Namib, from the Kuiseb River to the Orange

River, which forms the border of Namibia and South Africa. Although various parts of this 350-mile (565-km) stretch have been mined in decades past, most of CDM's present-day operations take place just north of the Orange River delta in the mining town of Oranjemund.

The diamonds ended up on the Namib coast the same way the sand did—as sediment carried by the Orange River from deep within southern Africa's hilly interior. The diamonds were formed tens of millions of years ago in underground veins in which carbon was superheated by volcanic thermal activity, then cooled. Geologists believe these deposits were broken loose in two major upheavals of the African plateau, one 70 million years ago, the other as recently as 2 million years ago. These geological rifts were accompanied by heavy floods in which tons of sand, gravel, and diamonds were carried to the coast by the Orange. Over the ensuing millennia, these sediments were carried up the coast by the northward-flowing Benguela Current and smashed into the coast by the Atlantic waves. In what amounts to a natural sorting process, winds blow the sand inland for miles, but the heavier sediments—including the diamonds—remain largely along the coast. Embedded in the shifting dunes, they can be uncovered by either the tossing and tumbling of sand and wind or by the scraping and scooping of heavy-duty steel.

Because the diamonds are not native to the coast, it is understandable that early South African prospectors concluded that the Namib's geology was unsuitable for gemstones. It was not until 1908 that August Stauch, a German railroad worker who had come to the colonial port of Lüderitz to benefit his asthma, discovered the Namib's wealth, much by accident. An amateur rock collector, Stauch had ample opportunity to pursue this hobby while supervising the crews that cleared the drifting sand from the coastal train tracks. One day, a worker brought him an unusually clear crystal that proved to be a diamond. Within weeks, in what was then called German South West Africa, a diamond rush was on. Boatloads of Germans and others—thousands, all told—flocked to the desert coast to make their fortune from the glittering gems that were touted as ripe for the picking. Many of the zealous prospectors died or were killed in the heyday of the diamond fever.

In the decade after Stauch's discovery, more than 5 million carats of diamonds were plucked from the Namib. Opulent boomtowns like Kolmanskop and Elizabeth Bay grew up almost overnight, only to be abandoned after the diamonds were mined out by the end of the 1930's. In these ghost towns today, huge homes with art deco trappings lie half buried in the dunes near the beach.

The desert's diamond mines are rich in both quantity and quality. In one recent year, for instance, CDM processed some 57 million tons of sand and gravel to extract more than 1.5 million carats. Moreover, more than 96 percent of the Namib's diamonds are of gem quality; in a typical mine, 70 percent of the stones are of the much less valuable industrial grade.

Whalebones in the Sand

Along the windblown shores of the northern Namib, the bones of whales, slaughtered decades ago by whalers, lie bleaching in the sun and surf. The bones of humans, too—some evidently killed for the gems they were carrying—have been found in the dunes along this coastline. But the hulking remains of wrecked ships, scores of which dot the ever-encroaching beach sands, are the vestiges that truly gave rise to the name of this stretch of desert: the Skeleton Coast.

Here, where the pounding ocean and the piling sands seem locked in a relentless battle of conquest, countless mariners have met their doom, running aground in the deceptively shallow waters. The thick fog that often shrouds these shores makes navigation along the Skeleton Coast all the more treacherous. Ever since the earliest ocean voyages four or five centuries ago, ships have been stranded up and down this coast for hundreds of miles. Modern-day wrecks are not uncommon—even radar can miss the flat beach sands.

A narrow strip of the duned Skeleton Coast—extending 300 miles (484 km) south from Namibia's northern border with Angola—was declared a national park in 1971. Notable for its shipwrecks, many of which lie entombed in the encroaching sands, and stunning vistas, Skeleton Coast Park is a protected haven for the desert's

wildlife. But it is a mere 25 miles (40 km) wide, and animals continuously come and go across the boundaries of the park—into interior lands that offer little protection to species on the move. Inland from the shore, the dunes give way to the low, rocky hills of the Kaokoveld. Here, the nomadic Himba peoples and their herds share the desert's bare provision with elephants, rhinos, ostriches, and a dwindling population of lions. All roam the riverbed oases and canyons that meander inland from the coast, through the dune sea, and into the gravelly flatlands, seeking water and grazeable vegetation. Many of these animals commonly travel hundreds of miles in a matter of days, seeking the land's fickle water supplies.

The bones of a Cape fur seal (*above*), perhaps killed for its pelt, bleach in the sun of the Skeleton Coast of the Namib. The seals breed on the coast, 120,000 and more congregating there each year.

Since fresh water in the Namib is so hard to come by, many animals must pass the desert's boundaries to find reliable water sources. One popular spot is another of Namibia's ten protected wildlife sanctuaries, Etosha National Park. For animals along the Skeleton Coast, the park is a 350-mile (565-km) trek inland, across the sea of desert dunes and to the far side of the near-barren Kaokoveld. There, the 8,600-square-mile (22,274-sq-km) flatland is a haven for thirsty animals who come from points throughout southwestern Africa. In many areas of the Etosha, spring-fed bodies of water, their shores lined with scrub trees, nourish a wide array of animal species throughout the year—among them cheetahs, wildebeest, rodents, elephants, snakes, birds, and lions—which gather to drink among the aquatic reeds and grasses.

In the national park's vast salt pans, or gentle depressions, however, the environment is desertlike most of the year—too hot and dry for most animals, and void of vegetation. But in the summer months of January through April, monsoon-season thunderstorms transform the dusty, cracked-clay floor of the largest such depression, the massive Etosha Pan, into an 1,800-square-mile (4,662-sq-km) shallow lake. Resident animals, as well as hundreds of thousands of migratory birds, are joined at the newborn 60-mile-long (97-km) lake by the throngs of animals that arrive from afar. For the wild creatures that endure the long, dry walk from the parched sands and rugged inland hills of the Namib Desert, abundant water such as this is rare in their homeland—or within any of the world's dry, fog-shrouded coastal deserts.

Its hull plates rusting away, a large freighter sinks into the shifting sands of the Skeleton Coast, where hundreds of ships—victims of shoals, gales, and fogs—have run aground over the centuries.

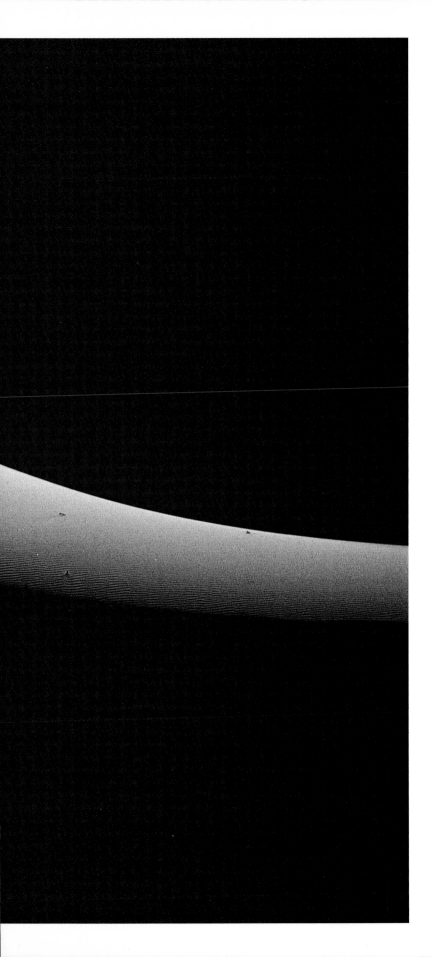

"Look out from the mountain's edge once more. A dusk is gathering on the desert's face, and over the eastern horizon the purple shadow of the world is reaching up to the sky. The light is fading out. Plain and mesa are blurring into unknown distances, and mountain-ranges are looming dimly into unknown heights. Warm drifts of lilac-blue are drawn like mists across the valleys; the yellow sands have shifted pallid gray. The glory of the wilderness has gone down with the sun. Mystery—that haunting sense of the unknown—is all that remains."

—JOHN C. VAN DYKE

Deserts cover nearly one-third of the Earth's land surface—from hot, subtropical latitudes to polar regions, and from fog-shrouded coasts to snow-peaked mountaintops 5 miles (8 km) above sea level. Aridity unites them all, and latitude bonds certain ones of them; but a seemingly endless array of flora, fauna, and physical features makes each desert unique in its own right.

The Desert Profiles highlight the geology, topography, climate, and life-forms of the world's 20 major desert regions; some are further subdivided into smaller desert areas. They appear in order of longitude, starting with the Sahara, through which runs the Greenwich meridian—0° longitude—and move eastward around the globe. Map coordinates and country names assist in locating the deserts on a world map.

TABLE OF CONTENTS

Sahara

35°N to 12° N latitude
17°W to 52° E longitude

Morocco, Western Sahara, Algeria, Tunisia, Libya, Egypt, Mauritania, Mali, Niger, Chad, Ethiopia, Somalia

The Sahara—Arabic for "desert," or "empty area"—is a predominantly flat realm of rock, gravel, and sand seas that blankets 3.5 million square miles (9 million sq km) of the northern third of Africa. It stretches 3,100 miles (5,000 km) from the Atlantic Ocean to the Red Sea and is about 1,200 miles (2,000 km) from north to south. The Sahara is the largest desert in the world, with aridity and temperature extremes to match its size, and little surface water other than, ironically, the world's longest river—the Nile, which flows 4,000 miles (6,400 km) from the mountains in equatorial Africa north to the Mediterranean. The rest of the Sahara is sparsely dotted by oases, which together make up less than 800 square miles (2,000 sq km).

The Sahara is bounded to the north by the Atlas Mountains and the Mediterranean Sea, to the west by the Atlantic Ocean, and to the east by the Red Sea. Its southern boundary is much harder to define. A semiarid region called the Sahel is the transitional zone between the desert and the savanna of tropical southern Africa.

History

Some 250 million years ago the Sahara was covered by ocean and then periodically inundated by seas; for long periods lakes and rivers kept the land green and fertile. Since the time when Africa was part of the supercontinent Pangaea, the Sahara has been subject to both geologic and climatic forces that have conspired to make it the vast desert expanse it is today.

Pangaea began to break up into plates 180 million years ago, bearing what we now know as the seven continents. Until 85 million years ago, the plate on which the African continent sits was part of this large landmass. It remained attached to the Arabian Peninsula until they broke up 24 million years ago, and the Red Sea formed between them; today they remain linked only at the Sinai Peninsula.

The African Plate began its present steady northward movement into Europe, simultaneously building up the Alps and the Atlas Mountains. This northward movement also maneuvered northern Africa into a dry tropical belt that encompasses the Arabian Desert to the east.

The Saharan region owes its aridity also to the collisions with other plates that over millions of years built up the Atlas Mountains and the plateaus of Spain. These shifts blocked moisture-laden air from drifting to and descending upon the increasingly arid plains and plateaus of northern Africa. In addition, the Sahara is surrounded to the north and east by relatively small bodies of water that can provide little moisture.

By about 2.5 million years ago, the stage was set for the pervasive desiccation of the Saharan region. Lakes and streams began to dry up, and rivers that had flowed from its mountains into closed basins dried up, leaving the wind to carry away their deposits into what became the sand seas. From that time, the climate fluctuated between wet and dry cycles about every 100,000 years. However, the wet periods were generally shorter than the dry. The last humid period occurred between 12,000 and 6,000 years ago, when the Sahara was covered by grassy savanna. In the 5,000 to 6,000 years since, the Sahara has been desert.

Topography

Much of the bedrock of the Sahara is Precambrian granite that is sheathed in sandstone and limestone resulting from a combination of erosion and deposition. These same forces ensure that the mostly flat landscape remains just that.

Within the layers of sedimentary rock, water has been discovered in aquifers far below the surface; much of it is "fossil water" thousands of years old. Originating in wetter areas hundreds and even thousands of miles away, this water, which seeped through porous rock and was trapped between layers of impervious rock, has flowed beneath the Sahara for centuries. It is estimated that these aquifers may hold up to 4 billion gallons (17 billion L) of water.

Exceptions to the rule of Saharan flatness are the sedimentary ranges of the Atlas Mountains in Morocco and northern Algeria, and the tablelands of the Tassili-n-Ajjer in eastern Algeria. Wind and water have carved deep canyons and left standing spires of sedimentary rock. Where the edges of plateaus in the sandstone ranges have been worn away by wind-driven sand, long walls known as *garas* remain.

At the center of the Sahara the Ahaggar Mountains, products of volcanic eruptions some 2 million years ago, rise 9,852 feet (3,000 m) above the black gravel plains that radiate from them. Elsewhere in the desert, blackened rock and soil are common; this discoloration is called desert varnish. Volcanic ranges to the south include the Aïr in Niger and the Adrar-n-Iforas, which straddles Algeria and Mali to the southeast. To the east of the Ahaggar, the Tibesti Mountains of southern Libya and northern Chad rise somewhat higher, to 11,204 feet (3,415 m), the highest point in the Sahara. A vast network of grooves covering 35,000 square miles (90,650 sq km) has been carved into the Tibesti by winds; some are ¼ mile (0.4 km) or more wide and some are filled with sand.

Almost 70 percent of the Sahara is covered by regs. These plains of dense and compact gravel are desolate and nearly waterless, the most hostile Saharan environments. Ranging in color from black to red to white, the gravel was deposited by ancient seas and rivers and remained after winds carried away the lighter sand, silt, and clay over thousand of years. In fact, even today, Saharan clay transported thousands of miles has on occasion dusted cities in northern Europe.

Somali village

The black reg known as Tanezrouft stretches seemingly endlessly west of the Ahaggar Mountains and covers 200,000 square miles (518,00 sq km). To the east, the Libyan reg spreads over 340,000 square miles (880,000 sq km). Much of the northern part of the Ténéré desert region in Niger is also covered by regs, as are vast expanses of the Sinai desert. Hammadas, flat stony plateaus, constitute about 10 percent of the rocky Saharan terrain.

Sand seas, called ergs, fill large depressions. Unlike the vast regs, the ergs blanket only about a fifth of the Sahara. These seas are composed of shifting dunes that reach heights of 1,000 feet (300 m). Chains of sand ridges up to 3 miles (5 km) apart spread like veins across the ergs. Where these chains cross, they make star-shaped formations known as *rhourds.*

Erg Chech, 600 miles (1,000 km) long, lies in the west, spanning mainly Mali and Algeria; to the north the Grand Erg Oriental and the Grand Erg Occidental blanket Algeria. In Libya, the Selima sand sheet spreads over 3,000 square miles (7,000 km). The Majabat al-Koubra, or Saharan Empty Quarter, lies to the southeast, and the Grand Erg of Bilma, where salt is mined, lies mainly to the south in Niger. In the northern Sahara, salt also carpets large areas known as chotts, which are shallow or dried-up lakes.

These arid expanses of rock, pebbles, and sand are broken up here and there by sources of water. Wadis, or oueds, are temporary riverbeds fed by precipitation in the mountains.

Climate
Rainfall is an erratic and infrequent phenomenon; over three-fourths of the desert receives less than 4 inches (100 mm) annually. Several years can pass without any appreciable rainfall at all.

The annual mean temperature ranges between 63° and 86° F (17°–30° C). Daytime temperatures can drop 100 F degrees (56 C degrees) after sunset. Because the layer of soil on the bedrock is relatively thin, heat that soaks into it during the day is quickly lost at night; thus nights are often very cold, with temperatures sometimes dropping to freezing. The lowest nighttime temperature recorded was 20° F (-7° C); the highest was recorded in Azizia, Libya, at 136° F (58° C). The hottest months are June, July, and August.

In addition to the scorching heat, hot winds known as *sirocco, khamsin, shahali,* and *harmattan* blow fiercely, especially in the spring and fall; they can be dangerous and make life insufferable.

Plants
The relatively rich variety of flora in the Sahara is the product of this region's contact with the Mediterranean region to the north and the tropics to the south. Nevertheless, vast expanses are almost devoid of vegetation.

Obtaining and retaining water are fundamental for all desert life. Many plants have extensive root systems that can seek out water in the deepest reaches of the soil, as well as small, thick leaves that minimize evaporation. On the rare occasions that it does rain, long-dormant seeds of annuals burst to life, blanketing the desert in vibrant colors; drought-resistant seeds are able to survive years in dormancy. Once sprouted, annuals complete their entire life cycle within weeks and even days.

Pockets of vegetation are more likely to occur in the mountain ranges where pools of fresh water form in catchments, along wadis, in depressions, and on sand dunes. Small shrubs are likely to grow in the depressions, and grasses grow on the dunes. This is less true in the regs and hammadas, which are virtually barren.

The appearance of *cram-cram* (*Cenchrus biflorus* and *Cenchrus echinatus*), a spiny tussock grass, marks the transitional zone between desert and Sahel, and it often grows close to the thorny *Acacia seyal* trees.

Shrubs include the *had* (*Cornulaca monacantha*), a small bush with bluish-green stems and small thorns. It grows in bunches, causing sand to collect around it. Milkweed (*Pergularia daemia*), another hardy plant, has a thick outer skin to minimize the loss of moisture and looks much like a small cactus.

A more unusual plant is the desert, or colocynth, melon (*Colocynthis vulgaris*). It takes root in sand mounds and has vines that bear inedible melons. These melons, once dried, can roll for miles driven by the wind, thereby dispersing their seeds over a large territory.

Several acacias, also known as thorn trees, thrive in the Sahara. The most common in the northern and central regions around the Ahaggar and Tassili ranges is *Acacia raddiana*; *A. seyal* grows in the south. Another type of tree, the impressive fat-trunked baobab (*Adansonia digitata*), also grows to the south in the Sahel.

Relics of earlier wet periods are found in the mountainous regions such as Ahaggar and Tassili and in the oases. Some Laperrine olive trees (*Olea laperrini*), standing 30 to 40 feet (9–12 m) tall, are believed to be 3,000 to 4,000 years old; their ripe age is evident in gnarled trunks of up to 9 feet (2.5 m) in width.

Animals
Petroglyphs such as those found in the Tassili-n-Ajjer ranges reveal that during wetter and more humid times, animals such as giraffes and elephants roamed the Sahara. Today, larger animals survive by retreating to the remotest parts of the Sahara.

The regal addax (*Addax nasomaculatus*), superbly adapted to life in the sand dunes, travels in small herds in the western Sahara, Mauritania, and Chad. This mostly white, heavy-bodied antelope with black spiral horns feeds on perennial grasses and *had* bushes, from which it obtains moisture; it rarely, if ever, drinks water. The gemsbok (*Oryx algazel*) has a larger body

Petroglyphs in Tassili-n-Ajjer mountains, Algeria

than the addax and stands 4 feet (1.25 m) high; it can run up to 37.5 mph (60 kph). It copes with the heat by allowing its body temperature to rise to 107.6° F (42° C); during the night the heat dissipates, and its temperature drops to a normal 98.6° F (37° C). Its light beige or white coat contrasts with its reddish-brown neck and shoulders, and its head is crowned by long horns.

Gazelles are among the larger mammals. They obtain moisture from plants and bushes and occasionally dig up roots. They retain fluids in part by producing highly concentrated urine. During the day, they remain in the shade of rocks or trees whenever possible. One of the most well adapted gazelles is the dorcas gazelle (*Gazella dorcas*). It can thrive in a wide range of environments, while the slender-horned gazelle (*G. leptoceros*) roams largely through the ergs. Other species include the dama (*G. dama*); Cuvieri's, or the Altas mountain, gazelle (*G. cuvieri*); and the red-fronted gazelle (*G. rufifrons*).

Another spectacular animal is the wild barbary or mountain sheep, known in the Sahara as the mouflon, or aoudad (*Ammotragus lervia*). It stands about 3 feet (1 m) high, has reddish-brown fur with long hair that cascades from the throat and chest, and carries backward-sweeping horns. Increasingly rare in the ranges of the Ahaggar, Tibesti, and Tassili-n-Ajjer, this adept climber stays close to pools that form in crevices and hollows; it feeds on thorn trees such as *Acacia ehrenbergiana* and *A. tortilis.*

Several carnivores have adapted to the rigors of desert existence. The small fennec fox (*Fennecus zerda*) has disproportionately large ears that radiate heat from its body. It is a nocturnal predator and hunts when its prey, often the gerbil-like jerboa, is active. The fennec lives in sand dunes, where it can burrow tunnels 30 feet (9 m) long and 3 feet (1 m) deep with its strong forelimbs. Other carnivores include the jackal (*Canis aureus*) and several hyaenas (*Hyaena striata, H. crocuta,* and *H. barbara*).

The largest share of smaller mammals is made up of rodents, of which there are 40 species. Like most small desert animals, they escape the daytime heat by burrowing below the sun-baked surface, where the soil is more humid and the temperature is many degrees cooler. The animals are nocturnal, searching for moisture-rich plants and seeds at night. They excrete concentrated waste products to minimize loss of fluids.

The fat sand rat (*Psammomys obesus*) is among the most common rodents and thrives in areas with halophytic, or salt-loving, plants. The jerboa (*Jaculus jaculus*), unlike the sand rat, which builds networks of shallow tunnels, has weaker forelimbs and digs short burrows that it closes off with a thin layer of sand; to ensure its safety from predators such as the fennec fox, it also prepares a short escape tunnel.

Small mammals found in rockier and mountainous areas include gundis (family Ctenodactylidae) and hyraxes (family Procaviidae). Shrews (*Crocidura*) are also found in rockier terrain, while elephant shrews (*Elephantulus*) live closer to the coast; they are among a number of insectivores found in the Sahara in addition to several kinds of hedgehogs (*Erinaceus, Hemiechinus,* and *Paraechinus*). The desert hare (*Lepus capensis*) and the porcupine (*Hystrix cristata*) are also frequent residents.

Birds that live in the Sahara must remain close to sources of water because they cool themselves by panting, thereby losing water through their breath. They are drawn to mountains and rocky outcrops where *gueltas,* or pools of water, form. Here they gather to drink and bathe, as well as to feed on the insects that swarm around these watery places. The trumpeter finch, house bunting, crag martin, and crowned sandgrouse are among those that are found in and around rocky hillsides and mountains. The crowned sandgrouse, like the chestnut-bellied sandgrouse (*Pterocles exustus*) and the spotted sandgrouse (*P. senegallus*), carries moisture to its young by soaking its breast feathers in water.

Larks and wheatears are numerous in the desert because they are able to remain relatively cool by shading themselves with rocks or plants, or by standing close to burrow entrances.

Many larger birds are increasingly rare. Vultures, which are found close to oases, include Rueppell's griffon vulture (*Gyps rueppelli*) and the smaller and somewhat more common hooded vulture (*Neophron monachus*). The ostrich (*Struthio camelus*), once frequently seen, has also almost disappeared. Falcons, bustards, hawks, and storks are still fairly common.

A wide variety of reptiles inhabit the far reaches of the Sahara. One

Wild barbary sheep

of the largest is the land tortoise (*Testudo kleinmanni*). Smaller reptiles include a gecko (*Tropidocalotes tripolitanus*) and the chameleon (*Chamaeleon chamaeleon*), and lizards such as *Acanthodactylus boskianus, A. pardalis,* and *Agama inermis*. Skinks, members of the lizard family, are well armed with desert gear; their eyes are sheathed in clear scales, and their bodies are covered in smooth scales that allow them to "swim" through the sand. Appropriately, two types are named the sandfish (*Scincus scincus*), which lives in the great sand seas, and the sand swimmer (*Phrynocephalus nejdensis*). Other reptiles include the spiny-tailed iguana (*Uromastix acanthinurus*) and the desert monitor (*Varanus griseus*).

Also at home in the sand is the light-colored horned viper (*Cerastes cerastes*), one of the most poisonous desert snakes. It lies beneath the sands waiting for its prey of rodents and birds, with only its horns betraying its location.

Insects are the most abundant of desert creatures. As in most deserts, ants and termites (Isoptera) are plentiful. Beetles, as well, are an important segment of the insect population; the most common are the family Tenebrionidae.

Many arachnids inhabit the Sahara. Scorpions are common, and although most are harmless, the fat-tailed scorpion (*Androctonus australis*) of the northern Sahara, the small yellow *Buthus occitanus* of the southern Sahel, and the Tibesti scorpion (*B. quinquestratus*) are highly venomous.

A group of arachnids called Solifugae are also known as false spiders, camel spiders, and wind scorpions. These frightening-looking predators are up to 5 inches (13 cm) long and are commonly found in the southern Sahara. They are nocturnal predators and feed voraciously on insects.

Namib Desert

15° S to 35° S latitude
11° E to 19° E longitude

Angola, Namibia, South Africa

The Namib Desert curves for 1,200 miles (1,935 km) along the southwestern coast of the African continent, from the Cape Province of South Africa northward along the coast of Namibia, to the southern part of Angola. It extends 80 to 100 miles (129–161 km) inland across the coastal plain to the foot of a mountainous rise called the Great Escarpment. The southern portion of the Namib merges with the Kalahari Desert on the plateau atop the escarpment.

The name *Namib*, which is derived from the Nama language, means "an area where there is nothing": the Namib encompasses more than 13,000 square miles (33,670 sq km) of nearly barren sand dunes.

Geology

The structure of the Namib Desert consists of a relatively smooth platform of bedrock of various types but all belonging to the Precambrian era, making them more than 560 million years old. Mica schist, quartzites, marble, and other metamorphic rocks, as well as granite and volcanic rocks, predominate. The platform rises gradually from the coast to about 3,000 feet (900 m) at the foot of the Great Escarpment. Scattered isolated mountains, called inselbergs (from a German word meaning "island mountains"), rise steeply and abruptly above the platform.

Large areas of this desert have no soil, just bedrock, while others are buried under sand. Close to the shore, decomposing phytoplankton have been blown inland from the South Atlantic Ocean, and the sulfur-rich crust they help form supports rich lichen fields. Farther from the coast the surface is calcrete—calcium carbonate that forms a rocklike layer.

In much of the southern half of the desert, the platform is blanketed by an expanse of sand originally deposited by the Orange River and other rivers that flow westward from the escarpment, never reaching the sea.

The sand dunes in this region run from northwest to southeast, with individual dunes up to 10 to 20 miles (16–32 km) long and 200 to 800 feet (61–244 m) high. Troughs between these lines contain smaller transverse dunes. The color of the sand changes from the off-white of the coastal dunes to the orange of the inland dunes to the brick red of the star-shaped dunes in the eastern part of the central Namib. The deepening color is caused by a coating of iron oxide that has accumulated since the sand was transported by water. At Sossusvlei, the star dunes tower 984 feet (300 m) above the ground, where patterns of cracked clay surround skeletons of camel thorn (acacia) trees.

The dunes of the central Namib are constantly on the move, driven by the prevailing winds. To the north of these dune fields, the Kuiseb River blocks the dunes' northern advancement. The river runs only intermittently, and reaches the sea only every ten years or so, but this is enough to sweep away the sand that blows into the riverbed and to prevent the northward spread of the dune field.

The bed of the Kuiseb River is carved deep into hard granites and schists and lies hidden beneath billions of tons of sand and silt. This bedrock acts as a barrier to seeping groundwater, and the sand shields any underground water from evaporation. As a result, a slow but dependable flow of water from sources to the east exists not far beneath the sandy desert surface.

The Kuiseb is one of a series of rivers that in the distant past carved their way hundreds of miles from the interior highlands to the coast. Today, they flow only whenever enough rain falls in the highlands. That does not happen every year, and even when it does, the water usually trickles away into the sand. But the water remains trapped under the sand, turning the dry riverbeds into "linear oases." Wildlife seeks out the permanent springs along these channels, and the accessible groundwater provides moisture for trees and shrubs. The major riverbeds support acacia trees and thickets that afford habitats for animals and birds.

At the northern end of the Namib is a region called the Skeleton Coast, where ancient seas deposited dark, gravelly material. Diamonds, agates, and other precious and semiprecious stones hide among the gravel washed down the river courses from the gold- and diamond-bearing formations to the east.

Climate

In the South Atlantic, the cold Benguela Current flows northward along the southwestern coast of Africa, chilling the air above it to

Upper Kuiseb Canyon, Namibia

the saturation point and producing fog. This fog is borne 31 miles (50 km) and more inland by the southwest sea breeze, creating a temperature inversion about 1,000 feet (300 m) thick, with fog below and hot, dry air above. Toward midmorning, the temperature of the lower part of the air rises enough to evaporate the tiny droplets of fog.

The prevailing sea breeze is too cold to hold enough moisture for rain clouds to form. Furthermore, the strong downward atmospheric currents of this high-pressure latitude prevent the moist air from rising high enough to create rain clouds. Any rain coming east from the Indian Ocean is caught by the mountains of the Great Escarpment.

The average annual precipitation at the coast ranges from 0.3 to 1.0 inches (9–27 mm) and is generally about 0.5 inch (13 mm). Precipitation increases gradually inland until it reaches nearly 7 inches (175 mm) at the foot of the escarpment. There is tremendous annual variation in precipitation, and in some years there may be no rainfall at all.

In summer, west winds prevail; this means that air coming from the ocean passes over the cold Benguela Current, cools, and crosses over the coastal plain without ever reaching the condensation point. In winter the easterly trade winds sweep over the Namib from the eastern highlands, but the greater part of their moisture has fallen when they reach the desert. Thus the western Namib Desert can be chilled by moist winds carrying fog inland from the Atlantic Ocean or roasted by furnace-hot east winds descending off the escarpment.

At the coast, temperature is almost constant, day or night, winter or summer. The difference between mean daily temperatures of the hottest and coldest months ranges only between 11 and 12 F degrees (5.9 and 6.6 C degrees). Average temperatures are usually between 50° and 60° F (10° and 16° C). Along the inland margins, summer temperatures normally reach about 88° F (31° C) in areas sheltered from the cooling sea breeze. Freezing temperatures occur occasionally along the inner edge of the desert. The surface of the sand or rock, however, has a great range of temperature, becoming very hot during the day and cooling at night.

The present climatic conditions seem to have prevailed, on and off, for 55 million years or more, making the Namib Desert possibly the oldest in the world.

Plants

The lengthy existence of the Namib has allowed the evolution of distinctive plants. There are six main vegetational regions of the Namib. These are the coastal, which has highly succulent vegetation that uses moisture derived from fog; the almost completely barren Outer Namib; the steppes of the Inner Namib, which are often barren but in wet years are covered with short annual and perennial grasses; the dunes of the Inner Namib, which have a surprisingly rich array of bushes and tall grasses; the larger river channels, along which large trees, particularly acacias, flourish; and the southernmost end of the desert, where a succulent bush growth occurs.

Along the coast, nearly everything depends on fog and dew. The rocky gravel plains take on a soft green hue after a fog bank drifts over them and drenches the resident lichens. The coastal fog does not provide enough water for seeds to germinate but does give some plants enough water to keep growing. Two species of dwarf shrubs, one in the dunes and one

on the plains, have specially adapted leaves that can take up fog water. A tall dune grass sends out roots up to 66 feet (20 m) long to take advantage of fog water in the top 0.04 inch (1 mm) of sand. Both of these plants flower and produce seeds regardless of whether or not rain has fallen, and shed seeds, flowers, and leaves that many animals use for food.

Lichens and algae also depend on fog and dew and are the only permanent vegetation near the coast. Some algae live under translucent quartz rocks, which let enough light through to allow photosynthesis and which trap condensation underneath them. One lichen, *Omphalodium convolutum,* lives freely and unattached in a small area of the desert; it blows about until it accumulates in drifts. After a thick mist it opens up, allowing the sun to shine upon its moistened green interior.

Another unique plant in the Namib is *Acanthosicyos horrida,* the *naras* melon, which bears a spiky globular fruit. The bush's stems, branches, and thorns carry out photosynthesis in place of leaves. The *naras* melon grows on lower dune slopes, and its roots tap water deep below the surface.

Many species consume the *naras* melon. Its prickly fruits are food for jackals, gerbils, lizards, and beetles. The plant provides food and shelter for mice, lizards, insects, and snakes. Ostriches eat the soft growing tips, and one species of lizard of the northern dunes even eats the thorns.

A curious Namib plant is the *tumboa,* or welwitschia (*Welwitschia mirabilis*), whose two gigantic leaves sprawl over the surface of the ground from its huge root crown. This slow-growing plant, actually a dwarf tree, can take 25 years to flower from seed. Its two leaves reach 20 to 29 feet (6–9 m) in

length; they grow at a rate of 4 to 8 inches (100–200 mm) each year and last for its entire lifetime. Some very large specimens are thought to be thousands of years old. Like the *naras* melon, welwitschias have male and female flowers on separate plants. The flowers are pollinated by the wind, and one medium-sized plant can produce 10,000 or more seeds. Only a few seeds are fertile; the rest serve as food for a variety of animals.

Where there is some water, lithops species grow. These "living stones" have thick fleshy leaves that look very much like pebbles; after a rain they produce short-lived, colorful flowers.

Animals

The Namib's dune sea teems with a multitude of insects and animals, all uniquely adapted to living in an ocean of sand. Even where there is little vegetation, insects live off the plant debris that blows in from the eastern highlands. Vegetable and animal debris blows down into the desert from elsewhere and accumulates on the leeward sides of dunes, where it is eaten by insects.

The plains and dunes of the Inner Namib support several varieties of antelope, especially gemsbok (oryx) and springbok, as

A gemsbok in the shade

well as ostriches and some zebras. Elephants, rhinoceroses, lions, hyenas, and jackals are found in the northern Namib, especially in the oases along the rivers that flow from the interior highlands. In the inland stony deserts, shallow lakes form after a rain, and these harbor shrimp, whose eggs can remain dormant for years but hatch and mature in the short-lived pools. The dunes of the Outer Namib provide habitats for various types of insects and reptiles, especially beetles, geckos, and snakes, but virtually no mammals. The shore area is densely populated by marine birds (notably flamingos, pelicans, and, in the southernmost part, penguins), a few jackals, some rodents, and a few colonies of seals.

The Skeleton Coast of the northern Namib, now a national wildlife park, is the domain of jackals, brown hyenas, desert elephants, and lions. The southern coast shelters seals, jackass penguins, cormorants, and gannets, while ever-present jackals and brown hyenas roam its beaches. They scavenge carcasses thrown up by the sea and hunt for fur seals. Desert lions stalk their prey under the cover of the noise made by wind and surf.

Desert-adapted elephants and black rhinoceroses live in the Namib on open gravel plains, in stony valleys, and even on the dunes. Both dig for water in dry watercourses or get moisture from bushes. Desert elephants need to drink only every three or four days during the dry season and are perpetually on the move, in search of the water holes. Their numbers have dropped precipitously because of poaching; only about 70 are alive today.

One well-adapted animal of the Namib is the golden mole, a totally sightless yet ferocious predator only 3 inches (77 mm) long. Named for its fine coat of pale yellow fur, the nocturnally active mole "swims" underneath the loose sand, an adaptation that enables it to live without burrows in the sliding slip faces of the dunes. It senses the vibrations made by its favorite prey: web-footed geckos, crickets, and beetle larvae.

Two species of gerbil are also found in the dunes, the dune hairy-footed gerbil and Setzer's hairy-footed gerbil.

At the shore towns of Sandwich and Walvis Bay, flocks of flamingos of up to 40,000 birds, as well as pelicans, can be found.

The gravel plains and sand dunes of the Namib do not support a wide variety of bird life; there are, however, ostriches and sandgrouse. They can get no moisture from their diet of dried seeds and have to drink daily. Adults visit water holes every day; the sandgrouse transports water to its young in its breast feathers.

Ostriches practice communal breeding, with the male actively involved; as many as three females contribute eggs, an average of eight each, and then the dominant female and her mate take over the job of hatching.

Other bird species include bustards and korhaans, or lappet-faced vultures; raptors, including red-necked falcons; and several species of larks, buntings, and chats. A few birds, including the Namib lark, desert chat, pied crow, and rock kestrel, nest in the desert.

Much of the available water in the Namib is in the form of fog, which condenses on the sand and rocks. Survival depends on being able to make use of this moisture. Since it will condense only on a surface colder than the air, a cold-blooded animal has an advantage.

Some two hundred species of beetles live on the dunes. Darkling beetles burrow into the sand at night and by morning have used up much of their body heat. They emerge from the sand and go to the crests of the dune slopes, where they raise their cooled backs to the sea and bask in the incoming fog. Water droplets form and run down the beetle's back to its mouth. A white variety of this beetle, which has the same water-gathering characteristic, is found only on the Skeleton Coast. *Camponotus detritus*, a large species of ant, sucks moisture directly from the dampened sand.

Many animals, such as gerbils, oryx, and hares, take in fog water indirectly by feeding on plants or other creatures, such as beetles, that obtain moisture from fog.

Several species of spider build amazing webs that extend well below the surface of the sand, and one, a nocturnal hunter, drags its captured prey down into its tunnel to consume it. One species, *Carparachne aureoflava*, the golden wheel spider, is known both for its glossy yellow hair and for its ability to flip sideways and roll down sand dunes when pursued by a wasp. On steep slopes the spider can move as fast as 5 feet (1.5 m) per second.

The sidewinding adder consumes fog water directly, licking condensation off its scales. These scales resemble the sand the sidewinder lives in, and its protruding eyes give it a good view even when it is almost completely buried in sand. Its sideways way of moving counters the tendency of loose sand to slip under its body: poising on two points, the snake repeatedly rolls to one side, marking the sand with parallel imprints.

The chief prey of the sidewinding adder, the web-footed gecko, has webbed toes, enabling it to walk on shifting sand dunes and to dig burrows in the sand. A total of six species of diurnal geckos are found in the Namib.

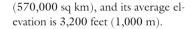
15° S to 30° S latitude
19° E to 28° E longitude

Botswana, South Africa, Namibia

Classified as a semidesert, the Kalahari is a huge arid landmass with an even greater area of grassland blending into it. Rich in vegetation, the Kalahari supports an equally rich variety of wildlife. Because of its remoteness and relative inaccessibility to most people, the Kalahari suffers less from the effects of grazing and settlement than do other deserts. The Bushmen inhabit the otherwise sparsely populated region and because they are seminomadic, they have not stripped the land as has happened in other deserts such as the Thar in India.

Topography

The Kalahari lies in a depression in southern Africa's central plateau and is flanked by the high plateaus and ridges of the Karoo basin to the south and the still higher plateaus of the Transvaal and Zimbabwe to the east. It covers two-thirds of Botswana and extends into neighboring parts of South Africa and eastern Namibia, where it runs into the coastal Namib Desert. Its total area is 220,000 square miles (570,000 sq km), and its average elevation is 3,200 feet (1,000 m).

Sand up to 300 feet (100 m) deep blankets most of the desert and is interrupted only by widely scattered outcrops of basalt or granite rock. The sand covers bedrock that includes some of the oldest rock formations known, some dating back over 3 billion years in the Precambrian era. The color of the sand ranges from red to gray and yellowish brown.

In the southwest quarter of the region, parallel chains of sickle-shaped barchan dunes stretch for miles across the plains. The dunes average 25 feet (8 m) high, with some rising to heights of 900 feet (300 m) or more. The average distance between dune chains is 700 feet (225 m).

The plains of the Kalahari were once the drainage basin for the now-dry Molopo and Nosob rivers; remnants of these former rivers exist today as sand-filled drainage channels and flat basins called pans. These pans number about a thousand, and during the rainy season they collect runoff from ephemeral streams that follow the courses of the ancient waterways. These pans are a primary, although temporary, source of surface water for wildlife and are usually surrounded by

N'haro Bushmen digging roots

denser vegetation than is found elsewhere. Pans come in different shapes and sizes, up to 3 miles (5 km) in diameter and 30 to 50 feet (10–15 m) deep; some of the largest are found in Makgadikgadi basin in the northeast. After the water evaporates, a layer of salty silt remains, which animals use as salt licks. Some pans are spotted with grasses or karroid bush (salt brush).

There are only three permanent water holes in the Kalahari and four others that provide water except during extreme drought. The rainwater that does not flow into a pan soaks quickly into the porous soil. Because the Kalahari has almost no surface water for most of the year, wildlife and vegetation must depend on water that has soaked deep into the soil underneath the dry riverbeds.

Climate

Annual rainfall in the Kalahari averages 18 inches (460 mm), ranging from 25 inches (640 mm) in the north to 5 inches (130 mm) or less in the southwest. Monsoon winds off the Indian Ocean bring rain in the summer between November and March, with peaks usually in January and February. There are also considerable, and unpredictable, variations in rainfall from year to year; some years there may be none for nine months at a time. When rain does fall, it is in the form of localized heavy downpours or short thunderstorms, sometimes so intense that they cause damage to both crops and man-made structures; rain can be accompanied by winds of up to 60 miles per hour (100 kph).

Relative humidity in the dry season sometimes falls to less than 10 percent. Hot dry winds tend to accelerate up to 10 miles per hour (16 kph) as the day progresses but calm during the night. Dust storms are rare, although dust devils and small whirlwinds can occur during the summer.

In January, the hottest month of summer, temperatures sometimes climb to 120° F (49° C), but during the winter months of April through September nighttime temperatures may drop low enough to form frost.

Plants

Plant life in the Kalahari takes the form of grass, shrub, bush, and woodland savanna. Vegetation becomes larger and more dense and woody from the dry southwest to the relatively moister northeast, reflecting the increase in rainfall.

Grasses, including those of the *Aristida* genus, grow between sand dunes and fringe the pans and drainage lines of ephemeral streams. *Stipa grostis*, an annual grass, is also common in much of the region. Acacias are among the shrubs and brush that make up the shrub savannas that predominate in the Kalahari. Their leaves resemble long, pointed thorns to minimize exposure to the sun. These plants have a dual root system that enables them to reach water, up to several yards away, both on or near the surface and deep underground. In areas of deep sand, the shrub *Acanthosicyos horrida* stabilizes

Blooming camel thorn acacia

dunes by sending its roots down 65 to 80 feet (20–25 m), while *Acacia hebeclada* offers shelter to rodents burrowing beneath its thorny cover. Annual halophytes, or salt-loving plants, such as *Atriplex* and *Suaeda,* grow at the edges of the pans.

While trees are often widely scattered in the savannas of the south and central Kalahari, in the northern parts of the Kalahari they are more likely to grow in small stands. The camel thorn (*Acacia eriolabae*) is widespread, and its pods, wood, and bark are valuable sources of fodder, firewood, and medicine, respectively. The fruits and leaves of the *motlopi*, or shepherd's tree (*Boscia albitrunca*), nourish game and livestock. One of the landscape's most impressive sights is the baobab tree (*Adansonia digitata*); some of the largest, standing 50 feet (15 m) high with trunks 100 feet 30 m) around, may be 4,000 years old.

Since the Kalahari has very little surface water, vegetation is a vital source of moisture. Among the most common species are the juicy *morama,* or gemsbok bean (*Bauhinia esculenta*); the *tsama* melon (*Citrullus vulgaris*), which looks like a small round watermelon with watery green pulp; and a hairy gray beetlike tuber with a hard crust called *leditsa, bi,* or water root (*Raphionacme burke*). The bitter-tasting *ga* root is one of the more unusual plants in that it stores water until rain falls; it then uses the stored moisture to grow vines that soon wither.

Other flora that have adapted to the desert include the succulents, among them the cactuslike *Euphorbia.* Another succulent, the pachycaulus (*Pachypodium namaquanum*), looks like a leaf-crowned, spiny elephant trunk. The plant turns slightly to the north to minimize its exposure to the sun.

Certain blue-green and green algae exhibit a rare adaptation to desert conditions. These tiny plants are found only under clear quartzite pebbles, a circumstance that gives them the name "window plants." The quartz traps water and blocks out all but 10 percent of the sun's rays.

Animals

The Kalahari is home to well-known large predators such as lions (*Panthera leo*), leopards (*Panthera pardus*), and cheetahs (*Acinonyx jubatus*). The brown hyena (*Hyaena brunnea*) is a common smaller predator. Many of the carnivores in the Kalahari eat fruit to obtain moisture and therefore are not completely dependent on sources of surface water. The bat-eared fox (*Otocyon megalotis*) digs for tubers and roots to supplement its main diet of termites, rodents, and insects; its large ears, which give it its name, allow excess heat to radiate from its body. Other small carnivores include the wild dog (*Lycaon pictus*), the small-spotted genet (*Genetta genetta*), the Cape fox or silver jackal, and the catlike caracal (*Felis caracal*).

Many of these predators are found close to the pans, as are most of the 22 species of antelopes that graze on their grassy fringes. As its name suggests, the small springbok (*Antidorcas marsupialis*) is able to jump great heights. The gemsbok (*Oryx gazella*), which obtains much of its nourishment from digging for roots and bulbs, is in turn a valuable source of moisture for the Bushmen, who strain the animals' stomachs for their precious fluids. The duiker (*Sylvicapra grimmia*) gets most of the moisture it requires from leaves, flowers, tubers, and fruits and can survive long periods without drinking water. Other antelopes include the steenbok (*Raphicerus campestris*),

Cape hartebeest (*Alcelaphus buselaphus*), blue wildebeest (*Connochaetes taurinus*), and eland (*Taurotragus oryx*).

Others living close to or around the edges of the pans are smaller herbivores such as the springhare (*Pedetes capensis*), the Cape hare (*Lepus capensis*), and the scrub hare (*Lepus saxatilis*).

At the edges of the pans, a wide range of animals have adopted subterranean lifestyles as a means of seeking shelter from the intense heat aboveground. The ground squirrel (*Xerus inauris*) uses its bushy tail to shade itself from the overhead sun. It digs burrows that are often shared with the suricate, or meerkat (*Suricata suricata*), and the yellow mongoose (*Cynictis penicillata*). The meerkats, whose comical racoonlike appearance belies their industrious habits, have a highly developed group structure similar to that of the North American prairie dog. A variety of gerbils, such as the pygmy gerbil (*Gerbillurus paeba*) and the bushveld gerbil (*Tatera leucogaster*), as well as the porcupine (*Hystrix africaeaustralis*), make their homes in burrows as well.

Insect burrowers include termites (*Trinervitermes* and *Hodotermes*), which eat mostly grass.

Termites play a very important part in the desert ecosystem as the main staple for such predators as the large and powerful aardvark, or ant bear (*Orycteropus afer*), and the aardwolf (*Proteles cristatus*). Termite mounds, which dot the Kalahari landscape in places, are a sign of underground moisture at a moderate depth. Other invertebrates include scorpions and spiders, some of which boobytrap their burrows to catch prey that wander over them; tenebreoinid beetles; and, occasionally, locusts.

The burrowing tendency of several reptiles is reflected in their names: Peter's worm snake (*Leptotyphlops scutifrons*) and the worm lizard (*Zygaspis quadrifrons*). Another type of lizard, *Eremias lugubris*, has adapted to desert conditions by developing colorful grainy scales that enable it to blend into the red Kalahari sand.

Aboveground, birds such as the sociable weaver (*Philetairus socius*) build massive nests composed of smaller individual nests, each with a separate entrance; a single colony may contain up to 500 birds. Ostriches (*Struthio camelus*), whose shells are used by Bushmen as containers, are fairly comon and avoid overheating by panting much like dogs.

Zebras and wildebeest in Etosha National Park, Namibia

30° N to 12° N latitude
35° E to 60° E longitude

Saudi Arabia, Kuwait, Qatar, United Arab Emirates, Oman, Yemen

The great Arabian desert is located primarily in the country of Saudi Arabia. The Rub al-Khali, or Empty Quarter, is called *ar-Ramlah,* or "The Sand," by the nomadic Bedouins who live there and is the largest uninterrupted sand desert in the world.

The Arabian Peninsula, which joins the northeastern corner of Africa to Asia Minor, is a wedge-shaped rectangle, with its widest area to the southeast. It totals about 1,000,000 square miles (2,600,000 sq km) and is known for its absence of water and its abundance of oil.

Geology

The Arabian Shield, the primary geological formation of the Arabian Peninsula, began to split off from Africa in the early Cenozoic era, about 65 million years ago. Spreading of the Earth's surface under what is now the Red Sea pushed the Arabian Plate to the north and east, where it collided with the Central and Eastern Iranian Plate and created mountains and volcanoes in what is now Iran.

The shield lies just inland of the coastal escarpment and is made up of Precambrian metamorphic and igneous rocks; it is dotted with extinct volcanoes. Their eruptions, which stopped in relatively recent geologic time, produced the broad black lava beds that characterize much of this section.

In the northeast and east, sedimentary rocks overlie the shield. Aquifers underlie the dry surface. These aquifers are a plentiful source of ancient fossil water.

The Arabian Peninsula's surface slopes gradually away from sharp mountainous ridges on the west and south to low-lying plains in the northeast along the Persian Gulf. A virtually unbroken escarpment runs along the southwestern coast that borders the Red Sea. The southernmost part of this ridge is the Asir range, which plunges down from 9,800 feet (3,000 m) to a narrow coastal plain. This plain comprises most of the habitable land along the southwestern edge of the peninsula.

The peninsula has no important rivers and as a result no river-cut harbors. It does have a network of dry watercourses, or wadis, that can fill suddenly during the rare but intense rainstorms.

Covering much of the peninsula, the Rub al-Khali, or Empty Quarter, is a barren wilderness of sand dunes. The largest dunes are in the eastern portion. Sometimes reaching heights of more than 800 feet (240 m), they can extend as far as 30 miles (50 km).

Climate

As recently as 17,000 years ago, the Arabian Peninsula experienced a cooler, more humid climate than it does today. However, global climatological changes have resulted in its present-day dry, hot, and windy environment.

Lying on the Tropic of Cancer, the Arabian Peninsula suffers intense summer heat, with temperatures occasionally reaching over 129° F (54° C) in places. In the winter the temperature often drops to freezing, except in the warmest coastal areas; in the interior of the country temperatures fall as low as 26° F (-3° C), and precipitation occurs as frost and snow.

A distinguishing aspect of the Arabian climate is the frequent winds. The maximum wind velocities occur from March to May and average 36 mph (60 kph). However, frequent high-velocity winds sweep over the peninsula, carrying vast amounts of dust and sand and, in cold weather, often causing frost damage to plants.

Except for the Asir and the east coast, the entire Arabian Peninsula is remarkably dry. What little rain there is generally falls between November and May; June through October is a long rainless period. On average, Saudi Arabia receives no more than 3 to 3⅓ inches (75–85 mm) of rain each year, and many areas go for several years without rainfall. When rain does occur, it often comes in torrents, which result in temporary flooding that passes quickly and leaves the land still parched. Rain in the Rub al-Khali can reach 3 to 4 inches (75–100 mm) a year. But this is only an average; droughts can last as long as 10 years.

The lack of rain in much of the country does not necessarily mean dry air: August and September can be quite humid. Along the Persian Gulf coast, the subtropical desert climate is extremely hot, with humidity reaching 90 percent.

Plants

Plant habitats in the Arabian Peninsula vary with the topography. Dates form the staff of life in this part of the world, and date palms grow almost everywhere in the inhabited regions. These trees provide food for humans and animals, fiber for ropes and mats, and material for building construction.

Although the peninsula is primarily desert, many areas do have sufficient water for a variety of plants. For example, extensive marshlands border the Red Sea. The mountainous areas in the southwest are covered with junipers (*Juniperus* species) at higher elevations, while various species of acacias (*Acacia* species) grow on the mountains' lower slopes. After the early spring rains, long-buried

seeds will germinate and bloom within a few hours; even the rockiest plains can produce late winter and early spring grazing areas for sheep, but these plants are short-lived. In some low-lying areas, enough water has collected to support dense communities of shrubs and acacia trees.

In the lowest elevations, below 1,000 feet (300 m), the foothills become much drier and more barren and are sparsely covered with small acacias, euphorbias, and some grasses. Various species of euphorbias have a bitter milky sap and large thorns to discourage browsing animals. Along the wadis, tall trees such as tamarinds (*Tamarinus indica*) and Christ's-thorn (*Ziziphus spinachristi*) send down extensive root systems to draw on the deep water stored in these normally dry river courses. Along the beaches, brackish water lies just below the surface in most places, so *Zygophyllum* and *Salsola* species, which are tolerant of salt, are common, and hardy grasses grow on mounds of blown sand.

Artemisias, plantago, gypsophila, heliotrope, anthemis, and other annuals respond to a good rain by growing rapidly and reseeding themselves. Annuals line hollows among the dunes and can

Date palms near the Dead Sea

be widespread over the more level sand areas.

The gravel belts in the desert areas are largely bare of vegetation because roots cannot take hold in and extract nourishment from pebbles and stones. In the rocky areas, the rainfall just runs off. In many parts of central Arabia, lack of water often inhibits the growth of herbs and grasses for several years in succession.

To the south of Kuwait, plains of wind-piled hummocky sand support the grass *Panicum turgidum,* which grows in wiry tussocks on small sand mounds. A zone of white coastal sand lies between the salt flats of the beach and the dunes of the interior, which form the threshold of the Rub al-Khali. The whole area is extremely barren and supports virtually no plant life. In fact, the high dunes that edge the Rub al-Khali on the west are remarkably free of plant life, in part because of their unstable surfaces.

An area of irregular rainfall near the Persian Gulf coast to the south and west of Qatar supports several salt-loving plants, but the salt flats farther south, known as *sabkhas,* are vast level areas, whose surfaces are devoid of vegetation and are often encrusted with salt.

Sedge, which grows in sandy areas, is a tough plant with deep roots that help hold down the soil; it is planted on dunes to try to stabilize them. Tamarisk trees are often found on the borders of oases, where they help prevent the encroachment of sand.

The eastern Rub al-Khali, although generally dry and barren, supports plant life on the giant dunes, including a sweet grass called *nasi,* which provides forage for the oryx.

The Arabian Peninsula has no native cacti, but the prickly pear has been imported from the Americas and thrives here. It is used by

nomads as livestock feed and as a source of fruit.

The hot and humid plains toward the southwest, in the province of Asir, are dotted with shrubs, palms, and acacia trees; along the higher ridges juniper trees catch the seaside fog as a source of water.

Animals

Desert insects include the fly, the malaria-carrying *Anopheles* mosquito, fleas, lice, ticks, roaches, ants, termites, and beetles, as well as predatory mantids that camouflage themselves as leaves, twigs, or pebbles. Swarms of locusts periodically descend as a plague in Arabia, devouring every plant in their path.

Arachnids include spiders and sapulgids, or scorpion-killers, which can grow up to 8 inches (20 cm) long. Scorpions also range up to 8 inches (20 cm) and are colored black, green, yellow, red, or off-white; their sting is poisonous and can even be fatal to children.

The Arabian Peninsula supports 130 species of butterflies. Most live in the mountainous regions, but even the desert areas have butterflies. Leopard butterflies have been caught in the heart of the Rub al-Khali. Such species as the desert white are the only residents of the driest regions and have a finely tuned survival mechanism. Some butterflies, for example, spend several years as pupae in an immobile and nonfeeding stage, waiting for the right conditions for breeding. They then emerge, mate, and lay eggs, which hatch quickly; in a matter of weeks the next generation reaches the pupal stage and may remain that way for years more. Some members of the blue butterfly family turn into cannibals; if food becomes scarce, at least a few will survive. The painted lady butterflies spread out in all directions and are not specifically adapted to any particular climate. If conditions suddenly become right for breeding, some specimens of this butterfly will breed and lay their eggs. But the new generation will leave the area, so that if it is not suitable for breeding again for many years, the species will survive.

In oases, pools contain small fish and amphibians such as newts, salamanders, toads, and frogs. Reptiles include lizards, snakes, and turtles. The dabb, a fat-tailed lizard, lives on the plains and can reach 3⅓ feet (1 m); it is a vegetarian and its tail, when roasted, is a Bedouin delicacy. Other lizards, including skinks, geckos, agamids, large desert monitors, and collared lizards, live in the sand. A salmon-colored lizard, the *dammusa*, eats black beetles and literally dives and swims in the sand dune surfaces. The poisonous horned viper and a species of cobra also inhabit the rocky parts of the desert.

Many of the larger mammals and birds have seen their numbers decline. Hunting from motor vehicles has taken its toll on many. Gazelles are almost extinct, and the oryx had disappeared from the Rub al-Khali by 1960. It is now, however, making a comeback, thanks to the Omani government, which reintroduced the almost-extinct Arabian oryx into the wild, using third-generation zoo-bred animals. The animals have formed a self-reliant herd and produced young.

Habitat destruction has also been a factor in southwestern Saudi Arabia. Within the 20th century, there has been widespread destruction of many wildlife species. Increasing human population has placed strains on water resources, fertile land, and the green valleys that formerly served as animal habitats or migration routes. Spells of drought, overgrazing, and extensive cutting of trees and shrubs for firewood and charcoal have disturbed plant cover and adversely affected plant reproduction. This, in turn, has seriously reduced wild animal populations.

In the desert plains the ratel—a badgerlike carnivore—the fox, and the civet cat live in territorial isolation. Wolves are widespread but not numerous. The hyena lives wherever sheep are herded, preferring escarpments that provide cover. Jackals are to be seen particularly at dusk, when they appear for water. There are hares, as well as golden sand rabbits. Small rodents include the mouselike jerboa, mice, rats, and porcupines, while small hedgehogs are found in the rocks. In Asir, troops of baboons live in the rocky outcrops.

Birds include bee-eaters, sparrows, weaver birds, crows, kites, falcons, hawks, vultures, wagtails, flamingos, seagulls, kingfishers, and owls. Birds such as the sand-grouse and Houbara bustard are becoming rare. Indeed, the bustard, a large running bird, has so suffered from hunting and the destruction of its habitat that it is almost extinct in Saudi Arabia.

The lion, ostrich, zebra, and several other species are now extinct on the peninsula. The Arabian ibex (*Capra arabica*), once abundant in the mountains, has fled northward. Other species, such as gazelles, which benefit from juicy plants and thus need little or no free water for drinking, have fled to the south.

Arabian Peninsula governments have started making serious attempts to preserve wildlife habitats. Asir National Park covers more than 1 million acres (400,000 ha). Animals within its borders include jackals, hyraxes, baboons, gerbils, jerboas, and bats, all of African origin. Rarer species include wolves, leopards, hyenas, ibex, and mountain gazelles. Birds include the endangered African bearded vulture.

41° N to 34° N latitude
55° E to 67° E longitude

Kazakhstan, Uzbekistan, Turkmenistan

The two largest deserts found in Central Asia are the Kara-Kum and the Kyzyl-Kum, in a region commonly known as Turkestan, located north of Iran and Afghanistan and east of the Caspian Sea in the Turanian lowland.

The Kara-Kum and the Kyzyl-Kum are separated by the Amu Darya river. The Amu Darya empties into the Aral Sea, as does the Syr Darya, which forms the northern border of the Kyzyl-Kum. The Kara-Kum, whose name means "black sand," lies to the south of the Amu Darya and is 90 percent sand desert. The Kyzyl-Kum, or "red sand" desert, starts just north of the Amu Darya. It is at a somewhat higher elevation than the Kara-Kum and is rockier with considerably less sand cover.

Topography

The lowland plains of Central Asia, including the Turanian lowland, are relatively young, in some cases dating from the early Quaternary period, about 2 million years ago. The Turanian lowland was once completely isolated from the rest of Asia by surrounding mountain ranges. Over time, sedimentary debris from weathering in the mountains to the east was deposited in the Turanian lowland. There are a number of dry river courses that parallel the present rivers and extend toward the Caspian and Aral seas. Alluvial plains associated with these ancient rivers occupy vast expanses of the lowland.

The Kara-Kum Desert, largest of the low-lying areas within the Turanian lowland, is a sand desert composed of beds of gray, layered sand several hundred feet thick. The Kara-Kum has several distinct types of dunes. Sand ridges are especially widespread; their length is 10 to 100 times their width or height. These ridges are stabilized by plants and are immobile, but sand can be blown out of them to form crescent-shaped barchan dunes in the surrounding areas.

In the center of the rockier Kyzyl-Kum are stone outcrops called inselbergs that rise to more than 3,000 feet (900 m); they are the eroded and weathered remains of ancient plateaus and mountains.

Large amounts of groundwater lie between 30 and 60 feet (9–18 m) below the surface close to the mountains. In the interior of the

Sand ridges in the Kara-Kum, Uzbekistan

desert the groundwater is closer to the surface and emerges in the form of springs and oases. Under the ancient alluvial plains the water tends to be slightly salty; the salinity increases toward the southern parts of the desert. In places there is a salty layer of water, above which are huge pockets of comparatively fresh water.

Mineral deposits in these desert regions include various metals, bentonite, potassium, sulfur, and petroleum. Much of the area near the Caspian Sea contains working oil wells, and there are numerous natural gas wells and pipelines in both the Kyzyl-Kum and the Kara-Kum deserts.

Climate

The climate of the Turkestan desert region is extremely dry and continental, with short but cold winters and hot summers.

In winter, cold air sweeps in from the Arctic and Siberia, and temperatures drop as low as -44° F (-42° C). In summer, the temperatures can reach 120° F (49° C), and the weather is dry and cloudless. The range between annual minimum and maximum temperatures is considerable—nearly 101 F degrees (56 C degrees) in the Kyzyl-Kum and 176 F degrees (98 C degrees) in the Kara-Kum.

Total precipitation in both deserts is sometimes less than 4 inches (102 mm) per year, falling mainly in the winter as snow and in the spring as rain. Augmenting the effects of the low amounts of precipitation are the high evaporation rates; in the Kara-Kum the annual rate of evaporation is 25 times the annual amount of precipitation.

The wind in the deserts of Turkestan blows from different directions depending on the season. The wind helps create *takyrs*, or bare clay patches, in both deserts. It keeps drifting sand from settling on their relatively smooth surfaces. Winds also help form salt pans by blowing the dry salty dust covering away until a damp layer of sand is laid bare. Evaporation causes a solid crust of salt to form on this surface even when the groundwater beneath is only slightly saline. Similarly, around the margins of the shrinking Aral Sea, the dry seabed gives rise to clouds of alkaline dust that are blown about by the nearly constant wind. Because the volume of water in the Aral is much less than it was even a few decades ago, the effect of the sea on the region's climate is less, and so the summer and winter temperatures are more extreme than they used to be.

Plants

Fossil remains from the region prove that the plant life in the Kara-Kum is ancient. There are many endemic groups of plants, and more than half of the species found are unique to the area. Plants in Turkestan have evolved in very dry conditions and in nearly complete isolation for the 2 million years since the Tertiary period.

Most of the surface of the Kara-Kum is sand with some forms of vegetation. The rest is divided into regions with little or no vegetation, and *takyrs* and salt pans. Both the *takyrs* and the salt pans often have relatively fresh groundwater underlying them, which allows various species of salt-tolerant plants, or halophytes, to grow in these areas.

Slightly salty groundwater is often found 16 to 33 feet (5–10 m) beneath the hollows between sand dunes. Here can be seen forestlike stands of *Haloxylon ammodendron*, the black saxaul.

Haloxylon persicum, the white saxaul, is the most common and characteristic plant in the Kara-Kum. This species, along with a sedge, *Carex physodes*, forms the most common plant combination on stabilized sands.

The sedge *Carex physodes* has long underground growths and is an important turf-forming species in the stabilized sand areas. The leaves die in May but remain on the plant until September or even the following spring. Other common plants include *Salsola, Calligonum*, and *Artemisia* species.

Semishrubs are common in the *takyrs* and form colonies with wormwood and saltbush. Oleaster and shrub willow are typical of the sandy regions, along with desert wheatgrass, lyme grass, and other grasses. *Ammodendron connolyi*, the sand acacia, is an important tree in areas where the sand is not stable. Sand acacia tolerates being covered and uncovered by sand, and can produce either long shoots or roots from its trunk, depending on how deeply it is buried.

Plants in the *Calligonum* genus have cylindrical leaves that fall off early and leave the branches bare. During the rest of the growing season, the plants carry out photosynthesis in their densely clustered annual shoots.

The spring rains bring forth a wide variety of ephemerals, including plants that grow from bulbs, such as wild tulips and alliums.

A caracal bares its teeth

Animals

Because of the long history of human settlement in this region, untold numbers of animals have been gradually removed from the Kara-Kum and the Kyzyl-Kum. In histories of the area, herds of thousands of saiga, or wild goat-antelopes; tarpans, or wild horses; and kulans, or wild asses (*Asinus hemionus*), are reported, but all have since disappeared—they may even be extinct. Herdsmen exterminated the carnivores to protect their flocks, and as a result rodents have bred without hindrance; today they are the most numerous mammals in the Turkestan deserts.

A few dzeren gazelles (*Gazella subgutturosa*) remain in the deserts; they seek shelter in the stands of *Haloxylon persicum* shrubs or in the dunes, where they eat the dry leaves of the *Carex* sedges. A common carnivore is a fox (*Vulpes vulpes flavescens*). It eats small mammals, birds, reptiles, insects such as sand cockroaches, and scorpions and tarantulas.

The spotted wildcat (*Felis ocreta*) is very common, especially near stands of shrubs where birds are nesting. During the day it lies in shallow hollows and ditches. Rarer is the dune cat (*Felis margarita thinobia*) and the desert lynx, or caracal (*Lynx caracal*).

A species of porcupine, *Hystrix hirsutiorostris*, lives in the dense stands of black saxaul and roams far afield in search of food, up to 6 miles (10 km) per night. It eats the fruit of *Nitraria* bushes in the saline areas, as well as the bulbs of wild tulips.

Many of the small desert animals in the Kara-Kum and Kyzyl-Kum do not drink water directly. Instead, they meet their needs for water by eating the parts of the plant that contain moisture. Most also conserve water by going out at night, when it is cool and the air is moist, and by staying in their cool, underground burrows during the day. They also conserve water by concentrating their urine, so they lose minimal amounts of fluid through excretion.

The local ground squirrel, *Spermophilopsis leptodactylus*, is extremely common. It stays within 300 to 500 feet (100–150 m) of its burrow when foraging for food. It can tolerate relatively high temperatures and is one of the few animals that will leave its burrow during the heat of the day. Its diet consists of the fruits of *Calligonum* species, parts of the spring ephemerals, and other geophytes. It can locate food very accurately by smell, even underground.

The desert hare (*Lepus tolai*) is a wide-ranging animal. In spring it eats the new growth and ephemerals; at other times it lives on the bark of shrubs other than *Haloxylon* or *Salsola*. It can be very damaging to shrubs because it will bite the young shoots off completely, and it interferes with the stabilization of dune sands because its favorite foods are the species that are planted in attempts at dune stabilization.

When the spring ephemerals flourish, wild pigs (*Sus scrofa*) occasionally migrate from the forests on the floodplains of the Amu Darya and wander through the sand areas.

There are three species of jerboas. One, *Dipus sagitta*, leaves its burrow only at night, closing over the opening with sand during the day. When it is alarmed and fleeing predators, especially owls, it can jump up to 6 feet (2 m) and then bury itself quickly in the sand. It eats fruits and the branches of shrubs as well as insects. The desert jerboa (*Eremodipus lichtensteinii*) has a similar diet and is also very common. The third species, *Paradipus ctenodactylis*, is widespread and occurs in large numbers,

but its habitat is restricted to shrub vegetation in slightly mobile sands that it can burrow into. It digs its burrow down to the wet layers of sand and gnaws on shrubs. This species of jerboa is dormant for 1 to 3 months during the cold season when there is no *Haloxylon* fruit available, awakening only when the *Haloxylon* comes out in the spring and the temperature rises.

The vole (*Ellobius talpinus*), a member of the rodent group, is found only in the southeastern Kara-Kum, near the oases. It eats the roots of shrubs, including *Haloxylon* and *Ammodendron*.

The tortoise *Testudo horsfieldi* can live in a density as high as 40 individuals per acre (100 per ha). They eat the young shoots of ephemeral plants during the spring rains and are active for 2½ to 4 months. After the rains stop and the vegetation dries out, the tortoises dig underground refuges in the sand and hibernate for the rest of the year. During their active season they lay eggs in the sand; although the development of the eggs takes only 3 months, the young tortoises do not appear on the surface until the following spring. When they do emerge, they are the favorite prey of many carnivores, including birds.

Wild boar, Turkestan Desert

Iranian Desert

31° N to 24° N latitude
53° E to 65° E longitude

Iran

Iran links the Middle East to South Asia, lying between Iraq on the west and Afghanistan and Pakistan on the east. The country occupies the eastern and larger portion of the great Plateau of Iran, a high, relatively level area that forms a geological bridge between the dry and grassy steppes of Central Asia and mainland Turkey.

Geology

The former seabed that is now the Iranian Plateau dates from the Mesozoic era and attained its current form during the Quaternary period, about 500,000 years ago. It was formed by the uplifting and folding effects of three giant plates pressing against each other: the Arabian Plate, the Eurasian Plate, and the Indian Plate. The squeezing and pressing resulted in considerable folding at the edges and some secondary folding in the interior, creating the present mountain ranges. The uplift and deformation of the plateau is an ongoing process that creates numerous faults. As a result, the area is subject to frequent and severe earthquakes as geologic forces make slow but powerful changes in the landscape.

The inland basins of Iran cover an area of over 300,000 square miles (770,000 sq km), more than half of the total land area of the country, and much of the present surface was once occupied by large lakes. These formed a continuous system that extended farther east into Afghanistan and Central Asia. In today's dry desert climate, only the lowest parts of the basins contain residual salt lakes or marshes, with extensive deposits of gravel,

sand, rock debris, and silt. This central basin is endorheic; in other words, all water flows into the basin and there is no outlet to the sea. The few streams flowing into these basins often disappear into salt marshes. As a result, salts and sediment have built up in the inland basins over the centuries.

To the east and south of Teheran is one of the best-known features of the Iranian Plateau: the Dasht-i-Kavir, or Great Salt Desert. The second large desert area is the Dasht-i-Lut farther south and east. The two salt deserts on the plateau make up about 25 percent of Iran's total land area.

Because water is so scarce, the people of Iran have created one of the most characteristic features of the landscape: *qanats,* Iran's underground irrigation tunnels. These underground watercourses draw water from springs, streams, and melting snow at the base of the hills and carry it into the flat desert plain.

Iranians have developed their own terminology for the features unique to their deserts. A *namak* is a salt lake, which can occur either as an open sheet of water or with a simple salt crust, without any mixing of silt or mud. *Kavir* is the name for an expanse of slime or mud, viscous rather than free flowing, with numerous patches or continuous thick layers of salt at the surface.

The salt crust of both *namaks* and *kavirs* forms polygonal plates on the surface. These plates develop as the water below the crust evaporates. The plates grow unevenly and arch upward. Sometimes the center lifts above the water surface, giving a hilly appearance; in other cases, the edges rise and the plates then look cupped.

The salt surface of a *kavir* can be from 4 to 8 inches (10–21 cm) thick, and below it can lie an expanse of salty, thick mud or slime.

The water in this mud comes from drainage channels where the water can flow more freely. These streams of ooze are usually narrow but deep, and they pose a significant danger to animals and humans crossing the surface of the *kavir*. These channels can be wide enough to engulf a whole group of people. Legend has it that entire caravans loaded with gold and gems perished in the Dasht-i-Kavir when they lost their way in dust storms and broke through the crust. Above the channels a hard salt crust forms that is indistinguishable from the rest of the landscape, so there is no indication that the channels are there. These channels remain liquid even in the hot, dry summer.

Earlier bodies of water filled the basin, as indicated by the occurrence of strand lines. On the landscape, where there were once the edges of a body of water, the former water levels are often defined by sharp breaks in slope—small, irregular cliffs 30 to 50 feet (9–15 m) in height.

The water surface was much larger during the earlier rainy periods, but even then the streams flowing into and out of the lakes were not powerful enough to cut through the outer mountains and create channels that reached the sea. This is one reason why there are no significant rivers flowing from the interior of the plateau.

The mountains consist primarily of crystalline metamorphic rocks, including schist and gneisses, and volcanic rocks, along with some Paleozoic and Mesozoic sedimentary formations. Toward the edges of the mountains, the bedrock dips under gravel, sand dunes, and loess deposits. Products of evaporation, such as calcium, magnesium, and sodium chlorides, are found. Sulfates tend to occur on the next level up the sides of the basin, while carbonates are found still higher. Iran's most important mineral deposit is its petroleum, which lies deep beneath the desert and mountain regions.

Climate

The area has an extremely continental and arid climate. The high degree of surface relief and folding, the tremendous variation in rainfall from year to year, and the fact that meteorological records have been kept for only a short time mean that the climate is not well understood. The country has many lakes, streams, and rivers, but most of them are shallow and dry up in the summer. Lake Urmia in the northwest of Iran, outside of the desert region, is the largest permanent lake and, like all of Iran's lakes, it contains saltwater.

Rainfall averages 5.4 inches (138 mm) a year, and almost all of it falls between October and March. The summer is totally dry.

The amount of precipitation varies greatly from place to place, depending on elevation and geography. Many areas receive less than 8 inches (200 mm) a year of precipitation, while some zones in the mountains and foothills have total precipitation (rain and snow) of from 7.8 to 19.5 inches (200–500 mm) per year. Only the mountain peaks and high ridges receive more than 39 inches (1,000 mm) per year. Most of it falls as snow during the winter. The wettest seasons are winter and spring in the north, with the rains stopping a few weeks later than in the south. The summer is rainless and hot, and fall is also very dry.

The daily temperature varies more than 30 F degrees (16 C degrees) during all seasons. Kuzistan, in the southwest, is the hottest region, with summer temperatures reaching 131° F (55° C).

The *shamal* is a regular wind pattern that occurs every year from February to October. It blows northwestward along the Zagros Mountains and the Iran-Iraq border. Another pattern, the "120-day wind," also originates during the summer. It is hot and violent and carries abrasive particles of sand. It blows from Pakistan toward Sistan and Baluchistan, damaging vegetation, carrying away the soil, and damaging the buildings and livestock with scorching heat and gusts of up to 70 miles an hour (112 kph).

Plants

Vegetation on the plateau is sparse and consists mainly of thorny shrubs, spindly tamarisk and acacia trees, dwarf palms, and hardy herbs such as giant fennel and salvia.

Grapevines and palms grow in the desert oases. Brush thickets sometimes grow on sand dunes, because the dunes can hold underground water. Lines of trees often mark the courses of the *qanats* in an otherwise barren landscape. Many parts of the Iranian Plateau are covered with a colorful but ephemeral blanket of wildflowers after the rains in March or April.

Vast areas of the inner Iranian plateau have almost no vegetation at all. In the saline plains, fine-textured soils with high salt content can support little life. Despite the high number of halophytic, or salt-loving, species, the plant communities have little variety. The groundcover is usually of one species, which grows sparsely over vast expanses.

Enormous portions of the saline flats are bare of higher vegetation. Trees such as *Halostachys caspica* and several *Tamarix* species sometimes grow near watercourses or on river plains with accessible water tables.

Reaumuria fruticosa occupies dry, salty ridges. Clusters of this plant typically develop on small ridges where the soil contains large amounts of soluble salts. The plants take in salt along with water. Then, salt glands in the leaves pump the salt out of the plant. As a result, a layer of powdered salt is often found below the shrubs.

Grasses and shrubby herbs found in the desert areas include *Artemisia herba-alba, Anabasis setifera, Ephedra strobilacea,* and *Haloxylon aphyllum.*

The Iranian Desert is home to a large number of tamarisk species. *Tamarix aphylla* and *T. macrocarpa* occur with *Prosopis spicigera* (a plant related to North American mesquite) and *Calligonum* species at the edges of sand and gravel deposits in the Dasht-i-Lut. The center of the Dasht-i-Lut has

Multicolored stratified rock in the desert mountains of eastern Iran

no vegetation at all and may be truly abiotic.

Animals

The number of animals in the desert varies greatly from season to season and year to year. The density of wildlife fluctuates with the growth of plants, which in turn depends on the amount of rainfall. After an unusually long dry period, the rodents disappear and there are only a few migrating birds.

Iran's native animals are diverse but are threatened by human activity. Jackals, rabbits, wildcats, and many species of small rodents are found on the central plateau. The onager (*Asinus hemionus*), an elusive breed of wild ass, lives on the central salt deserts.

Larger mammals and bird species are extinct or nearly so in many regions. Hyenas, leopards, caracals, cheetahs, and other animals were once common but are now rare. Wolves and foxes, however, are still common in most of the mountains. Wild dogs are abundant in the lower elevations. They subsist primarily on the plentiful gerbils and jerboas.

The open woodlands and artemisia semidesert are habitats for ungulates, or hoofed animals. One species of gazelle, *Gazella subgutturosa*, is common in some plains of the protected areas in Iran. Dorcas gazelles (*Gazella dorcas*) are also abundant in lower areas.

Rodents are common in the Iranian Desert. They include various species such as the ground squirrel *Spermophilopsis leptodactylus*, the gerbils *Rhombomys pimus* and *Meriones libycus*, and a jerboa, *Allactaga elater*. Two other species, *Calomyscus bailwardii* and *Meriones persicus*, live in rocky areas. Marmots (*Marmota caudata*), hares, and pikas are found at elevations above 10,000 feet (3,000 m). Porcupines and voles are found only in moderately arid regions. In addition, hamsters (*Cricetulus migratorius*) are found near farmland areas and on well-drained sites. The principal desert herbivores also include rabbits.

Rodents are able to survive in the desert by using several different strategies. Seed-eating species are active all year round in the open plains because food is available in every season. Hibernating species and those that are dormant during droughts are active only when enough green plants are available for food; the rest of the time they remain in underground burrows. These include ground squirrels and marmots. Species that eat underground plant parts are active only when the soil is moist; during wet periods they dig burrows near the ground surface. These animals include a species of burrowing rat.

A large number of reptiles live in the sandy deserts, including monitor lizards, agamids, and several snakes—many species are poisonous. Amphibians are also well represented, with many types of frogs and salamanders.

The tortoise (*Testudo horsfieldii*) is one of the most common reptiles and is found by the hundreds in the spring rainy season. These animals eat ephemeral vegetation in the loess region of the artemisia semidesert. This tortoise has two dormant periods a year: one during the winter cold and another during the summer drought. It is particularly abundant in areas of finer soil.

Iranian Desert arthropods include scorpions, which are found throughout practically the entire area. A common insect is *Hemilepistus aphaganicus*, a plant-eating wood louse, which is widely distributed in the desert areas of the Middle East.

A species of snail can be found living in the desert salt marshes.

Thar Desert

28° N to 23° N latitude
68° E to 76° E longitude

India, Pakistan

Ancient cities living and dead are evidence of lengthy habitation in the arid expanses of northwest India. As deserts go, the Thar is relatively young. Three rivers, the Ur-Jumma, the Saraswati, and the Sutlej, flowed through the region as recently as 3,000 years ago, when the annual rainfall was significantly greater than it is now. Today, however, rainfall averages less than 4 inches (102 mm) a year, the rivers have migrated west and east of the region, and empty lake beds await occasional downpours in the region known locally as *Marwar*, the place of death.

Also called the Great Indian Desert, the Thar is the easternmost extension of the Saharan-Arabian desert belt, which stretches across northern Africa and includes Saudi Arabia, Iran, Iraq, and Pakistan. The Thar Desert lies southwest of the Himalaya, mostly in the northwest Indian state of Rajasthan; its western edge runs a short way into the states of Sind and Punjab in Pakistan.

The desert covers about 175,000 square miles (453,250 sq km) and is bordered on the

Ancient Jodhpur, Rajasthan, India

northwest and east by the alluvial, or silt, plains of the Indus and Ganges rivers. The southeastern boundary is formed by the Aravalli Hills, which, because they block most of the summer monsoonal rainfall, are also a major factor in the existence of the desert.

Geology

History. India was formed about 100 million years ago when a portion of the supercontinent known as Gondwanaland separated and drifted north. About 60 million years later, India crashed into the Tibetan Plateau, forcing the crust up 5 miles (8 km) and creating the mountains of the Himalayan and Alpine ranges. The Indian Plate then moved underneath, raising the Tibetan Plateau.

The rivers that developed to drain the Himalaya, among them the Indus and the Ganges, carried silt from mountain erosion southward. The silt was then deposited on the plains that formed west and east of the Aravalli Range. Over time, for reasons that are still unclear, the Indus River system and some of its tributaries migrated northwestward across the flat plains, leaving behind the thick, dry deposits of silt that would later be blown into sand dunes.

Topography. The Aravalli Range is composed of granite, quartzite, and other igneous and metamorphic rocks. Just northwest from the mountains, the landscape is dotted with rocky outcroppings called inselbergs. Farther north and west, these features are replaced by steep-sided, flat-topped sandstone hills and plateaus, which eventually give onto a relatively flat plain of sand. The primary features of this region, which are the most dramatic landscapes of the Thar Desert, are the sand dunes. Most of the dunes are the U-shaped parabolic dunes. The height of these dunes ranges from 30 to 100 feet (9–30 m).

Less common are the linear dunes. Those that do exist probably started as parabolic dunes whose centers were eroded by the wind. Some sickle-shaped barchan dunes exist, but they are quite rare.

Climate

Average rainfall in the Thar varies greatly from 4 inches (100 mm) in the western portion up to 20 inches (512 mm) in the east; 90 percent falls during the summer monsoon season. Temperatures range from near freezing to 75° F (24° C) in the cold season (December and January) and over 120° F (49° C) in the hot season (May and June). The mean maximum temperature is 113° F (45° C) in May, with temperatures as high as 122° F (50° C) being recorded on occasion.

The monsoons are seasonal winds that control rainfall in much of Asia. Throughout most of the year, the winds are dry and blow out of the northeast. During the monsoon season, June through September, the wind directions shift and begin blowing from the southwest—directly off the Indian Ocean. The moisture-laden winds bring heavy rains and slightly cooler temperatures to most of India. However, by the time the monsoon reaches the Aravalli Range, much of the moisture has already condensed and fallen, and most of what little is left falls on the southeastern face of the range.

Great variations in the monsoons mean that average annual rainfall figures can be misleading. No two years are ever exactly alike—6 to 8 inches (153–205 mm) of rain may fall in one year and next to none in the following year. The daily patterns also shift: in some years the rain occurs in brief showers throughout July and August. In other years, one or two heavy storms will fill ancient salt lakes and even cause floods.

Plants

The Thar is located in an area that has witnessed thousands of years of human activity, which have taken a toll on the region's vegetation.

In modern times, nomadic and seminomadic groups graze herds of sheep, goats, and camels across the desert. The result of this activity is a land where little truly native vegetation still exists. Thorny shrubs and drought-resistant grasses are the norm, and then only in areas where the sand is relatively stable.

The plants most often found in this region are stunted trees and thorny shrubs such as *Acacia*, *Capparis*, and *Ziziphus* (commonly known, respectively, as acacia or gum-arabic tree, caper bush, and jujube); the cactuslike *Euphorbia caducifolia*; and tough grasses in the *Cenchrus* and *Aristida* groups. Acacias, caper bushes, and euphorbias are found on rocky hillsides, while *Prosopis*, which is related to the North American mesquites, and grasses grow in flat areas of thick sand. In the alluvial plains to the north, groundwater allows the growth of thickets of acacia and *Tamarix dioica* (tamarisk or salt cedar).

In the parts of the desert covered by deep sand, stable sand dunes support large stands of acacias and *Prosopis*. *Prosopis* and caper bushes grow between dunes. In the northern part of the sand desert, a succulent shrub known as *Haloxylon salicornicum* is common on the slopes of the dunes. Tough grasses such as *Panicum turgidum* grow on the tops of the dunes. As a rule, more vegetation grows on the windward side of a dune; while relatively less sheltered from the drying effects of the wind, it has a gentler slope that allows the plants a better grip on the soil.

In contrast, the shifting sands of young, active dunes are far too mobile to allow any plant to take root. Drifting dunes can also envelop established plant life in areas where desertification is hastened by overgrazing. *Prosopis juliflora* has been planted in some places in an attempt to slow this process, with limited success.

Animals

Animal life consists of mammals, birds, reptiles, and insects that are common to much of central and southern Asia. The desert is too young to have allowed the types of evolutionary adaptations found in older, more remote desert regions.

Mud houses in a Rajasthan village, northwestern India

One of the more striking species is the blackbuck (*Antilope cervicapra*). This medium-sized antelope has a dark back, neck, and face with a much lighter-colored underbelly and white rings around its eyes. Males and females have two long, spirally twisted horns. Blackbucks are constantly on the move, browsing in herds on grasses and cereal crops wherever they can find them.

The nilgai, or blue bull (*Boselaphus tragocamelus*) is one of the larger inhabitants of the Thar. It gets its name from the male's bluish-gray coat. This member of the bovine family has a heavy, horselike body—complete with a long mane—combined with a fine head, large rounded ears, and a short tail like that of a deer. The males have a pair of short black horns. Like the blackbuck, blue bulls form small roaming herds and graze primarily on grasses and crops. During droughts they browse on leaves and berries.

The sandy-colored Indian desert gerbil (*Meriones hurrianae*) looks very much like a mouse with a furry tail. The gerbil eats grass and sometimes seeds, leaves, flowers, and stems from a number of plants. It needs very little water and multiplies rapidly.

This tiny mammal is one of the major contributors to the process of desertification. Six gerbils can eat as much grass in one day as a sheep; in some areas, one acre of land will contain close to 100 gerbils. The gerbils also try to cool their burrows during hot weather by digging up surface sand to expose moister soil. The rodents can excavate more than 300 tons of soil per square mile (105 t per sq km) in a single day. Much of this soil dries up and blows away to form sand dunes.

The tailless Indian false vampire bat (*Megaderma lyra*) is grayish brown above with pale, whitish-gray underparts. Its body is 3 to 4 inches (8–10 cm) long, and each wing is up to 3 inches (8 cm) wide. It has long ears and a long, ornate nose leaf, a fleshy appendage on its nose that gives the bat its frightening appearance. Unlike other bats common to India, which eat either fruit or insects, the false vampire bat also includes small lizards, sparrows, frogs, and even other bats in its diet.

The great Indian bustard (*Choriotis nigriceps*) is related to the crane and plover. This bird stands up to 3 feet (1 m) tall, weighs close to 40 pounds (18 kg), and has a wingspan of up to 8 feet (2.5 m). It has a brown back, a white belly and neck, and a black cap that extends down the back of its neck. Breeding season starts after the onset of the summer monsoon; the birds wait to mate until they have migrated to areas where rain has actually fallen.

The name *bustard* evolved from Latin *avis tarda*, or slow bird. The bustard's stately walk and slow, lumbering takeoff have made it an easy and popular target, bringing it to the brink of extinction.

Lizards are the most common reptiles in the Thar. They include the fat-tailed gecko (*Eublepharis macularis*) and the desert skink, or Indian sandfish (*Ophiomorus tridactylus*), which eat insects; the predatory monitors (*Varanus griseus* and *Varanus bengalensis*), which eat snakes, other lizard species, birds, and rodents (the larger monitor, *V. bengalensis*, is big enough to catch and eat even large palm squirrels); and the Indian spiny-tailed lizard (*Uromastix hardwickii*), which is a strict vegetarian. All of these species also exist outside of the Thar Desert.

Insect life in the Thar consists of a variety of species, including locusts, crickets, beetles, grasshoppers, and termites.

Taklamakan Desert

33° N to 30° N latitude
77° E to 85° E longitude

China

The Taklamakan Desert lies in the center of the Tarim Basin of northwestern China in the Xinjiang Province. This barren and hostile terrain is one of the largest sand deserts in the world. The Chinese call it the Sea of Death because of the many lives that have been lost there.

Not always a desert of extremes, this region was covered by seas on several occasions. Plant and animal fossils and debris left behind eventually formed the oil deposits under the basin; these now constitute what is estimated to be one of the largest oil and natural gas reserves in China.

Topography

The Tarim Basin is almost entirely surrounded by massive mountain ranges: to the north it is bordered by the Tian Shan; to the west by the Pamirs; and to the south by the Kunlun Shan. The latter loom 19,300 feet (5,900 m) over the sandy dunes of the Taklamakan. Only in the north and east is the mountainous rim broken.

Taklamakan sand dunes, China

At the heart of the Tarim Basin, the Taklamakan sprawls 600 miles (967 m) west to east and some 260 miles (419 km) south to north at its widest point; it covers 105,000 square miles (272,000 sq km).

A few ephemeral rivers merge in the basin and become tributaries of the Tarim River, the world's longest landlocked river. It flows along the Taklamakan's northern edge from the west toward the Lop Nor salt lake in the east. These tributaries include the Yarkant, Kashgar, and Keriya rivers to the west and the Hotan to the south. Shallower streams issuing from the Kunlun Shan disappear into the sands 60 to 120 miles (97–194 km) into the desert, feeding the groundwater table that lies not far below the surface.

The Hotan is the only river that crosses the Taklamakan seasonally. Between June and September it can become torrential when it swells with the runoff from the Kunlun Shan. As it surges north, the water erodes its banks and sometimes spills over 3 miles (5 km) onto the desert floor. Eventually the Hotan joins the Yarkant and Aksu rivers, feeding into the Tarim River as it heads eastward to Lop Nor.

The Lop Nor lowland is the Tarim Basin's lowest point. At one time the Tarim River drained into it; for 20,000 years a lake of varying size endured the arid climate. Today what remains of this lake is a crust of salt, alkali, and gypsum that only periodically contains small amounts of water. The erosion of Lop Nor's crust by the wind has resulted in unique formations on the landscape. Yardangs, or salt ridges, cover up to 1,200 square miles (3,100 sq km) of the flat and barren terrain.

Small mountain chains rise above the surface. In the west, the Mazartags arc from east to west for 90 miles (145 km) and are about 2

to 3 miles (3–5 km) wide. While they average a height of about 1,100 feet (335 km), their highest peak is 5,363 feet (1,635 m). This range is composed of sedimentary deposits that were left by an ocean that covered the basin over 67 million years ago and have since been thrust up from the plains. These sediments are visible in two of its branches: the northern is composed of white dolomite and gypsum, and the southern of red sandstone. The Chöl Tagh is a smaller range averaging 600 to 800 feet (183–244 m). Both ranges are surrounded by swirling seas of sand.

The sand covering the Taklamakan, in places 1,000 feet (300 m) thick, is the product of weathering and wind erosion of gravel, clay, and silt deposited at the foothills by mountain streams. In the south and west, a 30-mile (48-km) *gobi*, or gravel plain, rings the desert where it meets the Kunlun Shan. Swept up by northeast and northwest winds in the basin, the shifting and largely southward-moving sand dunes of the Taklamakan are mostly crescent-shaped barchans. However, these winds also produce many other magnificent shapes such as stars and crosses, in a variety of sizes. Pyramid-shaped dunes can reach heights of up to 1,000 feet (300 m); chains of dunes are sometimes 500 feet (152 m) long and up to 1,650 feet (503 m) wide with distances of ½ to 3 miles (0.8–4.8 km) between them.

Climate

The Taklamakan's arid climate is due in great part to the mountains flanking it, which block the interior from moisture-laden winds. Moreover, the area is far removed from any large bodies of water. Precipitation, therefore, is almost negligible, averaging 1½ inches (38 mm) in the west and decreasing to ⅖ inch (10 mm) in the east.

In July, temperatures range from 75° to 80° F (24°–27° C), although they sometimes rise above 104° F (40° C). Winter temperatures average between 14° and 21° F (-6° and 10° C), sometimes dropping below -4° F (-20° C), partly because of the influence of cold air masses from Mongolia and Siberia that sweep into the Taklamakan and the Tarim Basin through its opening in the east. There are also considerable daily fluctuations in temperature.

The climate is also influenced by air currents that collide near the center of the region and whip dust up to 13,000 feet (3,962 m) into the atmosphere. In the spring, violent dust storms develop when the ground begins to warm, causing the air above it to rise, while at the same time northeasterly winds gain momentum. Such dust storms, called *kara-buran*, or black storms, leave the sky pitch-black and the Taklamakan blanketed in dust for months at a time. These hazardous winds also create the fantastic sand dune shapes that cover the desert.

Plants

Most of the Taklamakan is devoid of vegetation because the moving sands prevent most plants from ever taking hold. However, in areas where groundwater lies between 10 and 16 feet (3 and 5 m) below the surface, tamarisk (*Tamarix*) shrubs, reeds, and niter bushes can survive in hollows between dunes and even on their ridges.

More plants grow along rivers and deltas. A 2-mile (3-km) swath of vegetation runs along the banks of the Hotan River and includes reeds, Ural licorice, and dogbane up to 3 feet (1 m) tall, as well as poplars up to 22 to 33 feet (6–10 m) tall. Sea buckthorn, chee reedgrass, little cattails, false broadleaf tamarisk, and Japanese inula also grow in parts of this oasislike belt.

Farther from the river, these are gradually replaced by the hardier tamarisk and serpentroot.

On the edges of the Taklamakan near river valleys and deltas grow the Turanga poplar, willows, camel thorn, members of the Zygophyllaceae (caltrop family), and saltworts.

Animals

Most of the Taklamakan animals live along the more hospitable periphery and near the rivers. Gazelles, wild boars, wolves, and foxes inhabit the river valleys. The tigers that once roamed these areas until the beginning of this century have totally disappeared. Also rare now are the Siberian deer of the Tarim River valley and the wild Bactrian, or two-humped, camel, which is found in the Lop Nor region to the east.

The meridian sand rat, the common house rat, the field mouse, and the jerboa are rodents common to the Taklamakan. Larger mammals include various species of rabbit, the talimu hare, the spotted prairie cat, and the corsac, or sand fox. Insectivores include bats and long-eared hedgehogs.

Typical desert-dwelling non-mammals include scorpions, centipedes, sand eels, the talimu maned lizard, and the red sand snake. More unusual are the grass, common, and crucian carps that swim in the Hotan River.

The Taklamakan is also home to many birds, particularly in the Lop Nor region. Most common are the tufted lark and the Tarim jay; in areas close to rivers the gray crane, the long-footed sandpiper, the herring gull, and the cormorant can be sighted. The white-tailed land crow, the purple-winged starling, the plumed grizzle-winged woodpecker, tree sparrows, and various owls live where there are trees in which they can roost.

Gobi

37° N to 34° N latitude
90° E to 108° E longitude

China, Mongolia

The Gobi is the coldest, most northern desert aside from the Arctic. It occupies a vast arc of land 1,800 miles long (2,900 km) and 300 to 600 miles (484–968 km) wide, lying northwest of Beijing and north of the Nan Shan mountains of western China.

Mountains surround the Gobi on the south, east, and north, and these natural barriers remove virtually all moisture from the winds that reach the desert. As a result, the annual precipitation of the Gobi is less than 8 inches (203 mm) a year, with some regions, such as the Trans-Altai Gobi, receiving an average of less than 4 inches (100 mm). The Gobi also suffers from scorchingly hot summers and freezing winters.

Geology

The Gobi's plains date mainly from the Paleocene to Recent epochs, up to 65 million years ago, although some of the low, isolated ranges are older. In the central Gobi, the remains of Mesozoic era dinosaurs 65 million

Sheep roam rocky Gobi terrain

to 225 million years old have been found.

In the early Paleozoic era, around 450 million years ago, southwestern Mongolia underwent a tectonic plate collision, resulting in massive alterations to the geography. Some areas became submerged by shallow seas. From the late Devonian until toward the end of the Paleozoic, tectonic activity decreased and the region underwent a slow uplift as the area of the seas shrank. Finally, tectonic activity eased, by which time the marine basins had been reduced to shallow lagoons. Part of the Paleozoic formations is composed of marine deposits as thick as 20,000 feet (6,000 m).

In the Mesozoic era, which started 245 million years ago, the current relief of Mongolia began to form. Weak mountain-building processes continued the general uplift; lake and alluvial deposits accumulated in the Gobi during both the Jurassic and early Cretaceous periods. At the end of the Mesozoic and beginning of the Cenozoic eras, around 70 to 50 million years ago, tectonic activity died out.

The overall topography of the Gobi today is one of ridges and basins; the eastern Gobi has elevations ranging from 2,300 to 5,000 feet (701–1,524 m). On the western border of Mongolia the mountains rise over 10,000 feet (3,048 m), with some peaks much higher; one in the Tian Shan reaches 24,407 feet (7,439 m).

The center of the Gobi consists largely of dry rocky or sandy soil. Steppes (dry grasslands) surround this central area. Sand dunes are not common in the Gobi; they cover only about 5 percent of the desert area. Instead, most of the Gobi is stony desert. Most soils are rocky and covered with a coating of broken stone and gravel, which accumulates on the surface as the finer materials are blown away.

This is called desert pavement. The stones take on a dark appearance from the action of dew and dust, which dry out in the sun and wind; the result is a black patina called desert varnish. Calcium and gypsum crusts are also common.

The compact soil surface and the short heavy rains cause high runoff and water erosion. In the smaller areas of sand deserts the sand shifts constantly because of the wind. Wind speeds of up to 73 mph (118 kph) are not uncommon, and in sandy areas these lead to shifting dunes and sandstorms.

The Trans-Altai Gobi is among the driest regions of Central Asia. Years without rainfall are common. It is geographically more varied than the other districts of the Gobi, with hilly landscapes and high mountain ranges. There are also extensive plains of gravel, rock, and stone desert.

Climate

The Gobi's climate is continental and dry, with temperatures that can range from -40° F (-40° C) in January to 113° F (45° C) in July. Winter is severely cold; spring is dry and cold; and summer is hot. Temperatures are extreme—there is as much as 150 F degrees (65.5 C degrees) difference between the hottest day in summer and coldest night in winter. As a result of the amount of sunlight that reaches the desert surface, the daily maximum temperatures can reach above freezing even in winter.

Scanty precipitation falls in summer, in the form of occasional hard rain with thunder and lightning, and adds up to less than 10 inches (254 mm) in a normal year, but can vary from 3 inches (69 mm) in the west to more than 8 inches (203 mm) in the northeast. Although blizzards can occur, in winter there is often very light snow over most of Mongolia and the Gobi. The snow usually evaporates without melting, while the dry soil remains unfrozen.

The wind is persistent in the Gobi, blowing mainly during the day, and mostly from the north and northwest. In the sand dune areas, severe sandstorms occur even in July and August, the supposedly rainy months.

Surface rivers have very infrequent flow; mountain streams are confined to the Gobi's fringes and even then quickly dry up, as they disappear into the loose soil or the salty, enclosed depressions. Many rivers flow only in the summer. On the other hand, subterranean water is widespread in the river gravels.

Plants

Because of the high concentrations of salt and gypsum on the surface of most of the Gobi, plant growth is severely limited. Vegetation is sparse and short, and the variety of plants is small. Almost nowhere do plants cover more than 30 percent of the ground. Where there is groundwater or a river, poplars, tamarisks, and common reeds grow densely to form natural oases. In the drier sections, semishrubs and shrubs predominate.

Those species that prosper have adopted special characteristics.

Many species of wormwood (*Seraphidium* and *Artemisia*) that live in the Gobi have deeply divided leaves to minimize water loss from transpiration. Broomlike shrubs of the genus *Calligonum* and the salt-tolerant *Anabasis* have leaves that are slender and stiff, much like stems. Common horaninowia (*Horaninowia ulcina*) is almost leafless and is dependent upon its annual green branches for photosynthesis.

The leaves of the herb *Sassurea* and some wormwoods of the genus *Artemisia* have dense, fine hairs that reduce transpiration. Some kinds of flowering shrubs such as reaumuria and the closely related tamarisk (*Tamarix*) have leaves and stems with a waxy layer to reduce water loss. During extremely hot, arid periods they will preserve moisture by shedding leaves, or even branches, and becoming dormant until the next rainfall.

Little can survive in the sand and gravel deserts. The few species that do grow are grasses, bushes, and small shrubs that are drought tolerant, or xerophytic; they include *Calligonum* and saxauls (*Haloxylon*) and some *Aristida*, *Stipa*, and *Cleistogenes* grasses. On the mobile and semimobile dunes, *Mongolium calligonum* grows more than 5 feet (150 cm) high and is accompanied by milk vetch (*Astragalus*) and related species.

A few small bushes and shrubs find footholds in cracks or fissures in areas of detritus; as the water passes through in the brief and irregular rainy period, the salt in the soil is diluted and germination becomes possible. The main plants are Kashgar ephedra (*Ephedra przewalskii*), Siberian nitraria (*Nitraria sphaerocarpa*), reaumuria, and anabasis. The plants are all very short, under 16 inches (40 cm).

"Window lichens" appear on the bottom of transparent quartz pebbles. Dew and condensation of soil humidity at night after rains cause some water to accumulate at these points, enough to wet the lichen thoroughly and allow it to assimilate the water at daybreak.

Animals

The Mongolian deserts and desert steppes are refuges for some very rare and carefully protected wild animals: the Mongolian kulan, or dshiggetai (*Asinus hemionus*), the saiga antelope (*Saiga tatarica*), the dzeren gazelle (*Procapra subgutturosa*), and the wild camel (*Camelus bactrianus*). The wild Przewalski's horse (*Equus przewalskii*) lived at one time in the Gobi, but has not been seen there in the last few decades and may be extinct in its natural habitat.

The most common mammals in the Gobi are jerboas and gerbils; the area has no fewer than 11 species of jerboas alone. These rodents' hind legs are two to four times as long as their front ones, and they jump forward in powerful bounds. Jerboas have a camouflaged sandy-yellow back, a white belly, and a long whiplike tail for balance. Jerboas are unpopular with farmers because they destroy the grass as well as any crops and seedlings planted in oases.

A herd of Przewalski's horses

The other common rodent is the gerbil; seven or eight gerbil species live in the desert. Gerbils have sandy-colored backs and white bellies. Their burrows, which they dig near bushes, are complex, with many exits and a network of passages. Individual chambers are assigned to specific functions such as food storage. Gerbils breed very rapidly, having two to three litters a year, with six to nine young in a litter. They do not hibernate, but often migrate to a wintering place near their feeding grounds.

Most desert rodents do hibernate through the long winter and also store food in their burrows. Because rodents live in a small territory and have to make do with its local vegetation, when it rains, their numbers boom; when it is dry, populations decline through higher mortality and a reduced birth rate. However, rodents rarely drink and can survive on the little moisture contained in plants. In times of extreme drought their metabolism changes to reduce their moisture needs still further.

Gazelles, in contrast, roam widely, with no home territory, wherever the vegetation happens to be in good condition at the time. Even though grazing varies from place to place and year to year, the gazelles are able to maintain a stable population. Two types of gazelles, Przewalski's gazelle (*Procapra przewalskii*) and the goitered gazelle (*Gazella subgutturosa*) inhabit desert areas. They are small hoofed mammals, widely distributed in the northwestern area. They live on the plains of the steppes and in the stony deserts, where they eat the tender leaves and shoots of plants.

Carnivores include the Chinese desert cat (*Felis bieti*) and Pallas's cat (*Felis manul*). The rare Pallas's cat hunts the high plateaus, looking for small mammals, but

often lives in the desert grassland and stony deserts. It makes its lair in cracks of rocks or in the abandoned holes of marmots and, like many carnivores, lives singly.

Birds include eagles, hawks, and vultures. In addition there are sandgrouse, which fly very long distances to drink at a regular time of day. When they drink, the males also wet their absorbent breast feathers and transport water to cool their chicks and quench their thirst. Pallas's sandgrouse (*Syrrhaptes paradoxus*) also breeds in the Gobi. Occasionally the population becomes so large that the species seeks out new territory and spreads westward to Europe. One such eruption even led to a nesting in Britain. Their nests are simple hollows scooped out of the ground, in which they lay three or four eggs per clutch.

Grasshoppers live in the desert steppes and in the stony deserts, feeding on sparsely growing grasses. The next most common insects are beetles (order Coleoptera), as they can live off most desert plants.

The most common desert and semidesert reptiles are lizards, mainly species of *Phrynocephalus* and *Agama,* and of the genus *Eremias.* There are ten species of toad-headed agamid lizards. Unlike snakes, they have eyelids that close to protect their eyes from the wind and blowing sand, and can also close their nostrils for the same purpose. They emerge from hibernation in early April and mate in May or June. When danger threatens, they lie on the sandy surface, shake their bodies rapidly and kick up the sand, and then shuffle down into it to hide.

The ring-tailed gecko (*Crytodactylus louisiadensis*) is a nocturnal desert reptile. Additional geckos include other members of this genus, as well as the genera *Alsophylax* and *Teratoscincus.*

15° S to 32° S latitude
116° E to 145° E longitude

Australia

Australia has a greater percentage of desert area than any other continent; two-thirds of it is either habitable desert or semiarid.

History

Australia was once a piece of a greater puzzle that also included South America, Africa, India, Antarctica, and New Guinea. This ancient continent of Gondwanaland began breaking apart 100 million years ago. Australia, along with India, now rests on a plate that is moving slowly northward and pushing up the Himalaya in Central Asia. As a result of this movement, Australia has drifted into a subtropical zone characterized by extreme aridity, which it shares with the Kalahari in southern Africa.

Unlike neighboring islands with active volcanoes, Australia is relatively stable geologically; the greatest activity evidenced in its almost featureless surface has been the erosion over millions of years of once-high mountain ranges, which has reduced the average

Salt pan in the Western Desert

elevation of the continent to 1,000 feet (300 m).

Topography

Almost three-quarters of Australia is an arid plateau of Precambrian rock. The Outback, Australia's dry interior, sits on this plateau; at its heart is a broad region known as the Red Centre, named for its red sands. To the west lies the Western Desert; it makes up most of the central Outback. The extremely arid Simpson Desert is located in the central eastern lowlands.

Western Desert. The Western Desert extends 250,000 square miles (650,000 sq km) across the ancient plateau, and averages a height of 1,000 to 2,000 feet (300–600 m). For practical rather than scientific reasons, this large area is often thought of as three regions whose boundaries are drawn more or less arbitrarily: the Great Sandy Desert in the north, the Gibson Desert to its south, and the southernmost Great Victoria Desert.

Each of the regions in the Western Desert is a patchwork of different soils, although sandhills predominate in all of them. These sandhills are ridges that average a height of 50 feet (15 m). Spaced about 1,300 feet (400 m) apart, the sandhills are stabilized by the widespread spinifex grass. Shield deserts, plains of gravel common in the southwest, also sheath large areas of the Western Desert. Knolls made of this gravel are known as *rira.* "Breakaways" are *riras* with eroded bases and a top-heavy appearance; one of the largest, Mount Conner, has a tabletop 1.9 miles (3 km) long.

The few other formations and minor mountain ranges of the Western Desert are noteworthy because of the region's otherwise flat terrain. The most striking formation is Ayers Rock, or Uluru, one of the world's largest monoliths.

Rising 1,115 feet (340 m) out of the sandy plains, the imposing red mass is almost 2 miles (3 km) long. About 20 miles (32 km) to the west is another impressive rock formation of 36 rock domes, known as the Olgas, or Kata Tjuta. The ancient Macdonnell Ranges and the Musgrave Ranges are to the north and south of Ayers Rock, respectively.

Catchments, or pools, such as those found in the Macdonnell Ranges, are one of the most important sources of water. Water also collects for brief periods in salt pans, or depressions, and in river remnants called billabongs. There are no permanent rivers or streams; rather, the landscape is scarred by creeks and lakes that fill only after great downpours. The largest lake, covering 650 square miles (1,700 sq km), is fittingly named Lake Disappointment. Even when these lakes and streams fill, they do not come together to form a substantial flow of water, leaving the Western Desert with no connected drainage system. Instead, "native wells," once dug to access water tables, provide a more reliable source of water.

Simpson Desert. The Simpson Desert, in the eastern half of the continent, is composed of both sandy and stony, or "gibber," surfaces. The Simpson's straight, parallel sand dunes are the longest in the world and extend up to 125 miles (200 km). The gibbers are fragments of larger stones broken up by the expansion and contraction that result from hot days and cool nights. They range in color from red to purple to brown, and in size up to 1 foot (30 cm) in diameter. These sandy and stony plains are broken up by pans scattered throughout the south and east and by the 3,000-foot (1,000-m) Flinders Range in the south.

One large stony region is often called the Sturt Stony Desert, after one of Australia's famous explorers.

Drainage in the Simpson is consolidated and flows into salt lakes. The largest, Lake Eyre, spreads out over 7,550 square miles (19,500 sq km). When it fills—once or twice a century—it is transformed from a dry salt pan into a haven rich in wildlife. Another more permanent source of water is the underground Great Artesian Basin; 621,000 square miles (1.6 million sq km) in area, it lies under the lowland to the east of Lake Eyre and to the west of the Great Dividing Range that runs down the east coast.

Climate

Australia, with annual rainfall averaging 16.5 inches (420 mm) or less, owes the continuing aridity in the eastern interior to the blockage of moisture-laden Pacific winds by the Great Dividing Range. In the west, the moisture in oceanic winds is warmed and locked in by its passage over land. The interior must rely instead on rains that drift down from monsoons in the northern regions. This rain, however, is erratic and unpredictable, falling mostly during the summer months of December and January. Torrential and

A gum forest in western Australia

localized downpours sometimes result in catastrophic sheet floods that overwhelm the parched land. An extremely high and constant rate of evaporation ensures that whatever rain falls does not remain on the ground long.

In the summer, temperatures range from 80° F (27° C) to an agonizing 122° F (53° C). Ground temperature sometimes rises to 158° F (70° C). The intensity of the heat is mitigated only by the low humidity. During the winter months, temperatures range from 25° F (-4° C) to 80° F (27° C).

One result of these high daytime temperatures is that, as the hot air above the ground escapes from blankets of colder and heavier air above it, whirlwinds called willy-willies are formed. These columns of swirling air pick up materials such as plant seeds and strew them across the plains.

Plants

The hardy grasses of the Australian interior are among the many plants that have successfully evolved to endure harsh desert conditions. Many kinds of the spiky, silvery-green spinifex (*Triodia* and *Plectrachne*) grow outward from a central clump and form a ring that expands as older grass in the center

dies. Many species of animals make use of the spinifex. The grass known as woolly butt, or wire wanderrie (*Eragrostis eriopoda*), and twist-drill grass, which burrows its seeds into the ground, round out the list of other common grasses.

Communities of larger plants include the tough mulga, made up mostly of wattle, as species of acacia trees are called. The acacias are found in patches throughout the Western Desert. Species of wattles include mesquite (*Prosopis juliflora*) introduced from North America, and sweet acacia (*Acacia farnesiana*).

Mallee scrub, dominated by stunted bushlike eucalypts, or gum trees, grows at the edges of the deserts and displays some unique adaptations to the environment. To ensure their survival, eucalypts have buds that open immediately after a fire, as well as thick oily leaves that lock in moisture and protect them from the heat. The leaves hang downward to avoid as much solar radiation as possible. The white bark of the large ghost gum (*Eucalyptus papuana*) reflects the damaging rays of the sun. This gum grows along the drainage lines of creeks, as does the river red gum (*Eucalyptus camaldulensis*), which can extract up to one ton of moisture a day from water that has seeped deep underground.

Other trees include the desert oak (*Allocasuarina decaisneana*), which prefers sandy plains, and the native pine (*Callitris* species), found in rocky gorges. The blackboys, or grass trees (*Xanthorrhoea preissii*), resemble dancers with their thick skirts of long, fine needles above short, broad trunks.

Berries of the genus *Canthium,* wild figs (*Ficus* species), quandong fruits (*Santalum*), and tubers such as desert yams (*Ipomoea costata*), with their soccer ball–sized tubers, are found in wooded areas and are among the 50 or more species of edible plants.

Annual wildflowers of the Australian desert thrive after rainfall, creating a colorful carpet of blossoms; the brilliant red Sturt's desert pea (*Clianthus formosus*) and the pink *Cleome oxalidea* are two of the many that dot the usually dry landscape. The annuals soon wither once the available moisture is used up in this extravagant display; their survival, therefore, is dependent on drought-resistant seeds that can sprout after years of dormancy.

Perennials are more conservative in their use of moisture; many, like the butterfly bush (*Petalostylis labicheoides*), store nourishment in their roots and do not grow until it rains. Others, like the mulla mullas, also named pussytail and foxtail because of their fuzzy blossoms, have hardy stalks to withstand the effects of drought.

Other flowers include the succulent parakeelya (*Calandrinia* species), which has pink flowers, and the pigwood (*Portulaca oleracea*), a spreading succulent.

Simpler plants include lichens, growths of algae and fungi that live together and are ideally adapted to desert conditions.

Animals

The animals of Australia are the unique product of millions of years of isolation; some are found nowhere else in the world. Many of these are marsupials, or pouched mammals—a group for which Australia is famous. They make up the largest group of native mammals and range in size from the diminutive 2-inch (5-cm) long-tailed planigale (*Planigale ingrami*) to the towering 6⅓-foot (2-m) red kangaroo.

Well adapted to desert conditions, most marsupials require less food than other mammals; this is true for kangaroos because they expend less energy by hopping on two powerful legs than by walking on four. The mobile red kangaroo can efficiently attain speeds of up to 30 mph (50 kph). Less inclined to move around is the euro, or common wallaroo (*Macropus robustus*), which looks like a smaller version of the red kangaroo.

Smaller marsupials include the black-footed rock-wallaby (*Petrogale lateralis*), so named because it lives among granite boulders in the mallee scrub; the bilby, or rabbit-eared bandicoot (*Macrotis lagotis*); the fat-tailed marsupial mouse (*Pseudantechinus macdonellensis*); and the kultarr, or jerboa marsupial mouse (*Antechinomys spenceri*). The peculiar-looking marsupial mole (*Notorcytes typhlops*) is a product of extreme specialization. This earless and eyeless mole has front legs equipped with powerful claws for burrowing.

Further evidence of the unique character of Australian species is the echidna (*Tachyglossus aculetus*), one of the only two monotremes, or egg-laying mammals, in the world. Also called a spiny anteater, the echidna looks like a porcupine with a long snout that is ideally suited for unearthing ants. Another carnivore, the largest in Australia, is the dingo, or native dog (*Canis familiaris dingo*).

Bird species are also abundant in Australia: more than 700 exist. Millions flock to areas where there has been recent rainfall, where they feed on long-dormant crustaceans. Among these are the galah (*Cacatua roseicapilla*), which is a pink parrot, and the green parakeetlike budgerigar (*Melopsittacus undulatus*). Others include the little corella (*Cacatua pastinator*) and the zebra finch (*Taeniopygia*), named for the black-and-white stripes on its front. Unlike these colorful birds, the tawny frogmouth (*Podargus strigoides*) is well camouflaged to blend in with the bark of trees.

Larger birds include the kori bustard, or plains turkey (*Ardeotis kori*), and the scavenging wedge-tailed eagle (*Aquila audax*). The emu (*Dromaius novaehollandiae*), similar to the ostrich in appearance, makes up for its inability to fly by being able to run up to 30 mph (48 kph).

The 230 species of lizards living in Australia include the 8-foot-long (2.5-m) perentie (*Varanus giganteus*) and Gould's goanna (*Varanus gouldii*). Inhabiting the hummock grasslands, these harmless lizards employ a variety of physical and behavioral defense mechanisms to protect themselves. The thorny devil (*Moloch horridus*) is covered with frighteningly sharp spines, while the frilled lizard (*Chlamydosaurus kingii*) unfolds its large, bright-orange collar to intimidate potential predators. Other lizards such as the Centralian blue-tongued skink (*Tiliqua multifasciata*) and the shingleback (*Trachydosaurus rugosus*) hiss and open their jaws wide as a warning. Most of these lizards feed on insects. The thorny devil lizard alone consumes 1,000 to 5,000 insects daily.

The vast number of insects on which many lizards and other

Galah parrot

desert animals depend includes the ever-pervasive bush fly (*Musca vetustissima*), termites (*Amitermes* and *Drepanotermes*), grasshoppers, beetles, and the fat, juicy witjuti, or witchetty, grubs of the moths in the Cossidae and Hepialidae families. One of the tastier insects is the honey ant (*Melophorus bagoti*); once it fills its abdomen with honey it looks like a plump, translucent golden grape.

In order to protect themselves from sheet flooding after torrential rains, ants have developed an ingenious method of damming up their holes with soil, stones, and leaves. Other animals have also developed ways to cope with flooding in the desert. The wolf spider stuffs the hole of its burrow with available materials bound in its silk. As its name suggests, the trap-door spider constructs a door that shuts out water. Conversely, the water-holding frog (*Cyclorana platycephala*), which forms a cocoon to minimize water loss, leaves its burrow only when it rains so it can feed on insects and fill its bladder with water.

Additional subterranean desert dwellers are the blind snakes (*Ramphotyphlops*) and the desert banded snake (*Simoselaps bertholdi*), whose smooth skin allows it to slide effortlessly through the sand. While some snakes such as the woma, a type of python (*Aspidites ramsaui*), are edible, others, including the liru or mulga snake (*Pseudechis australis*), the fierce snake (*Oxyuranus microlepidotus*), the death adder (*Acanthopis antarcticus*), and the taipan (*Oxyuranus scutellatus*), are among the most venomous vipers in the world.

The desert hardyhead (*Craterocephalus dalhousiensis*), a small fish found only in an oasis in the Simpson Desert, and the tadpole shrimp (*Triops australiensis*) live in the few watery parts of the desert.

Great Basin Desert

46° N to 38° N latitude
121° W to 109° W longitude

USA

The Great Basin Desert, also known as the Sagebrush Desert, covers an area of between 158,000 and 190,000 square miles (409,220 and 492,100 sq km) in the western United States. The largest desert entirely within the United States, the Great Basin region derives its name from the fact that its various bodies of water have no outlet to the sea. The desert includes most of Nevada, some small areas along the California border, large portions of Oregon and Idaho, a fragment of Wyoming, and the northwestern portion of Utah.

The Great Basin is actually more than 150 different basins, separarated by long, narrow, roughly parallel mountain ranges that run generally north to south. These ranges vary from 60 to 120 miles (97–193 km) in length and 3 to 15 miles (5–24 km) in width and have an average elevation of 9,000 feet (2,743 m) above sea level. The valley floors, primarily deserts, average over 4,000 feet (1,219 m) above sea level and are wider than the ranges themselves. The Great Basin Desert

Tumbleweed swept up in a windstorm in the Great Basin

sustains lengthy periods of freezing temperatures in the winter and receives the majority of its annual precipitation in the form of snow.

Geology

History. The Great Basin region began to take its present form about 17 million years ago, when the Pacific Plate attempted to move past the North American Plate toward the northwest. The eastern edge of the Pacific Plate slid under the western edge of the North American Plate, giving rise to the San Andreas Fault. This action caused many more fractures in the landscape, and, as the plates continued to shift, some blocks dropped, forming basins, while others tilted. Great mountain chains, such as the Sierra Nevada, were formed as one edge of a rock mass rose while the other sank.

Toward the end of the last major glacial cycle, between 20,000 and 13,000 years ago, climatic shifts caused widespread changes in the region. Immense stream systems and lakes, such as Lake Bonneville, that had formed from the melting ice began to evaporate; only smaller bodies of water were left in the deeper basins. The Great Salt Lake of Utah is all that is left today of the old Lake Bonneville. A

drought that lasted from about 7,500 to about 4,500 years ago further reduced the amount of water in the area, leaving behind little more than flat salt and alkali plains, or playas. Other surface changes that took place during the glacial period include dune building caused by great winds that swept down from the glaciers.

Faulting, or the fracture and displacement of the Earth's crust, and volcanic activity continue in parts of the Great Basin region, as do plate movements, stretching the Earth's crust in an east-west direction. As a result, the area between the Sierra Nevada and Cascade mountains on the west and the Rocky Mountains on the east is being pulled apart. Geologists predict that in several million years this activity will create a new arm of the ocean extending northward from the Gulf of California.

Topography. The Great Basin is composed of many mountain ridges and isolated valleys, what geologists call the Basin and Range province. It has only a few rivers and lakes—mere remnants of their Pleistocene era ancestors—interspersed throughout.

The highest mountain in the area, White Mountain Peak, stands 14,246 feet (4,342 m) tall; several other mountains surpass 12,000 feet (3,657 m), and dozens more are over 10,000 feet (3,048 m) high. Mountain ranges in the Great Basin region generally have one steep slope and one fairly subtle slope, with steep-sided canyons slicing through them here and there. The ranges are deeply weathered, often containing streams, lakes, and cirques—deep indentations in half-bowl shapes left by small mountain glaciers. Occasional heavy rains cause flooding that carries eroded rock debris from the mountain slopes to the mouths of

canyons, where it piles up and forms alluvial fans that can be thousands of feet deep; where the mouths of several canyons from opposite sides of the long basins are close together, these fans merge to form *bajadas*, the Spanish word for these dry slopes. Dry falls, or dry waterfalls, become active when floods sweep through the area perhaps three or four times a decade.

Valleys lie between 1,000 and 6,000 feet (304–1,828 m) above sea level and are for the most part desert regions. Sand dunes occupy less than 1 percent of the Great Basin, but they are a spectacular feature of the region. The most notable is a strip 40 miles (65 km) long and up to 10 miles (16 km) wide, north of Winnemucca, Nevada, where sand averages 35 feet (11 m) deep. There are also huge sand hills in two areas of Nevada: one near Eight-mile Flat, in the central part of the state, and another near Lathrop Wells, in the south.

The Great Basin region contains few rivers, and with the sole exception of the Humboldt River none of them rise inside its borders. Of the rivers with east-west orientations, the Humboldt also covers the greatest distance, a span of almost 290 miles (468 km). Like the other rivers in the area, however, the Humboldt ends in a sunken valley that contains water for only a short period following the spring thaw and is dry the remainder of the year. Many rivers in the region, in fact, culminate in saline or alkali flats, where they evaporate.

The region's largest and most significant body of water is Great Salt Lake, in northern Utah. With a maximum depth of only 30 feet (9 m), Great Salt Lake is 80 miles (129 km) long and 30 to 35 miles (48–56 km) wide, and covers a total area of 2,360 square miles (6,112 sq km). Although fresh water flows into the lake from several rivers, the overall content of the water is seven times as salty as that of the ocean because of the lack of external drainage. As the river water evaporates, the minerals it carried to the lake remain, intensifying the water's salinity.

Useful rocks and minerals are distributed widely but sporadically. They include dolomite, a member of the limestone family; granite; and volcanic rock, mainly basalt, lava, and ash—some as much as 30 million years old. Some metals are found throughout the Great Basin, with Nevada and Utah ranking among the nation's leading producers of lead, silver, and gold.

Climate

Climates in the Great Basin vary considerably from north to south and from higher to lower elevations. Winters are generally quite cold, with heavy snowfall and blizzard conditions prevailing in the northernmost portions well into late spring. Snow accumulations range from 117.3 inches (3,007 mm) near Salt Lake City to 5.4 inches (138 mm) in Reno.

Average annual temperatures along the northern border of the desert range from 28° F (-2° C) to 80° F (20° C). The most extreme temperatures ever recorded in this region are -50.8° F (-46° C) and 116° F (46.6° C); some spots in the higher elevations have recorded temperatures below freezing in every month of the year.

The Great Basin is a rain-shadow desert; its aridity is largely due to the loss of moisture over the Sierra Nevada and Cascade ranges to the west and, to a lesser extent, the Rocky Mountains to the east. Precipitation occurs primarily during the winter, from December to March, as rain in the lower elevations and snow elsewhere, and in summer, during July and August, in the form of thunderstorms. Both

temperature and precipitation vary according to elevation and latitude. Coincident with the low temperatures, higher elevations may experience snowstorms at any time of year. Average annual precipitation ranges from 4 to 16 inches (102–419 mm) per year, most of which, at a ratio of 10 to 1 along the northern border, occurs as snow. High winds prevail in the same area during most of the year, particularly in the spring.

Plants

Elevation generally dictates plant life in the Great Basin, although climate and geology also play significant roles in its distribution. The arid conditions of the past few thousand years have produced an abundance of xerophytes—species that thrive in dry climates—such as sagebrush, saltbush, creosote bush, shadscale, and sulfur flower, while trees and other plants that require more moisture are primarily confined to the higher elevations. The unique nature of the landscape in this area also creates highly specialized plant and animal communities within the individual valleys and mountain ranges.

Valleys of the Great Basin that fall below the 3,500-foot (1,066-m) level—mostly in the southern

Common sagebrush in the Great Basin

part—contain vegetation similar to that of the Mojave Desert: burroweed, creosote bush, and prickly pear cactus and cholla cactus—the few cacti found in the Great Basin. Areas of particularly high alkalinity generally sustain only halophytes, or salt-tolerant plants. These include greasewood (*Sarcobatus vermiculatus*), with its distinctive bright green leaves; pickleweed (*Allenrolfea occidentalis*), a native of coastal areas; and glasswort (*Salicornia rubra*). Dominating the alkaline but moister soils of the lower elevations are shadscale (*Atriplex confertifolia*), hopsage (*Grayia spinosa*), winterfat (*Eurotia lanata*), and rabbitbrush (*Chrysothamnus*).

Sagebrush, the plant most closely associated with the Great Basin Desert, begins to appear at about 4,000 feet (1,219 m). A member of the sunflower family, sagebrush has a low tolerance for alkaline soils. Between 6 and 11 different species of sagebrush are found in the Great Basin region, particularly along the plains of the Snake River in southern Idaho. The most common is big sage, or common sagebrush (*Artemisia tridentata*), which under the best circumstances can attain the size of a small tree. Big sage is grayish

in color, with woody stems and tapered leaves, and bears yellow flowers in autumn. Also found in areas of sagebrush growth are many flowering plants of spring and early summer, including the sego lily (*Calochortus nuttallii*).

A small cone-bearing shrub called Mormon tea (*Ephedra*) is found at slightly higher elevations. As its name implies, the leaves of the plant can be used to make a beverage. Also near this elevation, at about 6,500 feet (1,981 m), is the lower tree line, where pinyon pine and juniper predominate. Juniper fares better in dry conditions than does pinyon; the latter does not grow at all in the northern portion of this region.

Beginning at around 8,000 feet (2,438 m), pinyon and juniper growth diminishes, and the forest becomes more varied. Here, such species as curlleaf mountain mahogany and limber pine abound. The hardy but short-lived quaking aspen is found at slightly higher elevations, particularly near water sources, and is one of the first species to appear in locations ravaged by fire. Some mountain forests produce ponderosa pine and whitebark pine, as well as Engelmann spruce, Douglas fir, and white fir. Found primarily on dolomite soils at the upper reaches of the Great Basin tree line is the bristlecone pine (*Pinus longaeva*), notable both for its ability to thrive in arid conditions and for its longevity: some of these trees are known to have lived more than 4,000 years.

At 11,000 feet (3,353 m) or so, temperatures are too low for tree growth. Eleven mountain chains in the Great Basin region, in fact, are tundra zones, incapable of supporting any plant life other than a few dwarf herbs. Yet even at these elevations, the species combinations are fairly specific to the individual ranges.

Animals

Animal life in the Great Basin is not as varied as in some other North American deserts, and the larger mammals primarily inhabit the upper elevations. Invertebrates include the wind scorpion (order Solifgae), a small arachnid related to both the scorpion and the spider but without either the venomous sting or the ability to spin webs. Generally growing to no more than 2 inches (5 cm) in length, the wind scorpion is nocturnal and feeds on insects, such as termites, and other arachnids, including scorpions.

Fish are severely limited by both the temperature and the salinity of the water, although some species of pupfish (genus *Cyprinodon*) are found in waters of up to 112° F (44° C), while others inhabit waters up to six times as salty as the ocean. There are about 100 different species and subspecies of reptiles and amphibians, including the harmless Great Basin gopher snake and the western whiptail lizard (*Cnemidophorus tigris*), which feeds on insects, lizard eggs, and young lizards.

Some animals, such as the sagebrush lizard, sagebrush chipmunk, sagebrush sparrow, sage thrasher, and sage grouse, are best identified by the plant life near which they are found. One of the most prolific birds indigenous to the area, the sage grouse, relies on the seeds of the sagebrush for a good portion of its sustenance. Another bird inhabiting the region, the poorwill (*Phalaenoptilus nuttallii*), is the western cousin of the whippoorwill. Aside from the poorwill's call of only two notes rather than three, it is distinguished from the whippoorwill by its smaller size. *Holchko*, the Hopi Indian name for this bird, means "the sleeper"; some members of the species hibernate rather than fly south for the winter season. More than 150 species of birds reside in, and as many as 300 visit, the Great Basin.

Basin areas are inhabited by large numbers of rodents, such as ground squirrels, kangaroo mice, kangaroo rats, pack rats, pocket gophers, porcupines, and voles, as well as various rabbit and hare species. The most common rabbit is the desert cottontail (*Sylvilagus audubonii*), but the black-tailed jackrabbit (*Lepus californicus*) and the white-tailed jackrabbit (*Lepus townsendi*)—actually hares—are also present. Long ears for dissipating body heat and long legs for traversing the desert make both jackrabbits well suited to this environment. The white-tailed jackrabbit dons a white coat in winter and a brown one in summer as a means of camouflage.

The beaver, almost extinguished by fur traders in the 19th century, now inhabits the moister terrains of some mountain regions. The ringtail cat (*Bassariscus astutus*), a relative of the raccoon, also dwells in mountainous areas, generally no more than ¼ mile (403 m) from a reliable water source. It feeds primarily on insects, arachnids, small rodents, and, if close to a cave, bats.

Lowland areas are home to the pronghorn (*Antilocapra americana*), a hoofed mammal similar to the antelope. Like the beaver, the pronghorn was near extinction in the 19th century, but its numbers have since increased. Pronghorn feed on the leaves of the big sage, as do elk, mule deer, and other deer, all of which are generally found at higher elevations than pronghorn.

Along with mountain lions, bighorn sheep (*Ovis canadensis*) inhabit even higher ranges of the Great Basin. One of the most distinctive animals of the region, the bighorn is related to domestic sheep.

Mojave Desert

38° N to 33° N latitude
119° W to 117° W longitude

USA

The Mojave Desert, smallest of the North American deserts, is situated in southeastern California, southern Nevada, a small area of northwestern Arizona, and a tiny corner of southwestern Utah. It encompasses an area of about 54,000 square miles (139,860 sq km) and forms a transition zone between the Great Basin Desert to the north and the Sonoran Desert to the south. The Mojave is bordered by the Sierra Nevada to the west and the Colorado River to the east.

Although a large portion of the Mojave is high above sea level, with most of its area lying between 2,000 and 5,000 feet (610 and 1,524 m), it also contains the lowest spot in the Western Hemisphere—Death Valley, 492 feet (150 m) below sea level. The Panamints—mountain ranges of between 5,000 and 11,000 feet (1,524 and 3,353 m) in elevation—border the Death Valley area on the west, while roughly parallel, north-south–oriented mountain chains culminating in dry, alkaline lake beds make up much of the eastern portion of the region.

Joshua Tree National Monument

Geology

History. As in most of the North American desert regions, some plains and plateaus of the Mojave Desert are of Mesozoic origin, meaning that their bedrock may be as much as 225 million years old. Mountains were formed primarily during the Jurassic period of that era, and faulting in the late Tertiary formed the basins of the Mojave.

Topography. At the end of the last ice age, around 10,000 years ago, the Mojave Desert contained many rivers and lakes. Today the Mojave is primarily a land of undrained basins, with two rivers—the Mojave, originating in the San Bernardino Mountains and terminating in an alkaline flat, and the Amargosa, beginning in the desert and ending in Death Valley—occasionally winding their way through the region. Water flowing from the mountain ranges often creates temporary lakes, or playas.

Rocks are primarily granites and gneisses of the Precambrian era. Soil is generally gray and has a high calcium carbonate content, which creates a hard, crusty type of soil known as caliche. Dunes of calcium carbonate are also found throughout the region, particularly in Death Valley.

Climate

Its southerly location, combined with lower basin floors, makes the Mojave generally hotter than the Great Basin, although temperatures vary according to elevation. Average air temperatures in July range from about 90° to 120° F (32°–49° C), with soil temperatures soaring to as much as 190° F (88° C). Average low temperatures, in January, vary from 33° to around 40° F (0.6°–4° C), but temperatures as low as 0° F (-18° C) have been recorded. More than half of the year is frost free.

Both elevation and longitude determine precipitation levels in the Mojave Desert, with higher elevations and more westerly areas receiving the most moisture. Most precipitation occurs from December to March—some of it in the form of snow, particularly in the higher western elevations—although summer thunderstorms, from July to September, are seen occasionally in the east. Average annual precipitation ranges from 1½ to 5 inches (38–128 mm); western regions may have as much as 5 inches (128 mm) a year, while those in the east receive around 2 inches (51 mm) a year.

The record for the longest period without measurable rainfall in the United States is 767 days, occurring in Bagdad, California, in the southeastern Mojave Desert. Death Valley, northwest of Bagdad, holds records for the lowest annual average precipitation in the United States, 1.6 inches (41 mm), and the second highest temperature in the world, 134° F (57° C). In July, humidity levels may be as low as 3 percent.

Plants and Animals

The Mojave Desert is home to a wide variety of plant and animal life. As a transitional area, it supports flora and fauna of both the Great Basin and the Sonoran deserts. Bur sage (*Ambrosia dumosa*) and creosote bush (*Larrea tridentata*), for example, which are typical of the Sonoran Desert, cover up to 70 percent of the Mojave Desert's surface in some areas. About one-fourth of the plant life, however, is endemic to the Mojave.

Animals are highly dependent on the plants in a particular region for a variety of needs, ranging from hiding places to food and water.

Joshua tree: Although low moisture in the Mojave Desert generally produces a predominance of shrub growth, the plant most closely associated with the region is the Joshua tree (*Yucca brevifolia*), which is found almost exclusively in the Mojave Desert. The largest yucca in the United States, the Joshua tree is found throughout the Mojave but grows primarily along the desert's upper reaches, in the area between the creosote bush–dominated plains and the pinyon pines and juniper trees of slightly higher elevations. Joshua trees grow to an average of 20 to 30 feet (6–9 m).

A member of the lily family, this often tree-sized yucca grows from a caudex, or wood-based stem, of up to 3½ feet (107 cm) in diameter and develops many branches terminating in clusters of long, slender, sharply pointed leaves. Joshua tree blossoms appear in spring, producing light green flowers 1½ to 2¾ inches (4–7 cm) long and large fruits with thin black seeds. The trunk of the Joshua tree contains a pithy substance that often disintegrates, leaving only a strong hollow outer shell.

Plants and animals associated with areas of Joshua tree habitation are some of the most interesting in the Mojave Desert. One such area is Joshua Tree National Monument

Joshua trees in bloom

in the extreme southern Mojave, where these plants receive necessary moisture partially from the runoff of higher elevations. Among the animals is the yucca moth (*Pronuba* species), which has developed an almost inextricable link to yuccas, particularly the Joshua tree. The female moth not only gathers and disseminates the plant's pollen, she also lays her own eggs deep within its ovary, ensuring that her offspring will have an adequate food supply as they develop. The relationship between the two is so intimate that as new species of the plant have developed, so have new species of the moth.

One of the approximately 25 bird species that nests in the Joshua tree is Scott's oriole (*Icterus parisorum*), a yellowish bird with a black head, tail, and wings that also feeds on the plant's flowers and fruits and builds its nests of the plant's fibers. Another is the ladder-backed, or Mexican, woodpecker (*Dendrocopos scalaris*), the only woodpecker in the desert with a black-and-white–striped face. For other birds, such as the screech owl (*Otus asio*) and the sparrow hawk, or American kestrel (*Falco sparverius*), the Joshua tree serves as a lookout post from which they search for food.

Four amphibian and 25 reptile species also inhabit the Joshua tree and other yuccas. One of the most notable is the desert night lizard, or yucca night lizard (*Xantusia vigilis*), a black-speckled, grayish-olive reptile about 1½ inches (4 cm) in length, not including the tail, that resembles a gecko. This tiny lizard feeds on ants, beetles, caterpillars, crickets, flies, spiders, and termites. The sidewinder (*Crotalus cerastes*), one of about a dozen rattlesnake species of the North American deserts, is also found in areas of Joshua tree stands. This 2½-foot-long (76-cm), sinister-looking

snake is well adapted to sand travel, looping and rolling its body over the sand rather than crawling through it. The sidewinder feeds on lizards and small mammals, which it locates even at night by way of a heat-sensing capability common to rattlesnakes.

Mammals of 28 different species—most of them rodents, but also a variety of larger animals such as coyotes, foxes, bobcats, and desert bighorn sheep—also frequent areas dominated by Joshua tree growth. All are found around the Joshua Tree National Monument, as well as in other parts of the Mojave.

Creosote bush: Below the Joshua tree belt, at elevations of about 3,000 feet (914 m) and lower, the vegetation of the Mojave Desert is composed mostly of shrubby undergrowth such as creosote bush (*Larrea tridentata*), sagebrush (*Artemisia* species), and shadscale (*Atriplex confertifolia*). Creosote bush prevails in areas receiving less than 7 inches (180 mm) of rain per year, while sagebrush and shadscale dominate areas receiving more than this amount. Other species found in areas of creosote bush include desert shrub (*Tetradymia spinosa*), goldenhead (*Acamptopappus sphaerocephalus*), Mojave yucca (*Yucca schidigera*), and white bur sage, or burroweed (*Franseria dumosa*).

Insects associated with creosote bush include the furnace heat lubber grasshopper (*Tytthotyle maculata*), the creosote bush grasshopper (*Bootettix punctatus*), and a number of bees (*Apis* species). The coachwhip snake climbs creosote bushes looking for the young birds and bird eggs on which it feeds. The desert tortoise (*Gopherus agassizii*), which is an endangered species, obtains both its moisture and its nourishment mainly from flowers, fruits, and herbs. The desert tortoise does drink water, however, sometimes increasing its body weight by 40 percent or more with one drink. Mammals that inhabit creosote bush–dominated locales include the antelope ground squirrel (*Ammospermophilus leucurus*), the Merriam kangaroo rat (*Dipodomys merriami*), and the western pipistrelle (*Pipistrellus hesperus*)—at 3 inches (8 cm) in length, the smallest bat in the United States and one of the smallest in the world.

Sagebrush and Shadscale: Alkaline areas of the Mojave Desert receiving more than 7 inches (180 mm) of rain per year are likely to sustain, in addition to sagebrush and shadscale, such plants as desert holly (*Atriplex hymenelytra*). A favorite of desert bighorn sheep, desert holly is a saltbush with green fruiting bracts and silver leaves. Also found in areas of sagebrush growth are the nocturnal desert long-horned grasshoppers.

Cactus: The main species are cholla and prickly pear, with some barrel and beaver tail varieties also present. Areas sustaining Bigelow cholla cactus (*Opuntia bigelovii*), a branching, heavily spined variety, are also home to birds such as the black-throated sparrow (*Amphispiza bilineata*) and the house finch (*Carpodacus mexicanus*).

The racer (*Masticophis flagellum*), a red or black snake growing to 3 to 6 feet (1–2 m) in length, also inhabits areas of cholla cactus growth, feeding on lizards, rodents, and other snakes. The racer also climbs plants such as cholla cactus in search of birds and bird eggs. Unlike most desert snakes, racers are diurnal, meaning that they are active primarily during the day, and can move through the desert at speeds of up to 8 miles per hour (13 kph).

Sonoran Desert

34° N to 22° N latitude
119° W to 111° W longitude

Mexico, USA

The Sonoran Desert is considered by many the most beautiful of the North American deserts. It covers 106,000 square miles (274,540 sq km) between the Mojave and the Chihuahuan deserts and is bordered on the west by the Pacific Ocean. Straddling the Gulf of California, the horseshoe-shaped Sonoran extends from near the southern tip of Baja California north into southeastern California, arches around the head of the Gulf of California into southwestern Arizona, and dips south again to cover most of the Mexican state of Sonora, from which it gets its name. More than two-thirds of its area is occupied by the Mexican states of Baja California and Sonora.

The combination of its low elevation, low latitude, and varied topography produces a range of climatic conditions that conspire to make it the hottest of all North American deserts.

Topography

Most of the Sonoran Desert, underlain by Precambrian granites and gneisses, lies at elevations below 600 feet (183 m); much of its land surface is composed of large, expansive basins. Many of these basins serve as internal drainages for seasonally flowing mountain streams and rivers. The Salton Sea, located in southeastern California, is the Sonoran's largest internal basin. The water level of the Salton Sea is 232 feet (71 m) below sea level, and it lies in the same trough that contains the Gulf of California.

The Colorado River snakes through the northern Sonoran and forms the border between California and Arizona. Río Magdalena, Río de Sonora, and Río Yaquí flow only seasonally from the Sierra Madre Occidental, the Sonoran's mountainous eastern boundary.

Rising above the basins and plains of the Sonoran Desert are short, isolated mountain ranges that run north-south. On the other side of the Gulf of California, a series of mountain ridges forms the spine of Baja California.

Pediments, or eroded bedrock surfaces, are found at the bases of steeper mountain slopes. Rivers flowing from the mountains deposit material beyond the pediments. When several of these so-called alluvial fans merge, they form bajadas, or gently sloping rocky plains. Playas, or ephemeral lakes, form where there is no outlet to the basins. In other areas, dry riverbeds scar the surface of the Sonoran and are further carved out by flash floods.

Plains of sand studded with dunes blanket parts of the nearly barren and extremely arid land near the head of the Gulf of California. The Algondones Dunes near Yuma, Arizona, stretch up to 50 miles (81 km) in length and are up to 5 miles (8 km) wide. Dunes also cover El Gran Desierto in northwestern Sonora. This region, subject to tremors and geological disruptions, lies close to the San Andreas Fault Zone. Evidence of volcanic activity is apparent in the black, lava-encrusted fields surrounding Mount Pinacate, east of El Gran Desierto.

Climate

In July, temperatures reach a mean maximum of 106.3° F (41.3° C); in some parts of the Sonoran they can remain at about 100° F (38° C) for up to 90 consecutive days. The soil can be up to 50° F (28° C) hotter than the air temperature. Because the air and ground release heat once the sun has set, it can become quite cold at night. Below-freezing temperatures occur in almost all parts of the Sonoran at some time; the January mean minimum temperature is a chilly 38.1° F (3.4° C).

Rainfall depends on topography and location, increasing with the rise in elevation from west to east. The western section of the Sonoran lies in the rain shadow of the Coast Ranges, which block most of the moisture heading inland from the Pacific. Rainfall here occurs mainly during the winter or early spring. The eastern portion receives most of its rainfall from summer thunderstorms from the Gulf of Mexico; it receives additional rainfall from western winter

Saguaro cacti in Saguaro National Monument

storms. Thanks to this biseasonal rainfall, the eastern areas of the Sonoran average 10 to 12 inches (254–305 mm) of rain a year. In comparison, some western areas receive as little as 2 inches (51 mm) annually.

Plants

Because the different combinations of elevation, rainfall, and other climatic conditions result in a wide variety of plant life, the Sonoran can be divided into seven subregions on the basis of vegetation.

The *Lower Colorado Valley* lies in an arc around the head of the Gulf of California and is the hottest, driest, largest, and lowest part of the Sonoran. Crossing its center is the valley of the Colorado River in California and southwestern Arizona. This expanse of sand and volcanic rock is mostly barren and only spotted with vegetation.

Plants are mostly limited to the bur sage (*Ambrosia dumosa*) and the hardy creosote bush (*Larrea tridentata* and *L. divaricata*). These plants cover up to 95 percent of the surface in some areas. Bur sage is a low, gray, brittle-looking plant also known as bur-robush or burroweed. At higher and cooler elevations to the north, these hot desert plants give way to the sagebrush that is characteristic of the cool Great Basin Desert.

Creosote bush is widespread throughout the Sonoran. An extensive and highly competitive system of roots draws almost all available moisture from the soil. The creosote bush averages a height of 3 to 6 feet (90–180 cm), although it can grow up to 12 feet (370 cm). Its branches bear multitudes of small leaves that fall off in times of drought. In response to rainfall, however, the leaves turn a vibrant green, and small yellow flowers bloom. At these times, seed production and growth kick in, only to

stop when conditions deteriorate; this unique stop-and-go process may occur several times during the year. After rains, its distinctive odor is strongest. Its leaves are eaten by a few animals, and some burrow beneath the sands that tend to collect around it; this tendency also makes it valuable for stabilizing desert soils.

Woody short trees with many small leaves include mesquites (*Prosopis glandulosa*, *P. pubescens*, *P. juliflora*, and *P. velutina*), the paloverde (*Cercidium*), and the gray-barked ironwood (*Olneya tesota*). The smoke tree (*Dalea spinosa*) is nearly leafless, with light gray bark and branches armed with spines; its purple flowers bloom in late spring and early summer. These trees grow primarily along washes, or dry riverbeds.

The desert hackberry and the Mexican jumping bean, a bush that produces fruit that "jumps" because of the movement of a moth larva inside it, also grow along washes. The spiny cat's-claw (*Acacia greggii*) and desert willow (*Chilopsis linearis*), another pair of wash species, are widespread throughout the Sonoran.

The *Arizona Upland* region rises to the northwest of the Lower Colorado Valley. Splayed over its face are several small mountain ranges, beyond which stretch plains. This area is especially rich in plant life because of its higher, and therefore cooler, elevation and because the bountiful rainfall it receives twice a year totals 12 to 14 inches (305–356 mm) annually.

Creosote bush, bur sage, and thorny ocotillos (*Fouquieria* species) flourish in its valleys; on the hillsides these give way to more diverse communities that include shrubs and trees, such as paloverdes, and prickly pear and cholla (*Opuntia*) cacti. The paloverde has a yellowish-green trunk and grows

many small, bright green leaves when moisture is available; the blue paloverde (*Cercidium floridum*) grows up to 30 feet (9 m) high and is named for its bluish-green trunk. In the spring it produces yellow flowers, as does the foothill paloverde (*C. microphyllum*). The trunks of these trees contain chlorophyll. The bark, instead of the plant's small leaves, can carry out most of the photosynthetic functions when needed. Other trees growing on the hillsides of the Arizona Upland include the mesquite and the ironwood.

By far the most distinctive plant found here is the saguaro cactus (*Cereus giganteus*). It grows exclusively in this area of the Sonoran Desert and dominates the vegetation and landscape around it. These enormous cacti thrive on the lower rocky slopes of mountains, where their shallow roots can take hold and absorb runoff. The hillsides also provide some protection from winds that can easily topple the top-heavy cacti. A very slow grower, it reaches an unimpressive height of only 6 inches in 9 years. At a height of between 15 and 25 feet (4.5–7.6 m), several branches grow straight out of the main trunk and then turn skyward at their "elbows." In the springtime, large

Sonoran Gila monster and cactus

white flowers crown the branches and at night are pollinated by bees, moths, white-winged doves, and long-nosed bats. Its juicy red fruit and black seeds are eaten by rodents, birds, and insects.

Among the smaller cacti are the prickly pear and cholla of the genus *Opuntia*. The prickly pear can grow in poor soil and has a wider distribution than any other cactus. Its flat, succulent branches bear bright red fruit. Another flat-branched cactus is the appropriately named beaver tail cactus (*Opuntia basilaris*).

The teddy bear cholla (*Opuntia bigelovii*) is deceptively named; the sheer multitude of its sharp spines gives it a fuzzy, soft appearance. Its short, moisture-filled joints break off easily and attach themselves to people or animals that pass nearby. The tall, treelike chain-fruit cholla has a woody trunk and pink or purple flowers. These produce fruits that grow flowers the next season, only to bear more fruits; this process repeats itself, and eventually long chains of fruit form that sometimes reach the ground.

Other cacti include the barrel cactus, named for its relatively short, stocky trunk. Some grow to 10 feet (3 m). The hedgehog cactus has dangerously long spines but bears exquisite flowers that are sometimes so large that they overwhelm the cactus itself. An extreme case is the comb hedgehog, which produces blossoms up to 6 inches (15 cm) in diameter, while the plant itself grows no higher than 9 inches (23 cm).

The *Plains of Sonora* subdivision in Mexico is wedged between the Lower Colorado Valley and the Arizona Uplands to the north and the Central Gulf Coast and Foothills of Sonora subdivisions to the south. This territory is composed of plains and mountains that are covered mostly by trees such as the foothill paloverde and the mesquite; large shrubs; and impressive, tall columnar cacti such as the organ-pipe (*Lemaireocereus thurberi*). The organ-pipe has numerous trunks measuring 5 to 8 inches (13–20 cm) in diameter growing directly out of the ground. They bear fruits the size of a fist that taste much like watermelons, hence their other name: *pitaya dulce* or sweet *pitaya*. Found close to organ-pipe cacti is the sentina, or old-man cactus (*Lophocereus schottii*). Its multiple trunks, which rise to 10 feet (3 m) in the air, bear spines along vertical ridges. The trunks are capped with gray spines that look like gray whiskers.

The *Foothills of Sonora* region lies to the south and east of the Plains of Sonora; parts of it reach like fingers into higher elevations to the north. Trees and large shrubs cover extensive tracts of the land. The trees include mesquite, the flat-crowned espino acacia (*Acacia cymbispina*), the ironwood, and the paloverde. Ocotillo (*Fouquieria macdougallii*) and organ-pipe cacti also abound.

The *Central Gulf Coast* is composed of two strips of land that face each other across the Gulf of California. Because several islands in the gulf share similar physical characteristics as well as vegetation and animal life, these too are included in the Central Gulf Coast region.

This region is home to unique and bizarre-looking plants such as the elephant tree (*Bursera microphylla*) and the boojum (*Idria columnaris*). The elephant tree, or *torote*, which grows to about 16 feet (5 m) in height, thrives in rocky terrain and has a thick trunk and branches and distinctive red sap. Its white flowers produce a bluish fruit.

One of the most peculiar plants found in the Sonoran Desert is the boojum, or cirio, often described as an inverted gray carrot. It can stretch 70 feet (21 m) into the sky. Its name comes from a Lewis Carrol poem that describes a mythical "thing" living on a desert island. These trees grow thin twiglike offshoots from the trunk and are crowned with small white flowers.

The cardon (*Pachycereus pringlei*), a towering cactus that houses many animals and looks much like the saguaro, is also common in the Central Gulf Coast region. It can reach 60 feet (18 m) or more in height and weigh up to 10 tons. The oldest specimens may be up to 200 years old. These imposing cacti also grow in large stands on several of the desert islands in the Gulf.

The *Vizcaíno* region lies on the western half of the Baja California peninsula, to the west of the Central Gulf Coast region. Moisture-rich fog that envelops the coast up to 31 miles (50 km) inland from June through August does little more than promote the growth of lichen and ball moss, or Spanish moss (*Tillandsia recurvata*), which grows on stones and in the upper branches of shrubs and trees.

For the most part, the Vizcaíno region is dry and barren; the landscape is dotted with elephant and boojum trees, as well as the peninsular ocotillo (*Fouquieria peninsularis*). Leaf-succulent vegetation includes several species of agave (*Agave shawii* and *A. deserti*). Various yuccas grow in the Vizcaíno, including the *datilillo* (*Yucca valida*), which grows to 20 feet (6 m) and looks much like the Joshua tree of the Mojave Desert.

The *Magdalena* region stretches south of the Vizcaíno region almost to the tip of the western coast of Baja California. Vegetation in this section includes various species of small trees, including mesquites. The palo blanco (*Lysiloma candida*) has a silvery-white trunk with smooth bark and is topped by a head of branches and bright green leaves. The pitaya agria, or galloping cactus (*Machaerocereus gummosus*), has thick, spiny branches that grow either vertically or along the ground in a tangle. Other cacti include the cardon and the caterpillar cactus, which actually advances across the ground as its trunk grows horizontally. As it grows and takes root, the older parts behind die.

Animals

The Sonoran Desert fosters a diversity of animal life that rivals that of its plant communities.

Bighorn sheep in its rocky habitat, Sonoran Desert

The desert pronghorn (*Antilocapra americana*) is among the largest animals of the Sonoran Desert. It is the sole member of a family of hoofed animals unique to North America. Both males and females carry permanent prong-shaped horns and run at speeds of up to 60 mph (97 kph).

Like the pronghorn, the bighorn sheep (*Ovis canadensis*) must have water every two or three days during the summer. It obtains much of its moisture from a diet of green vegetation and prickly pear cacti, yucca, and brittlebush.

The bobcat (*Lynx rufus*), along with the mountain lion and coyote, is among the most important predators in the Sonoran. It has a russet-colored coat with black spots and a short tail tipped in black, and it reaches a size of up to 2½ feet (76 cm) in length. The gray, fast-running kit fox (*Vulpes macrotis*) is another, much smaller predator, the size of an ordinary house cat. It lives in burrows in sparsely vegetated areas where it preys mainly on kangaroo rats, but also on snakes, lizards, and insects. The badger (*Taxidea taxus*) is a less graceful animal but makes up for this with its strong digging ability, which it uses to unearth rodents and a variety of reptiles. Growing up to 2 feet (60 cm) long, the badger is grayish brown and bears a distinctive white stripe that runs from its face to its back. The coatimundi, or chulla (*Nasua narica*), is a long-nosed relative of the raccoon and has the telltale banded tail that is often as long as its body. It is most common in mountainous and wooded areas and has a varied diet of rodents, lizards, berries, and roots. Carrying a similarly banded, long black-and-white tail is the ringtail cat (*Bassariscus astutus*). It lives in canyons and hilly regions.

The javelina, or collared peccary (*Tayassu tajacu*), is a distant relative of the swine and is found from the desert Southwest to South America. This herbivore travels in groups of about a dozen animals and uses its nose to unearth its meals of cacti and roots.

Numerous smaller mammals inhabit the Sonoran Desert, including two species of jackrabbit. The nocturnal herbivorous black-tailed jackrabbit (*Lepus californicus*) is 18 to 20 inches (46–51 cm) long, with ears equal in length to a third of its body length. The tan antelope jackrabbit, which has slightly longer ears, gets its name from its ability to hop at speeds of up to 35 mph (56 kph). It has a unique ability to "flash," or to change the color of its haunches by exposing its white underfur with a movement of its muscles; this trick is especially useful when the animal is trying to escape predators.

Squirrels include the Harris ground squirrel (*Citellus harrisi*) and the antelope ground squirrel (*Ammospermophilus leucurus*). Both scavenge for seeds on even the hottest summer days and have bushy tails, unlike the round-tailed desert squirrel (*Citellus tereticaudus*), which has a distinctive thin tail and lives in burrows.

Many of the Sonoran's larger mammals depend on the desert's wide variety of other rodents for food. These rodents include deer, pocket, cactus, and grasshopper mice, and pack and kangaroo rats.

Farther down in the food chain are a vast number of invertebrates. Many insects and arachnids are also vitally important in the pollination of plants, and thus they serve an important function for both animal and plant communities. Bees, flies, ants, and tarantulas are only a few of these. Beetles include the blister beetle, which secretes an irritating, blister-causing red fluid from its body. Some of the beetles, bees, and other insects, such as the cac-

tus dodger, live in close association with certain species of cactus.

The Sonoran is home to an equally dazzling array of reptiles. The desert tortoise (*Gopherus agassizi*), sheathed in its hard bony shell, is well armed against both dehydration and enemy attack. During the summer, it remains out of sight in a cool den, but after rainfall it comes out to feed on moisture-rich vegetation.

Some of the many lizards include the chuckwalla (*Sauromalus obesus*), the desert horned lizard (*Phrynosoma platyrhinos*), the banded gecko (*Coleonyx variegatus*), and the collared lizard (*Crotaphytus collaris*). The zebra-tailed lizard (*Callisaurus draconoides*) has long legs, a thin body, and a long tail that it curls up when running, thereby exposing the black and white stripes on the underside of the tail.

The desert iguana (*Dipsosaurus dorsalis*) grows up to 5½ feet (168 cm) long and has a tail that is double its body length. Its body temperature is higher than that of any other lizard, 107.8° F (42.1° C), and can rise to 115.5° F (46.4° C), which enables it to remain active during the day. The orange and black Gila monster (*Heloderma suspectum*) is one of only two poisonous lizards in the world; the other is the Mexican beaded lizard. However, this shy, slow-moving, and thick-bodied lizard is more likely to slink away from a confrontation than to be the aggressor.

The Sonoran Desert is home to a long list of snakes, including the Arizona coral snake (*Micruroides euryxanthus*), the western blind snake (*Leptotyphlops humilis*), the rosy boa (*Lichanura trivirgata*), and the gopher snake (*Pituophis melanoleucus*). The many rattlesnakes include the black-tailed rattlesnake (*Crotalus molossus*) and the small, 18-inch-long (46-cm),

buff-colored Sonoran sidewinder, whose scales are colored to blend in with the sand.

More than 25 species of birds inhabit the Sonoran. Several have developed a close partnership with the saguaro, in particular two birds of the woodpecker family, the Gila woodpecker (*Centurus uropygialis*) and the flicker. Where these birds peck nests into the flesh of the cactus, the saguaro forms a thick, protective scar, or callus. The Gila woodpeckers raise up to three broods every year in these well-insulated holes. These birds are 8 to 10 inches (20–25 cm) long and have black and white bars across their wings and backs; the male wears a red cap on his head. The flicker has brown bars on its wings and upper parts, and a black belly with white spots. The gilded flicker (*Colaptes chrysoides*) has yellow beneath its tail and wings, while the red-shafted flicker has red.

Several birds, and other animals as well, are quick to move into the vacated nests of the Gila woodpecker and the flicker. One of these opportunists is the elf owl (*Micrathene whitneyi*). At 5.5 to 6 inches (14–15 cm) long—the size of a sparrow—this reddish-brown owl is one of the smallest in the world

Black-tailed jackrabbit

and preys on scorpions and centipedes. The pygmy owl and screech owl also make their homes in saguaros, as does the 2-foot-long (61-cm) great horned owl, named for the tufts that rise above its ears. It preys on rabbits, rodents, and skunks. Other birds that make use of abandoned woodpecker holes are the ash-throated flycatcher, the Arizona crested flycatcher (*Myiarchus tyrannulus*), the purple martin, and the starling. Larger predatory birds such as the 20- to 24-inch-long (51–61 cm) red-tailed hawk prefer to nest on top of saguaros.

Other characteristic birds of the Sonoran are the yellow-gray verdin (*Auriparus flaviceps*), which nests in spiny bushes such as the cat's-claw acacia and mesquite. Similarly, the cactus wren (*Campylorhynchus brunneicapillus*) builds its nest within the protective spines of the cholla cactus. The cactus wren has a large brown body, black-spotted breast feathers, and a loud, grating cry. The white-winged dove (*Zenaida asiatica*), Scott's oriole, and Arizona hooded oriole, as well as a multitude of migratory hummingbirds (the black-chinned, the ruby-throated, the rufous, and the Costa's) can also be found in the Sonoran.

The roadrunner (*Geococcyx californianus*) is one of the few birds that remains in the desert in the summer. The roadrunner can run up to 15 mph (24 kph), and its long legs can cover 20 inches (51 cm) in one stretch. Its traction is aided by both forward- and backward-facing toes. It has a long slender body covered with brown-and-white–spotted feathers; more than half of its 2-foot (60-cm) length is made up of its tail feathers. This aggressive bird preys on insects, tarantulas, and rodents and does not hesitate to attack snakes and lizards.

Colorado Plateau

38° N to 34° N latitude
112° W to 109° W longitude

USA

The Colorado Plateau, named for the river that winds through this high tableland, is also referred to as the Painted Desert because of its multicolored, stratified sedimentary rocks and canyons. It is a semidesert that stretches primarily across southern Utah and northern Arizona, and spills over into parts of southern Wyoming, western Colorado, and northwestern New Mexico. The Colorado River system runs southwestward into the Gulf of California, 1,200 miles (1,935 km) from its origin in the Rocky Mountains. The Colorado Plateau has generally high elevations (5,000 feet or 1,524 m), with mountain ranges of up to 11,000 feet (3,350 m).

History and Topography

The magnificent topographical features of the Colorado Plateau are the result of millions of years of the Earth's crust being arched upward and of the sandstone plateau being slowly and persistently cut through by the Colorado River and other smaller rivers. These competing forces of uplift and erosion have left high plateaus and mesas girdling gaping canyons. The effects of this constant erosion continue: every day, the Colorado River runs reddish brown with the 500,000 tons of sand and mud it picks up as it winds toward the Gulf of California. Its greatest creation is the unparalleled Grand Canyon, the largest river-cut gorge in the Earth's crust. It runs 250 miles (400 km), is a dizzying 6,500 feet (1,918 m) deep, and is up to 20 miles (32 km) wide.

Northeast of the Grand Canyon is Monument Valley. The sheer walls of flat-topped mesas rim vast expanses of grass- and sand-covered plains that stretch to the horizon. Walls of sedimentary rock and chimneylike outcrops that have been spared the effects of erosion rise abruptly from the flat plains, some looking wafer thin and brittle in comparison with rounder, more solid hills that share the valley floor.

Near the southern edge of the Colorado Plateau in Arizona, fissures and crevices cut deeply into hills rounded and scarred by erosion. Distinct strata of sedimentary rocks range in color from gray and brown to tan and chalky white. Erosion has created other formations as well. One, appropriately named the Molar, is a top-heavy protuberance with a narrow base, like a big tooth; another, called the Angel Arch, is a massive natural bridge. Both formations are representative of the numerous unique landforms that abound in the Colorado Plateau.

The dramatic semiarid landscapes of these areas were once gentle, vegetated hills and plains; the change occurred during the late Pliocene when the mountains to the west that now ring the desert interior were pushed up to heights of as much as 14,000 feet (4,300 m). As a result of this process, the Cascade Mountains in Washington and Oregon and the Sierra Nevada in California were formed and now block moist Pacific air from descending onto the Colorado Plateau. To the east, the Rocky Mountains were created, duplicating the effect for weather systems originating in the Great Plains. The result is an arid interior land wedged between massive mountain ranges.

Climate

The lack of precipitation caused by the rain-shadow effect, combined with the effects of varying elevations, particularly in the area between the high mountains of Colorado and the bed of the Grand Canyon, has produced a range of climates described as similar to that of the icy polar tundra at the highest points and of the hottest deserts at the lowest. These extremes of temperature are a distinctive characteristic of the Colorado Plateau; it has the highest daily and seasonal variations of temperature on the continent, with extremes of 120° F (50° C) in the depths of the Grand Canyon and of -40° F (-40° C) on the exposed plateaus. Precipitation in the lowest and driest regions is less than 6½ inches (167 mm), peaking during the summer and often appearing as thunderstorms.

During the winter, precipitation, sometimes in the form of snow, falls on the plateaus; at lower elevations snow commonly lasts only one day. In summer, dust devils, whirlwinds that are produced when heat escapes from colder, heavier air, sometimes create mud storms when they mix with precipitation.

Plants

With changes in climate, elevation, and soil makeup, there is an accompanying progression of plant coverage and diversity from the dry southern lowlands to the moister northern uplands, including widespread shrub and grasslands, and pinyon-juniper woodlands. For ease of identification, the predominant vegetation is grouped into three general ecosystems: sagebrush, salt-desert scrub, and blackbrush. These are not distinct, and there is considerable overlap as many plants grow in varying numbers and densities in all three.

The grayish-green woody sagebrush, also known as common sagebrush or big sage (*Artemisia tridentata*), dominates higher-elevation landscapes of 4,265 to 5,900 feet (1,300–1,800 m). Part of its success in maintaining coverage of up to 70 percent of the terrain is due to its deep roots, which tap underground water resources, and its longevity; it can live up to 150 years. The hardy, pervasive sagebrush community thwarts the growth of other plants in many areas of the plateau region with chemicals that seem to repress or prevent seeds of other plants from germinating nearby. Sagebrush is an important winter forage shrub for cattle, sheep, big game animals, and game birds.

Perennial bunchgrasses and herbs such as cheatgrass (*Bromus tectorum*) and *Sitanion hystrix* are also important for wildlife, as are seed-bearing annuals. On the little

A formation called the Double Arch, Arches National Park, Utah

ground without vegetation, crusts of moss and lichen produce a cover that helps protect the soil from the damaging forces of erosion.

At lower elevations, the high salinity of the soil is a major determinant of the habitat. Layers of salt collect in valleys and lowlands after water that cannot drain away has evaporated. Marine shale outcrops, remnants of ancient seas, also contribute to the salinity of the soil. Here, shrubs, half-shrubs, and herbs of the family Chenopodiaceae, commonly known as salt-desert scrub, replace sagebrush as the dominant vegetation. Some of the most common include shadscale (*Atriplex confertifolia*) and winter fat (*Eurotia lanata*). These hardy plants grow only to about 20 inches (50 cm) tall and are widely spaced and patchy; at their highest density in the relatively moister uplands, they cover only about 20 percent of the ground.

In the saltiest, driest areas there is almost no vegetation. As in the higher-elevation sagebrush habitat, open ground between higher forms of plant life is covered with mosses and lichens.

The blackbrush (*Coleogyne ramosissima*) ecosystem borders the salt-desert scrub to the south, at elevations of 2,600 to 5,240 feet (790–1,600 m). The spiny, round blackbrush is well adapted to the dry, shallow, sandstone soil. A slow-growing shrub, very old blackbrush may reach a height of only 20 inches (50 cm). Like the sagebrush, it is sought out only as a last resort because of its spines and woodiness and its minimal nutritional value, and it also prefers not to share the landscape with other shrubs. Some of the few plants that can coexist with it are the ephedra, or Mormon tea (*Ephedra* species), the leaves of which can be used to make a drink; the desert peachbrush (*Prunus fasciculata*); the

spiny hopsage (*Atriplex spinosa*); and the turpentine bush (*Thamnosma montana*). Perennial grasses such as galleta (*Hilaria jamesii*) and three-awn (*Aristida* species) grow interspersed among the shrubs, as do annuals such as pin grass (*Erodium botrys*) and the flowering herbs *Gilia scopulorum* and *Gilia leptomeria*. Spring annuals liven up the otherwise dry landscape when they put on a lush display after the spring rains of rare wet years.

Animals

While some animals of the Colorado Plateau are found primarily in one or another of the three major plant communities, many are distributed throughout the desert in varying numbers, as they respond to changing patterns of vegetation. Many overlap with the other North American deserts.

The hoofed grazers, in particular, move through the regions during the winter seeking nourishment from shrubs, grasses, and herbs. These include the pronghorn (*Antiocapra americana*), the desert bighorn sheep (*Ovis canadensis nelsoni*), the mule deer (*Odocoileus hemionus*), and the feral burro (*Equus asinus*).

Other herbivores include rodents, which make up a large part of the animal population of the Colorado Plateau. The availability of seed-bearing annuals determines the rises and declines of populations of such rodents as the deer mouse (*Peromyscus*), the pocket mouse (*Perognathus*), the pocket gopher (*Geomys*), and the kangaroo rat (*Dipodomys microps*), all of which efficiently extract nourishment from the plants and their seeds. Other rodents include the white-footed mouse (*Peromyscus maniculatus*), the harvest mouse (*Reithrodontomys megalotis*), and the desert wood rat.

The white-tailed prairie dog (*Cynomys leucurus*) is a rodent unique to the Colorado Plateau. These animals, in collecting and storing seeds, may actually help to encourage further growth of shrubs, unlike the black-tailed desert jackrabbit (*Lepus californicus*), which has destroyed vast quantities of vegetation and often leaves much foliage uneaten on the ground.

Other small mammals include the ring-tailed cat (*Bassariscus astutus*), which lives close to sources of water. A relative of the racoon, it prefers to live in trees, caves, and places high above the ground. It has a varied diet of plants, insects, and birds, while the badger (*Taxidea taxus*) preys on rodents. Larger mammalian predators include the bobcat (*Lynx rufus*) and the coyote (*Canis latrans*), which profits from the great abundance of black-tailed desert jackrabbits.

Several of the birds of the region feast on the jackrabbit as well, including the golden eagle, ferruginous hawk (*Buteo regalis*), and western red-tailed hawk. The great horned owl (*Bubo virginianus*) is another striking creature, with large, piercing yellow eyes and elegant black, brown, and tan feathers. Other common birds include the

Great horned owl

western turkey vulture (*Cathartes aura*) and the Nuttall's poorwill (*Phalaenoptilus nuttallii*). The poorwill is an oddity among birds in that it not only nests on the ground, but also hibernates during the winter. Smaller birds include the sage sparrow (*Amphispiza belli*), the sage thrasher (*Oreoscoptes montanus*), and the horned lark (*Eremophila alpestris*).

The diets of several birds and mammals either consist of or are supplemented by some of the almost 1,000 species of insects and other invertebrates that thrive in the more vegetated areas of the Colorado Plateau. They include spiders (Araneida), mites and ticks (Acarina), aphids and squash bugs (Hemiptera), cicadas (Homoptera), beetles (Coleoptera), and flies and gnats (Diptera). Some, such as the Mormon cricket (*Anabrus simplex*), the webworm (*Aroga websteri*), and the tent caterpillar (*Malacosoma*), have ravaged areas of sagebrush vegetation.

The harvester ant (*Pogonomyrmex* species), on the other hand, plays a beneficial role in the Colorado Plateau ecosystem. It is one of the most important and abundant desert dwellers, and a dedicated and productive forager of plant materials and seeds. Its mounds dot the terrain; often ant rings—wildflowers that have sprouted from seeds left at the entrances of its burrows—grow around the mounds. Its digging, tunneling, and transporting activities build up the soils of the plateau; harvester ants can move up to one ton of soil per acre (360 kg per ha) a year.

A variety of other animals, including reptiles, can be found burrowing beneath the landscape. The gopher snake (*Pituophis melanoleucus*) is common to all North American deserts, while the Mesa Verde night snake is found only in the Colorado Plateau. Unlike most other snakes, the gopher snake is unusually active during the day. This huge nonvenomous snake uses its length of up to 6 feet (2 m) to constrict its victims, which include various rodents and birds; it makes a show when disturbed by hissing and hitting its tail against the ground. It burrows using its nose, as does the shovel-nosed snake (*Chionactis* species), which, unlike the gopher snake, is nocturnal and much shorter, usually only 1 foot (30 cm) long. Its scales are designed to allow it to glide easily through sand. Other reptiles include the plateau whiptail lizard (*Cnemidophorus tigris*), whose name is descriptive of its quickness and long tail, and the northern side-blotched lizard, or brown-shouldered uta (*Uta stansburiana*).

Another burrower is the common scorpion (Scorpiones), which catches its prey with its powerful claws and disables it with its curled, venom-tipped tail. Truly a creature of the desert, it can survive months without water.

Not all animals of the Colorado Plateau have had to adapt to water deprivation; quite a few have taken advantage of the presence of the Colorado River and its related river systems. The canyon tree frog (*Hyla arenicolor*) lives along canyon streams, where its rough, camouflaged brown or gray skin blends well with the rocks along the water's edge. On the other hand, the smooth-skinned spadefoot toad (*Scaphiopus* species) stays wet by living underground in burrows, where it encases itself in a secretion that holds moisture in and dryness out. After a rainfall, it climbs up to the surface to breed amid a cacophony of mating calls. Often mistaken for an amphibian is the fierce-looking but harmless desert horned toad (*Phrynosoma platyrhinos*)—actually a lizard.

Chihuahuan Desert

33° N to 23° N latitude
108° W to 98° W longitude

Mexico, USA

The Chihuahuan Desert is situated primarily in the Mexican Highland sections of north-central Mexico and the southwestern United States, with 80 percent of its area in Mexico. It is the most southerly of the North American deserts, and receives an average of only 8 inches (205 mm) of precipitation per year. Its size may be determined either by annual precipitation or by the extent of certain vegetation and animal life, with a generally accepted average area of 175,000 square miles (453,000 sq km).

Geology
Rock formations range in age from Precambrian to Quaternary, with Mesozoic sediments especially found in the plains and plateaus, indicating activity over a long span of time. Volcanic activity during both the Tertiary and the Quaternary periods contributed greatly to the overall topography.

With its lowest elevation occurring at 1,000 feet (305 m) along the Rio Grande and its highest at nearly 6,600 feet (2,012 m) in

Mexico, the Chihuahuan Desert has a relatively high average elevation of 3,750 feet (1,143 m), with 50 percent of its area above 3,900 feet (1,200 m). The Chihuahuan is also characterized by internal drainage systems and by caliche, a soil type in which calcium carbonate has accumulated to varying thicknesses in semiarid regions.

There are relatively few dunes in the Chihuahuan Desert. Many, such as those found at the White Sands National Monument near Alamagordo, New Mexico, consist of gypsum granules, while others are formed of the more common quartz (silica) sand.

Climate
Because of the rain-shadow effect created by the Sierra Madre Occidental and Sierra Madre Oriental ranges, the Chihuahuan Desert plateau receives little precipitation. Annual averages range from 3 to 20 inches (77–513 mm), with the higher elevations generally receiving slightly more rainfall than the valley floor.

Summer is the rainy season, with 65 to 80 percent of the annual rainfall occurring between mid-June and mid-September in the form of brief but turbulent thunderstorms. The period from January to May is quite dry.

Temperatures in the region are directly related to elevation and topography. In winter, the area may have freezing temperatures for as much as 72 hours. El Paso, Texas, at 3,920 feet (1,195 m) above sea level, has a mean annual maximum temperature of 77° F (25.1° C) and a mean annual minimum of 49.5° F (9.7° C). The coldest mean maximum and minimum for El Paso are 56.3° F (13.5° C) and 29.5° F (-1.4° C), both recorded in January. The hottest mean maximum, 95.3° F (35.2° C), was recorded in June, and the hottest mean minimum, 68.9° F (20.5° C), in July.

Plants
Vegetation in the Chihuahuan Desert largely depends on geology, elevation, and soil type, and the variety is greater in the Mexican portion than in the U.S. portion. Lichens and grasses are common to most of the area, as are perennial shrubs such as the creosote bush. Various species of yucca and agave are also characteristic of the relatively high, cooler elevations of the Chihuahuan Desert.

The creosote bush (*Larrea tridentata*), named for the pungent aroma of its resinous leaves, is the hardiest and the most common shrub in the Chihuahuan Desert. It generally grows from 2 to 9 feet (60–270 cm) tall, although some grow as high as 12 feet (360 cm). Creosote thrives in hot, arid climates and a variety of soils that few other perennials can endure. This is primarily due to its extensive root system, which spreads out some distance from the plant itself and uses most of the available soil moisture. The roots of the creosote bush also excrete a poison that further limits the growth of other plants in the vicinity. Although the leaves are poisonous to sheep, some other animals, such as pronghorns,

Cacti and hardy desert vegetation grow between rocks in Texas

reptiles, and small rodents, feed on them without adverse effects.

Tarbush, black brush, or *hojase* (*Flourensia cernas*), a woody legume that grows to between 3 and 6 feet (90 and 180 cm) tall, is closely associated with the creosote bush. Tarbush grows primarily in limestone soils and is found in low foothills, mesas, and plains of dry sand or adobe. Also growing in areas of limestone is a low-branching shrub known as the guayule (*Parthenium argentatum*), which has a high rubber content.

Mesquite (*Prosopis glandulosa*) occurs in the creosote bush dunes, where it helps stabilize the sandy soil, and in washes. Ocotillo (*Fouquieria splendens*), a candlewood often mistaken for a cactus, occupies rocky areas of the Chihuahuan Desert. It is a favorite of hummingbirds.

Saltbush (*Atriplex canescens*), a shrub that reaches a height of 3 to 6 feet (90–180 cm), is found in slightly alkaline soil. Two varieties of acacia, *Acacia vernicosa* (varnish leaf acacia) and *Acacia constricta*, are also found on the washes of the Chihuahuan Desert.

Leafy succulents such as agaves and semisucculents such as yuccas are found in the higher elevations of the region. Members of the amaryllis family, agaves are used to make baskets, mats, ropes, and sandals; some varieties are found in beverages including mescal, pulque, and tequila. Some produce only one flower stalk during their lifetime, dying immediately thereafter.

The century plant (*Agave palmeri*) yields a plumelike flower stalk that grows over a foot a day. The plant has a life span of 7 to 20 years. Another agave common to the Chihuahuan Desert is the lechuguilla (*Agave lecheguilla*). Its sharp, upward-pointing leaves are surprisingly strong and are capable of tearing the flesh of humans and animals. The lechuguilla grows as tall as 10 feet (3 m), living an average of 3 to 4 years.

Several species of yuccas, including *Yucca filfera*, *Y. torreyi*, *Y. carnerosana*, and *Y. elata*, are found in the Chihuahuan Desert, with *Y. elata* particularly conspicuous in grasslands and in the transitional areas between grasslands and deserts. Growing 6 to 15 feet (1.8–4.5 m) tall, *Y. elata* has an extensive root system that makes it one of the few plants able to survive in the gypsum dunes of southeast New Mexico.

Prickly pears (*Opuntia*) are the most abundant cacti in the eastern portions of the desert, with some hedgehog, nipple, and pencil cacti scattered throughout the region. Larger cacti such as the barrel cactus (*Ferocactus*) and cholla are also found in a few areas, although the larger columnar types appear only in the southernmost reaches.

Small trees may be found along tributaries and rocky inclines, and some larger varieties grow in the eastern portions of the region.

Animals

Many species have adapted to the high daytime temperatures by becoming nocturnal. Some, such as reptiles, become diurnal during the cooler seasons. Insects include flies, mosquitoes, and gnats (Diptera); bees, wasps, and ants (Hymenoptera); squash bugs and mealybugs (Hemiptera); grasshoppers (Orthoptera) of sometimes tremendous size; beetles (Coleoptera); and butterflies and moths (Lepidoptera). The tarantula hawk (*Hemipepsis* species), for example, is a large wasp about 1½ inches (3.8 cm) in length. The female of the species is quite troublesome to spiders, particularly tarantulas: she paralyzes her prey and returns with it to her burrow, whereupon she lays her egg and leaves the larva to feed on the spider.

Of the arachnids, the desert tarantula (Theraphosidae)—a large, hairy spider approximately 6 inches (15 cm) in length—is the most common in the region. Although the tarantula's potent venom can subdue an animal as large as a mouse, it is not generally a danger to humans except when the toxins in its abdominal hairs cause itching and burning. Tarantulas first mate at about 8 to 10 years of age, after which the female often kills the male. She lives longer than many other spider species, however, often to the age of 25 years.

With its decorative topknot and masked face, Gambel's quail (*Callipepla gambelii*) is one of the more interesting birds to inhabit the Chihuahuan Desert. Also known as the desert quail, this bird is able to live its entire life without water, as long as it can find moist vegetation. It feeds primarily on legumes such as mesquite and acacia, supplementing its diet with seeds and wild herbs. The black-throated sparrow (*Amphispiza bilineata*) is a small seed-eating bird found in areas of saltbush and other low shrubs. Like the desert quail, it can survive entirely without water, provided that succulent plants and insects are plentiful.

Most other birds in the region are predators and scavengers, feeding primarily on insects and spiders. One of the more ominous birds is the turkey vulture. Its wings, although not particularly useful for flying, are adequate for hovering while it sniffs out carrion. Even young turkey vultures have virtually indestructible stomachs, capable of digesting bone and hide in a matter of days.

Reptiles and amphibians in the Chihuahuan Desert obtain most of their moisture from plant fluids. Two of the more distinctive of these creatures are the tiger salamander (*Ambystoma tigrinum*), an amphibian that often breeds in the watering tanks of cattle, and the western whiptail lizard (*Cnemidophorus tigris*). Some other species of the whiptail lizard are all female and can reproduce themselves without the participation of a male. They seem to produce a chemical that allows them to lay fertile eggs that develop, with only one set of genes, into exact duplicates of themselves.

The chuckwalla (*Sauromalus obesus*) is 5 to 7 inches (13–18 cm) long. It can change its usually reddish-black skin tone to blend in with its surroundings. It prefers rocky areas, feeding primarily on

Two chuckwallas bask in the sun

creosote bush, desert hollyhock, and ephedra, as well as some flowers and fruits.

Several varieties of rattlesnake are abundant in the Chihuahuan Desert. These include the Mohave (*Crotalus scutulatus*), western diamondback (*C. atrox*), rock (*C. lepidus*), and black-tailed (*C. molossus*) rattlesnakes. One snake species of the Chihuahuan Desert that is not found in the other North American deserts is the copperhead (*Agkistrodon contortrix*).

Small mammals include rodents such as mice, rats, and squirrels; rabbit and hare species, such as the Audubon's cottontail and the black-tailed jackrabbit; and a variety of bats. Like birds and reptiles, most of these animals procure their life-sustaining moisture from the food they eat.

The Mexican free-tailed, Brazilian free-tailed, or guano, bat (*Tadarida brasiliensis*) is about 4 inches (10 cm) long and dwells in caves in large groups. Most bats rely on insects for their sustenance, but the Mexican long-nosed bat also feeds on the nectar and pollen of night-blooming flowers. It is particularly fond of century plant pollen, which it disseminates during its frenzied nighttime feedings.

Carnivorous mammals in the Chihuahuan Desert include bobcats, coyotes, and at least two species of fox—the kit fox and the gray fox. The coyote, a close relative of dogs and wolves, eats bats, cottontails, javelina (a type of wild pig), kangaroo rats, mule deer, and squirrels. The kit fox (*Vulpes macrotis*), which grows to about 30 inches (76 cm) long, is a nocturnal animal, retreating to the cool comfort of an underground den when the temperature starts to climb. It feeds primarily on rodents and has adapted to desert conditions by growing tufts of fur on the bottoms of its feet.

Atacama Desert

17° S to 32° S latitude
82° W to 68° W longitude

Chile

The Atacama is located on the Pacific Ocean coast of South America, near the center of the continent. It extends 600 miles (970 km) south from the border of Peru to the area near Copiapo, Chile, with an average width of about 90 miles (145 km). The Pacific coastal mountains, the Cordillera de la Costa, lie to the west, and the Cordillera Domeyko, foothills of the Andes, to the east. The desert's average elevation is about 2,000 feet (600 m).

Paradoxically, this region lies next to the globe's largest body of water, but it may be the driest place in the world. Rain is virtually nonexistent; some places have never recorded any at all, while in others a downpour of 0.4 to 0.8 inch (10–20 mm) may occur only once in a decade. Although the Tropic of Capricorn passes through the Atacama, the region does not resemble anything tropical. Instead, it is an arid wasteland. Even along the ocean the coast looks dreary: the mountains fall in a wall of reddish-brown cliffs 1,500 to 2,000 feet high (450–600 m), sometimes sloping,

Río Loa valley, Chile

sometimes steep, but always barren and apparently endless. There is no coastal plain; towns, isolated from the interior, cling precariously to sea-eroded terraces at the bases of cliffs that rise to the rounded summits of an ancient 3,000-foot-high (914-m) coastal plateau.

Geology

History. The history of the Atacama extends back some 190 million years to the formation of the western Andes during the Jurassic period. Sediments were folded and lifted as the Nazca Plate and the South American Plate collided at the western edge of South America. In the early Tertiary period, 65 million years ago, active volcanoes spewed out copper, iron, silver, molybdenum, and manganese ores.

Later in the Tertiary period the Andes uplift continued, accompanied by further outbursts of volcanism. The main Andes separated from the older coastal ranges and the depression formed between them. In the Quaternary period, global cooling crowned the Andean summits with ice, and glaciers carved into what is now the desert. The depression between the Andes and coastal ranges forms a natural resting place for sediment from the Andes. In the Atacama, sediments washed down during the Tertiary and Quaternary periods created the rich nitrate deposits of the Tamarugal Plain and Carmen salt flat.

The coastal ranges, or cordilleras, form a ridge between the Atacama Desert basin and the Pacific coast. These mountains consist of Paleozoic and Mesozoic granites and metamorphic rocks that were uplifted during the Andean folding phase, but they have smooth shapes and flattened summits, since they are older than the Andes.

Topography. The depression between the two ranges creates a high plain at an elevation of more than 9,900 feet (3,000 m). Farther to the east there are numerous volcanic cones, some exceeding 16,000 feet (4,900 m). Along the northeastern frontier is the Atacama Plateau, more than 13,000 feet (4,000 m) high.

Three permanent river systems flow through the Atacama Desert: the Río Loa, Río Grande de Atacama, and Río Vilama, which among them supply 500,000 tons of water daily. The Loa, the longest Chilean river, is the only one that reaches the Pacific, with a greatly reduced flow, after pursuing a tortuous course of 275 miles (444 km) from its main source. The Grande and the Vilama disappear into the desert after losing much of their flow to irrigation in the San Pedro de Atacama area.

Overall, the desert consists of a series of salt basins interspersed with areas of sand and lava. It has salt pans at the foot of the coastal mountains on the west and alluvial fans sloping from the Andean foothills to the east; some of the fans are sandy and covered with dunes, but extensive gravel accumulations are more common.

Salt Lakes: Over thousands of years, salt has built up in salt lakes called *salars*. A *salar* is an immense salty, marshy area with shallow water. Crystallized salts settle on the bottom of the *salar* and form mounds of white or gray salt along the shore. Many *salars* are surrounded by salt plains more extensive than the lake itself.

Usually open water is only a few inches deep, and even large *salars* are seldom more than 3 or 4 feet (about 1 m) deep. As the salt accumulates on the bottom, the water level rises and spreads over a greater area, which in turn allows faster evaporation. Some crystals combine to form a solid bottom layer, while others mix with sand and clay to form a salty quicksand.

Most striking is the color of the waters of the *salars;* they can be blue, turquoise, emerald green, or silvery gray, sometimes at different points within the same *salar*. The pink waters are the most distinctive, since their color appears very unnatural. The colored lakes are considerably higher in salts than the transparent ones; some of the color is attributed to bacteria and dissolved salts. The minute powdery sulfur bacterium *Lamprocystis roseopersicina*, which thrives in the alkaline water, clouds it with clumps of pink cells. *Salars* also have pronounced odors, some of rotting (sulfur dioxide) and others of hydrogen sulfide.

Underlying the desert is the Pica aquifer, which feeds the groundwater. This groundwater, in the Antofagasta Province, originally fell as rain or snow a hundred years ago in what is now Bolivia, and ever since has been flowing westward underground toward springs in the Atacama.

Mineral Deposits: Early prospectors in the Atacama found a substance they called *salitre*, a name that usually denoted saltpeter, or potassium nitrate, which was used in making gunpowder. In fact, the new find was sodium nitrate, also useful as an ingredient in explosives but more important as fertilizer. The Atacama has the world's largest known reserves of sodium nitrate. The existence of the mineral is a testament to the dry climate: it is easily soluble in water; rain would have washed it away.

Sodium chloride (table salt), iodine salts, and sodium nitrate are still extracted from saline deposits called caliche. There are also rich deposits of copper and other minerals, including atacamite, a rare copper ore.

Climate

The outstanding features of the Atacama climate are an almost complete lack of precipitation, low humidity with resulting high evaporation under an unclouded sun, and a marked difference between the temperatures of day and night. Records in the province of Antofagasta show no real rainfall at all in coastal towns, just scattered freak showers that occur seven or more years apart.

Farther inland there is no precipitation until elevations of about 11,000 feet (3,350 m) are reached, at distances of 120 miles (190 km) or more from the coast. Above this elevation there is the summer rainy season, with rain, sleet, hail, and snow between January and March of some years. Heavier precipitation seems to occur in an irregular seven-year cycle.

Temperatures are relatively lower than those in similar latitudes, with an average summer temperature around 65° F (18° C). The mean daily temperature for the hottest month is 89° F (32° C) in February and for the coldest, 28° F (-2° C) in June.

Because cold air from the surrounding peaks settles into basins during the night, temperatures at sunrise are much lower than on higher slopes. Sunlight is curtailed by mountains to east and west, and evaporation causes further heat loss. Even the salty lakes are frozen during the morning throughout much of the year, despite their tropical latitude.

Rainfall: The Atacama Desert is part of the larger arid Pacific shoreline region of South America. The cause of the lack of rain originates in the Antarctic. The Peru, or Humboldt, Current brings cold water from the Antarctic; air masses passing over this cold water lose their rain while they are still over the ocean. Once an air mass reaches the warmer land it forms a thermal inversion, where a layer of warm air overlies a layer of cold air. This system creates abundant fog—the *camanchaca*—along the coast, as well as clouds, but no rain. The result is a shoreline temperature 10 F degrees (5.5 C degrees) cooler than is normal for the latitude. What precipitation does fall runs off as floods of occasionally damaging force because the bare surfaces do not retain water.

Evaporation is high throughout the region, because of the dry air and the great amount of sunshine and wind. The temperature varies widely over the course of a single day; the difference may be up to 50 F degrees (28 C degrees).

Prevailing winds blow from the west and attain considerable force during the afternoons and evenings. Up on the Atacama Plateau the wind is always strong, often mixing with snow and dust.

Plants

The Atacama's plant life is sparse, in places almost nonexistent, and what there is has adapted to an extraordinarily dry environment. Near the coast, varieties of cacti as well as shrubs and spiny brambles are kept alive by coastal fogs.

The desert coast at Antofagasta

In the northern desert region, vegetation has adapted to salinity and lack of rain. Tamarugo (*Prosopis tamarugo*), a spiny acacia tree related to the mesquite, does well in the dry interior desert. The hardy tamarugo can survive on the little moisture it gleans from the ground and from the Pacific fog. The tree occurs in limited areas and reaches its greatest abundance in the Salar de Pintados, an ancient lake bed that is highly saline and for the most part covered with a thick crust of sodium salts. Tamarugo is able to survive here because the entire plain is underlain by groundwater; the deep-rooted trees can reach groundwater 16 to 39 feet (5–12 m) below the earth's surface.

About 90 percent of the desert is devoid of higher plants most of the time. However, seeds of certain plants lie dormant, waiting for the rare rains. One important class includes lichens, which grow partially buried in the soil. In shape and color they look like the sand grains around them. Dew is their only regular water source.

In the few years with sufficient rainfall the ephemeral vegetation creates the phenomenon of a "flowering desert" in areas that are for many years devoid of any plant life. A rain brings forth color from a red *Calandrinia* species and blue and white from annual *Nolana* species. The dormant plants are of two main types: therophytes, which survive the rainless years as dormant seeds, and geophytes, which do so in dormant bulbs and tubers. Dwarf *Skytanthus arcutus* have spirally coiled fruits. Dispersed by wind, they pile up in heaps near obstacles.

Some lichens roll about, moved by wind or water and nourished by dew. *Rocella cervicornis* is found 30 miles (50 km) inland in regions with regular dew or fog formations. It is found in many desert regions devoid of other vegetation and as a component of plant communities such as cacti or herbaceous hills.

Along the coast, the condensation of fog water is vital to plant survival. In the fog forests just north of the Atacama boundaries, evergreen foliage trees are enveloped with a thick coat of mosses and covered by lichens hanging down from the branches. Moisture-loving shade plants and ferns cover the soil. The plants condense the fog water on their leaves, which then drips to the ground. The amount of water condensed by tree leaves can be as much as 60 inches (1,500 mm) per year. Condensed fog water runs down to the ground, enabling flora to survive dry periods without fog. Since the coastal mountains block the fog, the region east of them is devoid of vegetation.

In some areas of the Atacama, coastal oases shrink to gray-green patches of lichens (*Anaptychia leucomelaena* and *Ramalina cerruchis*) and algae (*Trentepohlia polycarpa*), while others support succulents, such as a variety of *Oxalis*, species of *Alstroemeria* and *Nolana*, *Calandrinia ruizi*, *Zephyranthes albicans*, *Plantago limensis*, and other annuals. Steeper rock slopes support stands of the columnar cactus *Eulychnia iquiquensis*.

Soil cacti are another feature of the Chilean fog desert. These plants are partly buried in soil, and the volume of subterranean parts is considerably greater than that of the aboveground organs and only really visible when they flower. These are mainly thick, fleshy, succulent tubers with thin root necks. The roots spread out just below the surface to take up water.

Animals

The absence of abundant plant life, along with the Atacama's geographic isolation, precludes an abundance of wildlife. Most of the water is so full of chemicals as to be unfit for any animal to drink.

The Andes have restricted the possibilities for animal migration, and the northern desert has proved a formidable obstacle to the southward migration of tropical Andean fauna. As a result, the most abundant animals are rodents. Chinchilla, degu, and mountain vizcacha are Andean rodents famed for their furs.

In the more vegetated areas, the only survivors of the Paleocamelids (predecessors of camels) are the guanaco and vicuña and their domesticated relatives, the llama and alpaca. The latter is known for high-quality wool.

Aquatic birds, including flamingos and ducks, abound in the salt marshes. Vicuñas frequent the shores where sweet water springs enter. It is not uncommon to find good drinking water beside the shore and bitter saline water just a little farther away.

On the coastal rocks of the Pacific, giant troops of sea lions congregate, and on the islands near the coast millions of birds nest. Important guano birds include the cormorant and *Sula variegata*; these live on steep slopes and summits, while the flatter areas are colonized by pelicans. The seabirds and mammals feed mainly off the shoals of sardines they find.

Aquatic life is abundant in the *salars*, supported by insects at their edges. Much of the water enters from beneath the *salar* bottom, but there are also cold and warm springs along the sides. One *salar*, the Salar de Ascotán, is known to support fish up to 2⅓ inches (6 cm) long, in part because this *salar*'s water contains less salt than others. The geographic isolation of the region accounts for the complete absence of both poisonous reptiles and spiders.

37° S to 50° S latitude
73° W to 68° W longitude

Argentina

Patagonia is a dry, cold, windy region of southern Argentina that extends from the Río Colorado some 1,200 (1,900 km) miles south to Tierra del Fuego. It has an arid climate, with only a few rivers that cut wide, deep canyons across a series of descending plateaus. The Patagonian Desert covers most of the region, which is almost all of the southern portion of the country of Argentina. It is the largest desert in the Americas, with an area of about 260,000 square miles (673,000 sq km).

Topography

Patagonia descends from the eastern slope of the Andes to the Atlantic coast in a series of broad, flat steps. Tectonic activity related to the uplift of the Andes created the area's gigantic platforms and coastal terraces. As a result, the coastline has cliffs along most of its length. These low cliffs tend to rise toward the south, where they reach heights of over 150 feet (45 m). Eastward-flowing rivers cut the landscape, some of them originating in glaciers in the Andes. These rivers have created broad valleys and steep-walled canyons that cross the terraces.

Westerly winds sweeping across the southern half of South America drop most of their precipitation on the high Andes. As a result, a rain shadow on the east side of the mountains causes an arid to semiarid climate in the interior of Argentina. The dry zone begins in the Andean northwest and extends along the eastern slopes of the Andes to the south but does not include Tierra del Fuego. The rain shadow covers a central desert area with a rim of semiarid, or steppe, climate. The steppes have about twice the amount of annual precipitation as the arid zones, but evaporation exceeds precipitation in both zones, keeping them treeless. Most of the arid region suffers from strong winds that carry abrasive sand and dust; the windblown dust creates a continuous haze that considerably reduces visibility.

Geology

During late Paleozoic times a marine basin covered Patagonia; this central basin was bordered by continental areas at the northeast and southwest. Much of the area was covered periodically by glaciers during the Carboniferous and early

Cloud-capped peaks rise above Los Glaciares National Park, Argentina

Permian periods, 330 to 290 million years ago.

The glacial evidence and the presence of the distinctive plant species *Glossopteris* and *Gangamopteris* in lower Permian deposits indicate that Patagonia was then part of the supercontinent Gondwanaland during the late Paleozoic, along with Antarctica, South Africa, India, and Australia.

In the early Jurassic, around 170 million years ago, marine sediments were deposited in the central Patagonian basin. By the middle Jurassic, the ocean had withdrawn and the layers took on a continental rather than marine character. Finally, in the Eocene, 40 million years ago, extensive volcanic activity took place, setting the stage for the landscape of the present.

Today, the Patagonian steppe rises in a succession of wide terraces that reach a height of 4,000 to 5,000 feet (1,200–1,500 m) near the foot of the mountains. Much of the surface is covered with tracts of a peculiar type of rounded gravel, 200 feet (60 m) deep in places, that lay under the sea a few million years ago. The pebbles are cemented together by soil rich in alumina clays. Toward the west, the gravel is replaced by granite and reddish porphyry—a type of igneous rock— and in many parts, particularly near the Chico and Santa Cruz rivers, there are broad sheets of volcanic basalt. South of the Río Negro, the plains are much more irregular, and volcanic eruptions have occurred in this area down to fairly modern times. Recent sheets of basalt cover the tableland east of Lakes Buenos Aires and Pueyrredón. The plains have spread to within 50 miles (80 km) of the coast along the Chico and Santa Cruz rivers and reach almost to the coast south of the Coig and Gallegos rivers. In places, plateaus of basalt are among the most common features of the

landscape. The hollows of the plains often contain broad shallow lakes, which have high concentrations of soda and other mineral salts and are the feeding places for giant flocks of flamingos.

Argentina has poor river drainage because it has only a gentle slope down to the ocean from the Andes. The rivers that cross Patagonia from west to east tend to diminish in volume as they cross the dry desert areas. The Colorado and Negro rivers can have major floods after spring melting of snow and ice in the mountains. In the south, the Santa Cruz River flows eastward out of the glacial Lake Argentino in the Andean foothills to the Atlantic.

Other geographic features of Patagonia include a series of basins, some of which contain lakes, that lie between the Patagonian Andes and the desert plateau, and volcanic hills in the central plateau west of the city of Río Gallegos. Glacial ice in the past extended beyond the Andes only in the south, where large moraines now mark the extent of soil and boulders left behind by the glaciers.

The arid and semiarid Patagonia begins at the Precordillera foothills in the west, and the elevation of the land gradually decreases toward the Atlantic. The land is cut by transverse valleys running from west to east. Other forms shaped by water and wind erosion can also be found within the region.

Gravel pavements and bare areas of compacted soil are the principal results of wind erosion. The most aggressive and active features are the *lenguas*, or "sand tongues." In these, sand is transported and deposited in narrow strips parallel to the wind direction. While the widths of the strips do not change markedly, their progression downwind may be quite rapid, sometimes exceeding

1¼ miles (2 km) a year. The "tongue" consists of an active frontal dune, usually of coarse sandy material; a central area where sand transportation is greatest but accumulation is temporary; and the area of origin, where large amounts of blowing sand prevail. Erosion pavement, or a denuded area with compacted soil, is all that is left behind. The predominant direction of movement is west to east in most of Patagonia, except in coastal regions and areas where local topography changes the direction of the wind.

Patagonia's mineral resources include oil fields near the town of Comodoro Rivadavia and iron ore deposits at Sierra Grande. The province of Río Negro also has deposits of manganese, tungsten, fluorite, lead, and barite, the principal ore of barium. Neuquén Province has deposits of copper, gold, vanadium, and zinc-lead ore. Chubut Province has uranium and manganese in modest quantities. There are also deposits of gypsum and a clay known as kaolinite.

Climate

In Patagonia the seasons are well defined. Winters—which, because Patagonia is in the Southern Hemisphere, cover the months from June through September—are not as cold and summers are not as hot as in similar latitudes north of the equator. On the desert plateau, however, the climate can turn quite rough. The mean annual temperature is around 46° to 48° F (8°–9° C) in northern Patagonia and is only slightly lower, about 41° F (5° C), at the southern tip of South America. The northern zone has annual mean temperatures between 54° and 68° F (12° and 20° C). Maximum temperatures recorded vary between 106° and 113° F (41° and 45° C), and minimum temperatures range between 12° and 23° F (-11° and -5° C). The cold season lasts for four months in the semidesert and five months elsewhere; the coldest month is July.

The ever-present characteristic of Patagonia is the wind, which blows all year round from the mountains to the sea. The prevailing winds from the southwest are dry, cold, and strong. A person driving along over unpaved roads with a tailwind of 37 mph (60 kph) is constantly blinded by the car's own dust clouds.

Patagonia is subject to heavy snows in winter and frosts throughout the year; spring and autumn tend to be noticeable but quite short. Average annual precipitation

The Patagonian Desert meets the Atlantic Ocean at the Valdés Peninsula

ranges between about 4½ and 8 inches (115 and 205 mm), although as much as 18½ inches (474 mm) has been recorded. In the central area of the desert there is less precipitation and more sunshine than on the coast or in the Andean cordillera.

Along the east coast, a cold ocean current flowing northward from the Falkland Islands creates the sea mists that often cling to the coast of Patagonia.

Plants

The plant cover in Patagonia seldom looks green. Yellow, gray, and brown are the dominant colors year-round. A high proportion of the flowers are yellow also.

Treeless Patagonia begins immediately to the east of the Andes foothills, first with a narrow steppe zone of such tussock-grass species as *Festuca pallescens* and *Stipa speciosa*. On moist sites introduced central European species, such as dandelions (*Taraxacum officinale*), white clover (*Trifolium repens*), and Kentucky bluegrass(*Poa pratensis*), are also found.

Where the land is drier, the vegetation becomes more like that of a semidesert, dominated by the cushion-plant growth forms that are well adapted to a windy climate. First come large, loose, but spiny cushions of *Mulinum spinosum*. In the true semidesert the cushions become lower and denser, with the total area of ground covered by vegetation falling to 30 to 40 percent or less.

The arid region of the Patagonian Desert comprises two zones, each with its own characteristic vegetation. The northern area consists of open brushland, which is covered with widely spaced thickets between 3 and 7 feet (1 and 2 m) high. Grasses flourish in the sandy areas, while salt-tolerant grasses and shrubs are common in the salt flats. In irrigated areas it is possible to grow crops such as peaches, plums, almonds, apples, pears, olives, grapes, hops, dates, alfalfa, and aromatic herbs. Willows, tamarisks, and poplars flourish along the water canals in Chubut Province.

In the second zone, covering the southwesternmost parts, the vegetation is low and very sparse and needs almost no water. The plants—commonly cushion-shaped shrubs and semishrubs—are scattered, stunted, and of a type that can withstand a dry habitat. The cushions are formed by numerous dense branches, and the shoots and leaves of the plants are often spiny. Common species are *Brachyclados caespitosus, Oreopolus glacialis, Junellia tridactylites, Junellia patagonica,* and *Nierembergia patagonica.* Additional types of vegetation include dwarf shrubs only a few inches tall, with small leathery or thorny leaves (for example, *Nardophyllum, Nassauvia,* and *Verbena* species).

Two species of barberry, *Berberis cuneata* and *B. heterophylla,* are the tallest shrubs found in the most arid parts of the desert. They also attract notice by being a deep green color, in contrast with the rest of the vegetation in the region. Barberries are usually found only as isolated individuals or small groups, although along the borders of the terraces and in some flat valleys a continuous strip of the plants may be seen, possibly because of groundwater sources. Their sweet fruits were known to early explorers as Magellan's grapes.

The mild winters make it possible for succulents and cacti to live in the desert. Several cacti are found and represent the southernmost members of the family. *Maihuenia patagonica, Austrocactus* species, and *Pterocactus* species are the most frequently found. *Maihuenia* forms large patches no more than 8 inches (20 cm) high but sometimes 3 feet (1 m) in diameter. It has beautiful clusters of large white, pink, or tobacco-colored flowers in the summer. Small, nearly spherical stems of *Pterocactus* species mimic the brownish-pink color of the sandy soil.

Low perennial herbs grow under the protection of grass tussocks or spiny shrubs. Most of them produce buds at the end of the growing season that wait until the next growing season to sprout. Plants that produce tubers seem to be more common than those that produce bulbs or corms. A few ephemerals are able to complete

Lilies bloom in the Patagonian Desert

development with only rudimentary leaflets and complete the list of plant species.

Animals

Patagonia has fossils of animals that are unlike any alive today. The ancient life in Patagonia developed into unusual forms because the present land connection of the Isthmus of Panama between South America and North America is of fairly recent geological origin. Near the beginning of the age of mammals, about 65 million years ago, South America became an island continent separated from the rest of the world. The creatures living on the continent were stranded there, and they developed into unique and individual forms.

In a later geological epoch the Isthmus of Panama arose and once again provided a land bridge between North and South America. Such creatures as cats, dogs, bears, mastodons, horses, peccaries, camels, and many others crossed this bridge to South America. Many of these animals have survived on both continents, although sometimes in different forms, and many that came from North America have survived only in South America. Modern wildlife includes the guanaco, a relative of the llama, which are both related to the camel; the *nandu,* or rhea, similar to the ostrich; several kinds of armadillo; and the vizcacha, a burrowing rodent similar to a prairie dog but as big as a small pig.

In the Patagonian Desert itself, vertebrates are comparatively rare. Mammals, birds, and insects have apparently not evolved to be closely associated with the different species of plants as have the reptiles; this may be because reptiles are less mobile and can interbreed more closely.

As in many other deserts, rodents are numerous. Similar to

North American prairie dogs, tuco-tucos emerge from their mazelike burrows at night to feed on roots and grasses. Their musical calls sound like something beating on tiny anvils, a series of clinks and trills. These small rodents have grayish fur, short tails, small ears, long claws for digging, and bright orange front teeth. In areas where sheep graze they have been largely driven out of existence.

The guanaco is the only large hoofed herbivore. These llama relatives are noisy, typically yelling at intruders. They prefer to drink water and have the curious habit of depositing their dung only in certain fixed places.

Predator species are surprisingly numerous; they include the red fox (*Dusicyon culpaeus*), gray fox (*Dusicyon griseus*), puma (*Felis concolor*), another cat called the Patagonian colocolo (*Felis colocolo*), Geoffroy's cat (*Felis geoffroyi*), a ferret (*Lyncodon patagonicus*), a species of skunk (*Conepatus humboldti*), and a marsupial animal (*Lestodelphis halli*).

Because temperatures vary so widely and because there are so few natural refuges, most animals live underground, digging their own burrows or using burrows of other species. Because there are few large natural caves, there are few species of bats in Patagonia. Most of the bird species are cursorials, that is, they prefer to run away from danger rather than fly. The two species of rhea, including *Pterocnemia pennata pennata*, are unable to fly. This grayish bird lays a large clutch of greenish eggs in a ground nest; the eggs are considered a delicacy.

Another common group of birds is represented by the Patagonian tinamou (*Tinamotis ingoufi*) and the elegant tinamou (*Eudromia elegans*); both birds can fly, but prefer to walk.

Patagonia also has plovers, sandpipers, and flycatchers, which are also mainly walkers. Other birds include one species of mockingbird and several types of finches.

There are large numbers of birds of prey but none of the species is endemic. Important species include the buzzard eagle, crested caracara, great horned owl and other owls, as well as falcons and hawks. Two species of vulture, the Andean condor, the crested caracara, and the *chimango* are eaters of carrion.

One bird not usually associated with deserts is the penguin. Patagonia's coast plays host to hundreds of thousands of Magellanic penguins, which come ashore in September to mate and raise their young in huge rookeries. The penguins remain on shore all summer and, in April, return to the ocean, where they spend the winter feeding on fish and squid.

Invertebrates found in Patagonia include winged bugs known as *vinchucas*; bloodsucking insects that are transmitters of American trypanosomiasis; scorpions; and 14 kinds of spiders, including one, called *Mecysmanchenius*, not found elsewhere. Rivers and lakes tend to have few fish, but some have been stocked with salmon and trout.

Elegant tinamou, Patagonia

68° N to 90° N latitude
All degrees of longitude

USA, Canada, Greenland, Iceland, Norway, Sweden, Finland, Russia

The Arctic is a vast area of ice, land, and sea that crowns the Northern Hemisphere from approximately 68° N latitude to the North Pole. Unlike Antarctica, it has at its core not a landmass but a body of water. The world's smallest ocean, the Arctic Ocean, covers 5.5 million square miles (14.3 million sq km) and is dotted with a collection of archipelagoes and several large islands along its perimeter. It is encircled by the landmasses of North America, Eurasia, and Greenland, a ring broken up only by seas and straits that allow its waters to mix with those of the Atlantic and Pacific.

Much of the land in the Arctic is rugged, mountainous terrain encased by immense glaciers that plunge into this frozen sea. However, most of the Arctic's flat inland surfaces beyond the timberline consist of marshy tundra, a treeless area dominated by low vegetation.

In the regions north of the tundra there are barren expanses of rock and gravel left by the crushing movement of ancient glaciers as they moved across the surface. Sand and silt deposited by meltwater in valleys carved by these glaciers, as well as on the coastal plains, are swept into dunes by the harsh Arctic winds, one of the few features the Arctic shares with more "typical" deserts.

Climate and Topography

The Arctic is defined as a polar desert because its land area has mean annual precipitation ranging from 4 to 6 inches (100–150 mm). Precipitation falls mainly in the form of light snow during the autumn but can remain on the ground for long periods, blown into high banks by the wind.

The climates in the Arctic fall into one or the other of two zones, polar or arctic, on the basis of the severity and duration of temperatures. Mean temperatures in the polar, or ice cap, zone never rise above 32° F (0° C). Mean temperatures in the arctic zone always stay below 50° F (10° C).

During the brief summer months, when 24 hours of sunlight warm up the surface, the Arctic tundra is transformed into a wet, marshy land. As the thaw peaks in July, runoff from melting ice cannot drain into the frozen layer of ground known as permafrost. It collects in boggy pools and lakes, and is left standing by low rates of evaporation.

Permafrost can consist of frozen water, soil, sand, or rock; it is defined by temperature, not content. The colder the temperature, the deeper and more extensive the permafrost becomes. Oil exploration has revealed that some areas of permafrost are over 2,000 feet (600 m) deep in Alaska, northern Canada, and Siberia.

Permafrost is easily damaged. It is afforded some protection and insulation by a relatively thin layer of soil and vegetation called the active layer. Between 8 inches (20 cm) and 3⅓ feet (1 m) deep, this layer thaws in the summer; as it soaks up runoff from melting ice it becomes a spongy and boggy blanket. This continued freezing and thawing expand small areas of damage into gaping wounds.

Seasonal warming and cooling and the related expansion and contraction of the active layer produce unique polygonal shapes, called patterned ground, that extend across the Arctic tundra surface. In this process, heavier soil particles are sorted from lighter ones and are pushed to the edges of these polygons. On slopes, the normally regular polygons are stretched into dramatic dark streaks.

Pingos, large mounds or domes of ice covered by peaty soil, are also products of the freezing and thawing of the permafrost. From a distance they look like miniature volcanos, rising up to 250 feet (75 m) in height and 1,640 feet (500 m) in diameter. They usually form in flat areas and are the result of groundwater welling up beneath the permafrost.

Plants

The combination of cold temperatures, harsh driving winds, sterile soils, and the short summer growing season limits the variety of plant life that can survive in the Arctic. To compensate for these inhospitable conditions, most vegetation grows low to the ground and has surface roots adapted to the makeup of the soil. The distribution, abundance, and coverage of plant life decrease and become more spotty the farther north one goes, as the relatively more fertile and wet tundra is replaced by the dry, barren fell fields and rock deserts, before they in turn give way to the bare sea ice.

The taiga defines the southern boundary of Arctic vegetation. This irregular line coincides roughly with the timberline. Its northern edge is marked by rivers and lakes, and supports communities of heaths, sedges, herbs, mosses, and lichen.

Sedges (*Eriophorum*) are by far the dominant plants and create a dense carpet of vegetation called the tussock tundra. Grasslike, although not true grasses, sedges are also called cottongrass or Arctic cotton. These tough plants have a fibrous, flexible stem capped with dense balls of single or multiple fluffy white flowers. *Eriophorum vaginatum* is the most common of the sedges. Wood rushes (*Luzula*)

are another group of grasslike plants that thrive in drier, fine-grained soils in the north.

True grasses such as *Arctophila* and *Arctagrostis* prefer wetter areas and grow at the edges of pools and lakes. The bluegrasses (*Poa*), red fescue (*Festuca*), and brome (*Bromus*) attract animals that feed on their tussocks.

The dwarf birch (*Betula nana*) has gray bark coated with a highly flammable resin and small leaves that explode with color in the fall. Along with willows and heaths, the dwarf birch makes up the bulk of the shrub tundra in many regions. Although larger and woodier than other Arctic plants, these shrubs are limited by wind and weather to heights of only a few feet. Willows (*Salix* species) grow along riverbeds and are extremely slow growers. Their true age is often disguised by their thin, young-looking trunks suspended only an inch or two off the ground; some are over 500 years old.

Heaths of the Ericaceae family, one of the most prodigious plant families, are creepers and have small thick leaves and woody stems. Many of the heaths have leaves that remain green year-round. A number of heaths produce berries, including the tundra bilberry

(*Vaccinium uglinosum*) and the crowberry (*Empetrum nigrum*), an important food for many animals. Most heaths have colorful and abundant flowers similar to those of the rhododendron and azalea.

In the drier, more northerly regions, fields of stone and rock replace tundra. Landscapes are dominated by cushion plants such as *Dryas integrifolia* and *Saxifraga oppositifolia*, prostrate shrubs such as *Salix arctica*, and rosette species such as *Saxifraga*, *Draba*, and *Minuartia*. Wildflowers are surprisingly plentiful and include the white, purple, and yellow flowers of the saxifrage family, the primrose (*Primula*), and the gentian (*Gentiana*). One of the more noticeable wildflowers is the bright yellow Arctic poppy (*Papaver*), which has fine hairs on its stem to protect it from the elements. Even buttercups and blue forget-me-nots are not uncommon in the polar desert.

Lichens live in the most barren and rocky areas. The acids produced by these plants allow them to carve into rock and take hold. Although extremely slow growing, lichens have proven to be hardy survivors of the Arctic cold. The apparently invincible reindeer moss, actually a lichen, is so tough that scientists theorize that it may be

able to grow in space because it has withstood exposure to gamma rays 1,000 times the level that would kill a human.

Animals

The Arctic landmasses are close together and have allowed migration from one to the other, and so animal species found on one continent are likely to be found on the others ringing the Pole.

Many Arctic animals have adapted to their environment in several ways: many grow white coats during the winter as camouflage, and their fur or feathers are thick and water-repellent. Fur often coats the entire body surface, including the feet, to allow a good grip on the ice. Low body temperatures and metabolism during hibernation enable many to survive the long, cold winters, while others flee altogether, migrating to warmer, more hospitable climates in the south.

The polar bear is one of the few animals that remains in the region the entire year. It can tower 12 feet (over 3.6 m) tall when erect; males weigh up to 1,000 pounds (450 kg), females a little less. Despite its size, it is graceful and quick. The fur is thick and oily to protect the bear from the wet and cold, and a membrane shields the eyes from the glare of the sun and snow. Usually a loner, the polar bear stays close to the coasts, where it feeds on the ringed and the bearded seals. When other food is scarce, the polar bear eats berries and lemmings. During the winter, the female wanders inland, digs a snow cave, and goes into a state of semihibernation, during which she gives birth to up to three cubs.

The brown bear (*Ursus arctos*) is found in the tundra and mountains and hunts mainly ground squirrels and rodents, although it supplements its diet with plants

Cotton grass blows in the Arctic winds on Wrangel Island

and other small animals. Another bear, the closely related barren ground grizzly, will wander across a region of 100 square miles (260 sq km) in search of food.

The wolf (*Canis lupus*) is a large predator that ranges throughout the north. It weighs between 85 and 115 pounds (38 and 52 kg) and has gray or white fur. Wolves live in packs of 2 to 15 members and have one of the most highly developed social structures outside of primates.

The Arctic fox (*Alopex lagopus*) is a common small carnivore that hunts mostly lemmings. It also scavenges seal meat left by polar bears. Smaller than the red fox, it has a brown summer coat that turns completely white in winter.

The coats of the least weasel (*Mustela rixosa*) and the short-tailed weasel, or ermine (*Mustela erminea*), also turn white in the winter. Their small sizes belie their fierce and aggressive natures, and although they feed mostly on rodents, they will not shy from attacking larger animals. The wolverine, or glutton (*Gulo gulo*), is another member of this family.

The large herbivorous barren ground caribou (*Rangifer tarandus*) has long, thin legs and a large body; both males and females have large sets of antlers. Strong swimmers, caribou also have large hooves superbly suited for walking across the soft tundra and digging through ice in search of food. Caribou move across the plains in large herds of up to several thousand, grazing on lichen.

Another migrant herbivore is the prehistoric-looking musk ox (*Ovibos moschatus*), which has a metabolism comparable to that of a camel. These large animals have long shaggy coats of dark brown or black fur and horns that grow from the center of the forehead and curl up at both sides of the head.

The largest group of herbivores subsists on a varied diet that includes grasses, sedges, seeds, tubers, and insects. The most important of these burrowing microtenes are the vole (*Microtus*); the small brown mouselike lemming (*Dicrostonyx*); the brown and white collared lemming (*Lemmus*); and the bog lemming (*Synaptomys*). Lemmings are one of the most significant sources of food for predators of all types; when their populations crash after cyclical population explosions every 5 to 7 years, predator populations suffer as well. Behavior linked to migrations after such population outbreaks has given rise to myths about their suicidal tendencies.

The Arctic hare (*Lepus arcticus*), another common herbivore, is found in the higher regions of the Arctic, where its white winter coat blends in well with the snow and ice. It locates plant matter by smell and unearths it with its sharp teeth and claws.

Some of the few Arctic birds that remain in the tundra during the winter also turn white. Among these are the chickenlike ptarmigans of the grouse family, whose feathers, in summer mottled brown and white, cover their feet as well. Their chicks can hop around only hours after they hatch, giving them a better chance to flee from predators. The willow ptarmigan (*Lagopus lagopus*) and rock ptarmigan (*L. mutus*) are found in the willow shrub of the tundra and in the rocky fields, respectively.

The short-eared owl (*Asio flammeus*) and the snowy owl (*Nyctea scandiaca*) also remain in the Arctic through the winter. The immense snowy owl builds its nest on the ground, where the female tends to her young while the male hunts. Lemmings are their main source of food; when their populations drop, the snowy owl will

migrate as far south as Louisiana in search of nourishment.

Migrants make up the majority of Arctic birds. These include the common pectoral and semipalmated sandpiper (*Eriola*), golden plover (*Pluvialis dominica*), and black-bellied plover (*Pluvialis squatarola*), which are generally found close to bodies of water, where they feed on insects. Skuas and jaegers look much like gulls and have the aggressive, predatory tendencies of hawks. The skua, also known as the great skua or eagle guard, is the only bird that breeds in both the Arctic and Antarctic.

A bird common in the Antarctic, but absent in the Arctic, is the penguin. However, several Arctic birds resemble penguins, including the puffin, or sea parrot (*Fratercula*), which has a black back and wings, white breast, and a large stubby yellow bill tipped with bright orange. These birds flock in great numbers to the cliffs of the Arctic coasts.

Waterfowl such as swans, geese, and ducks are also found along the coasts, as well as around lakes, rivers, and pools in the tundra in the summer. Some of the larger waterfowl are the white whistling swan (*Olor columbianus*), the Canada goose (*Branta*

Barren ground caribou

canadensis), and the black brant (*Branta negris*). Ducks include the white-winged scoters (*Melanitta deglandi*), the common eider (*Somateria mollissima*), the king eider (*Somateria spectabilis*), and the old-squaw (*Clangula hyemalis*).

Eagles and hawks—also known as buteos—search the ground from the sky for prey such as rodents and smaller birds. One of the more common is the rough-legged hawk (*Buteo lagopus*). The peregrine falcon (*Falco peregrinus*) can plunge from the sky at a speed of 200 mph (320 kph). The raven, solid black and close in size to hawks, can also be seen in the skies above the tundra most of the year.

The Arctic has a small share of songbirds, which include the Lapland longspur (*Eremophila alpestris*) and the snow bunting (*Plectrophenax nivalis*). One of the first birds to return from the south in the summer, the small black-and-white snow bunting lives in the northern highlands of the Arctic, while the longspur prefers the tundra and fell fields.

An important source of food for Arctic birds are insects, such as mosquitoes and blackflies, that thrive in the marshy soils and damp meadows of the tundra.

Most Arctic insects contain little water and manufacture substances such as glycerol and sorbitol that act as antifreeze. The Arctic beetle (*Pterostichus brevicornis*) can survive harsh temperatures of -22° F (-30° C), while the wingless springtail (*Collembola*) lives in the snow and ice of the far north. In these higher regions, insects support themselves on algae and mosses; even mosquitoes and blackflies are mostly plant eaters and are not as dependent on mammal blood as their temperate relatives. Other invertebrates include mites and a few snails and slugs. Reptiles and amphibians are entirely absent.

Antarctic Desert

68° S to 90° S latitude
All degrees of longitude

Antarctica

Extending from the South Pole to 68° S latitude is the continent of Antarctica. This ice-covered landmass is the coldest, windiest, and highest continent on Earth. It is also the driest, with average precipitation even lower than that of the Sahara. Nearly all of its moisture is locked in snow and ice and cannot evaporate or nourish life.

Antarctica encompasses an area 1½ times that of the People's Republic of China, with nearly 99 percent of its 5.4 million square miles (14 million sq km) permanently covered with ice that averages 8,000 feet (2,400 m) thick. During the austral winter, the ice shelves that border more than one-third of the continent's coastline actually double its total ice coverage. Three-fourths of the Earth's fresh water supply can be found in this virtually uninhabitable area. The 1 to 2 percent of land that is not covered with ice year-round is made up of *nunataks*, or high peaks, and oases, such as those found in the McMurdo dry valley area.

Geology

Originally a part of the supercontinent called Gondwanaland, the tectonic plate containing East Antarctica began separating from South Africa, Madagascar, India, and Australia during the upper Cretaceous and Tertiary periods, between 110 and 55 million years ago. The Antarctic Peninsula was still connected to South America by a narrow isthmus until about 25 million years ago, when the two continents parted, creating the Drake Strait. The South Georgia and South Orkney islands, which are considered part of Antarctica,

are remnants of this isthmus. Much of West Antarctica, on the other hand, appears to have resulted from subduction and volcanic activity both before and after the separation from the supercontinent.

The Antarctic continent has an average elevation of more than 7,500 feet (2,300 meters). East and West Antarctica are divided by the Transantarctic Mountains, a vast chain that extends some 3,000 miles (4,800 km) from the Weddell Sea to the Ross Sea.

Under the snow and ice of East Antarctica is bedrock of Precambrian age, 570 million to more than 3 billion years old. West Antarctica has a surface area only half that of its eastern counterpart and is composed of mostly sedimentary rock and glacial deposits from the Mesozoic and Tertiary periods. In many places they are covered by rocks of the Quaternary period. Also on the West Antarctic plateau are the Ellsworth Mountains, which contain the highest peaks on the continent: Vinson Massif, at 16,863 feet (5,140 m), and Mount Tyree, at 15,495 feet (4,723 m). This range is composed of sedimentary rocks.

At least five Antarctic volcanoes are still active. Mount Erebus,

12,447 feet (3,794 m), is on Ross Island, with others in the Transantarctic Mountains and the islands surrounding the peninsula. Dry areas, although few and far between, are also found in the region. The largest of these is the McMurdo Oasis, encompassing 965 square miles (2,500 sq km).

Climate

The average annual temperature is always below freezing: -76° F (-60° C) on the ice sheet and 14° F (-10° C) along the coast.

Winter extends from April to September, with July temperatures averaging -94° F (-70° C) on the continent and -13° F (-25° C) on the coast. To date, the lowest temperature ever recorded, -129° F (-89.2° C), occurred in July 1972 at the former Soviet Union's Vostok base, situated at 78.5° S latitude.

Antarctic summer lasts from mid-December to mid-January, with January temperatures averaging -40° F (-40° C) on the ice sheet and 28° F (-2° C) on the coast. Fall and spring are also short, from February to March and October to November, respectively.

Most of the negligible precipitation falls in the form of winter snow on the western portion of the

continent within 120 to 190 miles (200–300 km) of the coast. The water equivalent of snowfall in West Antarctica ranges from 8 to 20 inches (200–500 mm); East Antarctica receives an average annual water equivalent of 2 inches (50 mm). The lowest annual accumulation recorded was 0.27 inch (7 mm) in 1970.

High winds are fairly constant in the Antarctic, averaging over 40 mph (64.5 kph) much of the time. Winds were recorded at 200 mph (323 kph) at the French Dumont d'Urville base in July 1972.

Plants

Brutal weather conditions, gale-force winds, and limited fresh water supplies keep plant life in the Antarctic to a minimum. There are no trees on the continent and very little life of any kind is known in its ice-covered interior. Near the coast and in the dry valleys, grass, algae, moss, and lichens constitute practically all the land vegetation on the continent. Two types of flowering plants—Antarctic hair grass (*Deschampsia antarctica*) and Antarctic pearlwort (*Colobenthos subulatus*)—grow in small clumps on the western shore of the Antarctic Peninsula. Mosses and liverworts live in such moist areas; lichens thrive on stones and rocks in more arid terrains.

Vegetation flourishes along the coast. *Verrucaria*, a lichen, grows on rocks submerged beneath the sea level. But plankton, the primary food of the krill that sustain most marine life in the South Polar Ocean, is the most significant form of vegetation.

Animals

The weather conditions that limit plant life on the continent of Antarctica make animal life there even more scarce. Some microscopic invertebrates, particularly the

A leopard seal in the snow covering an ice floe

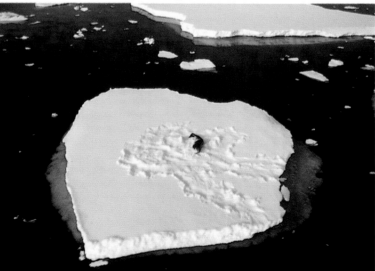

tiny mite *Gamasellus racovitzai*, occur in the soil and on the plants on the continent and its surrounding islands. Ticks, lice, and spiders are also found there, as well as the wingless springtail (*Cryptopygus antarcticus*). A midge (*Belgica antarctica*), a maximum of ½ inch (13 mm) long, is the largest native animal on the continent.

The surrounding South Polar Ocean, however, supports one-fifth of the planet's marine life. Fish, crustaceans, birds, and seals make up most of the animal population that inhabits the region during the summer mating season. Whales are also found in the coastal waters.

The shrimplike krill (*Euphausia superba*) is a small crustacean that provides sustenance for almost all the animal life in the area. Larger organisms include the squid, the starfish, and the icefish, whose blood contains natural antifreezes that help it survive the frigid temperatures.

There are about 12 species of birds living on and around Antarctica. One of these is the largest and longest-lived of the albatrosses, the wandering albatross (*Diomedea exulans*), with a wingspan of up to 12 feet (over 3 m) and a life span of 80 to 85 years. Other albatrosses are the black-browed (*D. melanophris*), gray-headed (*D. chrysostoma*), and yellow-nosed (*D. chlororhynchos*).

Another member of the same seabird group is the petrel, with its dense plumage and webbed feet. The snow petrel (*Pagodroma nivea*) and the Antarctic petrel (*Fulmarus glacioides*) are two of the few animals that actually breed inland, favoring the *nunataks* that project upward from the glacial ice. Other types, such as the giant petrel (*Macronectes giganteus*), prefer the western coastal areas of the Antarctic Peninsula.

Cormorants are also common in the Antarctic. Of these,

the blue-eyed shag (*Phalacrocorax atriceps*) lives on the Antarctic Peninsula and on the islands of Scotia Arc, and the king shag (*P. albiventer*) on Kerguelen Island. They feed on crustaceans, fish, mollusks, and squid. Gulls found in the Antarctic include the southern black-backed (*Larus dominicanus*) and the sheathbill, the only Antarctic bird that does not have webbed feet. The snowy sheathbill (*Chionis alba*) and the black-faced sheathbill (*C. minor*) feed on everything from insects and plants to dead animal carcasses. The Antarctic skua (*Catharacta maccormicki*) and the brown skua (*C. lonnbergi*) eat penguin eggs and chicks, krill, and small fish. The Antarctic tern (*Sterna vittata*) keeps to the peninsula and the islands, subsisting on a diet of plankton and small fish. The Kerguelen tern (*S. virgata*) eats insects and their larvae, as well as small mollusks.

The seven species of penguins belong to three main families. Most breed and raise their young on ice floes that break off from the larger continental ice sheets and ice shelves. They come ashore occasionally, but only onto the subantarctic islands. The pygoscelid, or brush-tailed, penguins include the Adélie, chinstrap, and

Crabeater seal, Antarctica

gentoo; the eudyptid, or crested, penguins are the macaroni and the rockhopper; and the aptenodytid, or royal, family has the emperor and king penguins.

The adult Adélie (*Pygoscelis adeliae*) weighs about 11 pounds (5 kg), and grows to 27.5 inches (70 cm) tall. Like most penguin species, the male and female alternate nesting duties during a 35-day incubation period. They feed on krill and fish larvae. At 27 inches (69 cm) tall and 10 pounds (4.5 kg), chinstraps (*P. antarctica*) are the smallest pygoscelids and feed primarily on krill. The gentoo (*Pygoscelis papua*) is the fastest swimmer of all the birds, racing 13 to 17 mph (21–27 kph) and diving to 328 feet (100 m).

In the eudyptid family, the macaroni penguin keeps primarily to Heard Island and South Georgia. With an average adult weight of 5.5 pounds (2.5 kg) and height of 22 inches (56 cm), the other eudyptid, the rockhopper, is the smallest of the penguins.

The emperor penguin is both the largest and the heaviest of the penguin species and never visits land during its entire lifetime. After mating, the male emperor, unlike the males of other penguin species, incubates the eggs for up to three months, while the female goes to feed herself. Like the male emperor penguin, the king carries its egg on its feet and covers it with a fold of abdominal skin called a brood patch. The king parents, however, share the chore of incubation in 15-day shifts.

The most common mammals to frequent the Antarctic coast are the seals. The two types of seals are the phocid, or true, seals and the otariids. Most Antarctic seals are phocids and have no external ears. Of these, the crabeater (*Lobodon carcinophagus*) rarely visits land and feeds primarily on krill. Females

grow to 10 feet (3 m) long and weigh up to 660 pounds (300 kg). Males are somewhat smaller. Their main enemies are the killer whale and the leopard seal.

The elephant seal (*Mirounga leonina*) is not only the largest seal but also one of the largest mammals: males grow to 15 feet (4.6 m) and can weigh 8,800 pounds (4,000 kg); females, which form harems of 20 to 30 for each male, can be 9 feet (2.7 m) long and up to 2,000 pounds (900 kg). Elephant seals take their name from their long noses, which act as resonating chambers.

Leopard seals (*Hydrurga leptonyx*) are ferocious, but their diet consists mainly of shrimp. The females, at 10 feet (3 m) and 770 pounds (350 kg), are larger than the males.

Ross seals (*Ommatophoca rossi*) are the rarest and smallest, with both males and females attaining 7.5 feet (2.3 m) and 440 pounds (200 kg). They have long rear flippers and feed primarily on squid, although they eat some cuttlefish and krill. Male and female Weddell seals (*Leptonychotes weddelli*) grow to 10 feet (3 m) and weigh 880 pounds (400 kg). They feed on fish, squid, and some crustaceans. They can dive to 2,000 feet (600 m) and stay under water for over an hour; they breathe through holes and cracks in the ice that they often make with their own teeth.

Otariids, the other major group of seals, include fur seals and sea lions. They have visible earflaps and move well on land. The male Antarctic fur seal (*Arctocephalus gazella*) averages about 6.5 feet (2 m) long and weighs 275 to 440 pounds (125 to 200 kg), while the female is somewhat smaller. Their coats have two layers: one of short, soft hair for insulation and the other of longer, coarser hair for added warmth.

High-Altitude Deserts

Atlas Mountains
36° N to 28° N latitude
11° W to 3° W longitude
Morocco, Algeria

Alps
48° N to 44° N latitude
3° E to 17° E longitude
France, Switzerland, Germany, Italy, Austria

Mounts Kenya and Kilimanjaro
1° S to 3° S latitude
37°30' E longitude
Kenya

Himalaya
38° N to 28° N latitude
73° E to 98° E longitude
Pakistan, India, Tibet, Nepal, Bhutan, China

Rocky Mountains
65° N to 15° N latitude
150° W to 98° W longitude
Canada, USA, Mexico

Andes Mountains
10° S to 52° S latitude
80° W to 68° W longitude
Colombia, Ecuador, Peru, Chile, Argentina

At the tops of the highest mountains and plateaus of the world lie some of the most arid and forbidding regions. Isolated from one another, and the products of different geological forces, the high-altitude regions each have unique physical characteristics. However, deprived of life-giving moisture to varying degrees and subject to a combination of similar climatic conditions, these regions have many traits in common, and their flora and fauna, while distinct, also share adaptations to life with reduced oxygen and high exposure to solar radiation. These regions include the Rocky Mountains in North America; the Andes in South America; the Atlas Mountains and several isolated peaks in Africa; the Alps in Europe; and the Himalaya, the Tibetan Plateau, and related mountain ranges in central Asia.

The Regions

The Rocky Mountains extend 3,000 miles (4,838 km) down the western side of North America. The highest point of this range is Mount McKinley in Alaska at 23,320 feet (7,108 m).

The Andes are the southern extension of the Rockies. They stretch 4,500 miles (7,258 km) down the western coast of South America, varying in width from 100 to 400 miles (161–645 km). They reach their highest point in Argentina at Aconcagua, 22,834 feet (6,960 m) above sea level.

On the other side of the Atlantic, north of the Sahara in northwestern Africa, the Atlas Mountains sweep 1,200 miles (1,935 km), forming the northern border of Algeria and spanning most of Morocco. They are composed of the Middle Atlas, the High Atlas, and the Anti-Atlas ranges; the highest peak is Mount Toubkal in Morocco, which stands 13,661 feet (4,164 m) tall. In east-central Africa, two isolated volcanic peaks rise far above the plains: Mount Kilimanjaro in Tanzania, at 19,340 feet (5,895 m); and Mount Kenya, or Kirinyaga, in Kenya, at 17,040 feet (5,194 m).

The mountain ranges of the Alps and the Himalaya are linked in one massive belt that stretches across Europe and Asia. The Alps extend over 80,000 square miles (207,200 sq km) and stretch 800 miles (1,290 km) from east to west. Mont Blanc, at 15,781 feet (4,810 m), is the highest summit in this chain, with the Matterhorn a close second at 14,803 feet (4,512 m).

Impressive as these peaks are, they pale in comparison with those of the Himalaya and their associated ranges, which average a height of over 20,000 feet (6,096 m). These ranges are part of the world's greatest mountain system, which extends 1,200 miles (1,935 km) from north to south and 2,000 miles (3,225 km) from east to west. The Himalaya, the name of which means "Abode of Snow" in Sanskrit, are the longest, highest, and most extensive high-altitude region in the world. Rising from the northern plains of India, these highlands form a bow-shaped arc around the southern edge of the Tibetan Plateau. They are home to the highest mountain peak in the world, Mount Everest, 29,028 feet (8,848 m) high.

Mt. Kilimanjaro looms over fever trees in Arusha National Park, Tanzania

Mountain Building and Shaping

These mountain systems are the products of millions of years of competing forces of crustal uplift and erosion. The continents on which mountains now rise lie on the somewhat rigid plates that constitute the Earth's crust. These plates move across the globe over the mantle—the viscous layer of material that separates the crust from the Earth's core. Mountains are formed when two plates collide and cause the earth's crust to buckle. Their appearance is further modified by fracturing and folding movements.

During the last 500 million years, there have been three major mountain-building periods, two during the Paleozoic Era and one that bridged the Cenozoic and Mesozoic eras. The Andes, the Alps, the Rockies, and the Asian mountain system were formed in the last paroxysm. The Andes began to take shape 400 million years ago and continued growing until about 70 million years ago, at which time the Alps and Rocky Mountains began to form. The Alps are the product of movements of several plates and are successors to a previous mountain system. The Himalaya are among the youngest mountain ranges in the world and underwent their principle building phase only about 40 million years ago.

Individual mountains form quite quickly by volcanic activity, as hot lavas from beneath the surface burst through vents in the crust. Mount Kilimanjaro in Africa, Mount Vesuvius in Italy, and Mount Pinatubo in the Philippines are examples of volcanic mountains, both dormant and active.

Countering the forces that have raised these mammoth mountains from the once-flat surface are forces that work to make them flat again. The oldest mountains, such as the 400-million-year-old Urals in Russia, have been whittled down, polished, and rounded over millions of years by glaciers and by stream erosion.

Between 5 million and 10,000 years ago, massive glaciers moved across the Northern Hemisphere during the Ice Age, leaving flattened and gouged peaks. In the tropical and temperate mountains of the Southern Hemisphere, such as the Andes, glaciers are still found at high elevations, and continue to grind away at the faces of the mountains.

The effects of water erosion over time are greater, although less spectacular, than those of the glaciers. As water cascades down mountainsides, it cuts deeply into rock and also acts as a solvent to break the bedrock material down further. Wind, powerful at high elevations, has also helped to shape the landforms; sand-bearing winds in arid regions are highly effective at grinding down rock.

Characteristics of High-Altitude Deserts

In addition to being subject to the forces of erosion and geological turmoil, all high-altitude regions share low temperatures, thin air, strong winds, and high levels of solar radiation.

Cold temperature is one of the most important climatic factors. Because mountains reflect the climates of their surrounding lowland areas, those close to the Equator will not experience seasonal temperature changes, while those in temperate zones will. On the other hand, mountains in equatorial tropical zones experience great daily and even hourly variations in temperature. On a smaller scale, temperatures can also differ greatly from one location to another within a small area. These microclimates, which are also affected by slope and aspect, or exposure to the sun, influence plant and animal communities as well.

Another limiting factor for life—especially animal life—is that air becomes thinner at higher elevations; in fact, atmospheric temperature declines because there are fewer molecules to conduct the sun's heat. Even the increased solar radiation does not compensate for the rarefied, or less dense, air.

Mountaintops are also often encased in clouds. As moisture-bearing clouds rise, they are forced up over the mountains and are thus cooled until they have to release their precipitation. Thus, rain or snow falls on the windward side, leaving the leeward side dry. This side, as well as the terrain beyond it, remains arid and is continually barraged by harsh, dry winds, while the windward side of the mountain may experience intense flooding and erosion.

Mountain environments occur in bands dictated by elevation. Most precipitation falls at a maximum of about 9,850 feet (3,000 m); above this point, both the windward and leeward sides of the peaks become increasingly dry and, as a result, barren.

Downslope from these high alpine deserts of rocky summits and ridges lie vast perpetual snowfields. Here, almost constant freezing temperatures ensure that snow never or very rarely melts; therefore, the moisture contained in the snow is not available for plants.

The snow line marks the lowest elevation at which there is permanent snow; it lies highest on mountains at the Equator and nears sea level at 75° N and S latitude, only about 1,400 miles (2,200 km) from the Poles.

Farther downslope lies the alpine tundra, an ecosystem characterized by low-growing shrubs, sedges, grasses, heaths, herbs, and mosses similar to those of the Arctic tundra. Here, moisture is more readily available, and vegetation is correspondingly denser.

Below the tundra lies the krummholz, the transition zone between tundra and the highest vestiges of forest. The German word for "gnarled wood," krummholz consists of dwarfed trees stunted by the adverse climatic conditions of higher elevations. Growth is inhibited by winds that become stronger and more damaging with increasing elevation.

Plants

Like other deserts of the world, high-altitude deserts have a short growing season—mainly because of temperature, however, not precipitation—that gets shorter with increasing elevation. In response, plants grow and mature quickly. As a result, few are annuals; most are perennials that store nourishment in their roots and stems to survive the winter months. Their seeds can remain dormant for long periods until temperatures rise enough for them to germinate. Some flowering plants, such as rhododendron, have even adapted by forming their flower buds the previous growing season and protecting them from winter cold with a tough outer husk. High-altitude plants are also more dependent on the wind than on insects for pollination.

In response to the cold and to driving winds, vegetation is small and stunted and grows close to the ground. Most plants extend only a few inches above the surface to minimize resistance and exposure to the wind. Many alpine plants produce a red pigment called anthocyanin, which absorbs heat while protecting the foliage from the damaging ultraviolet rays of the sun. Hairy or woolly leaves are another adaptation that protects against exposure to cold, wind, and solar radiation while locking in critically needed moisture.

Like all desert vegetation, alpine plants must be able to withstand aridity. Although snow and ice blanket much of the high-altitude terrain, the moisture in them is inaccessible until it melts. The presence of snow is a mixed blessing. On the one hand it provides plants beneath or behind banks with shelter from temperature extremes and exposure to the wind; it is also a source of moisture once it melts. On the other hand, when it does not melt, it prevents all growth other than that of the hardiest mosses and lichen—a growth of algae and fungi. To draw

High-altitude Patyong Valley, western Tibet

moisture from the ground, most plants have large root systems up to 2 feet (60 cm) long.

The temperature of the soil is also crucial. Soil temperature may vary from location to location, even between sites only inches apart, producing microclimates more subject to its influence than to atmospheric temperature. Spots that receive greater exposure to the sun or are protected by boulders and snowbanks from the elements are relatively fertile locations.

With increasing elevation, conditions become more and more inhospitable. One of the few trees that can survive the harsh climate at high elevations is the twisted and gnarled bristlecone pine of California's Sierra Nevada. These trees are considered to be some of the oldest living things on Earth—some are believed to be as much as 4,000 years old.

Dwarf shrubs are common. For the most part, however, plant life can be described as herbaceous perennials. Vast expanses of steppes and plateaus at high elevations, while cold and arid, are blanketed by meadows and grasses.

During the short spring and summer, mountainsides are covered with flowering plants that blanket the soil, sand, or rock in dazzling colors. Although some may not bloom for several years because of adverse conditions, at other times they transform the landscape with their blooms. Characteristic alpine flowers include potentillas, anemones, aconites, saxifrages, irises, asters, gentians, buttercups, crocuses, primroses, poppies, and bilberries.

At higher elevations are found cushion plants and mosses, often in thick mats. Tough, primitive lichens, which grow on rocky surfaces, are especially suited to high-altitude existence. They come in a wide array of colors. Green algae, or snow algae, envelop themselves in a red gel-like coating and live on the surface of snow, giving it a pink hue.

The hardy lichen and moss are the last holdouts below the zone of perpetual snow, which surrenders to exposed and barren ridges and rocky peaks totally devoid of life.

Animals

Unlike alpine vegetation, which is rooted in place, animals of high elevations are mobile and have the freedom to respond to changing seasons and climatic conditions by moving to lower elevations and more protected and secure locations. Although each group is the product of virtual isolation from the wildlife of other mountain peaks and plateaus, animals of high elevations share similarities and some basic adaptations to their environment.

These animals meet the demands of alpine conditions in numerous ways. Alpine fauna tends to be larger than that of lower elevations; the larger the heart and lungs, the better they are able to pump blood and process the little oxygen that is available in the rarefied air. In contrast, the hearts and lungs of smaller alpine animals have to work much harder and faster to do the same job with the same amount of oxygen; to maintain this rate, they must eat almost continuously to refuel themselves. Both large and small animals have increased numbers of red blood cells, which can carry greater concentrations of oxygen through the blood. Metabolism also drops so they can use limited energy sources more efficiently.

A reduced rate of metabolism and nourishment stored in the form of fat allow animals to hibernate during the cold winter months. They remain warm and protected in burrows below the surface of the earth or in deep crevices and holes in rock. While out and about, dark-colored fur and feathers absorb heat and at the same time shield the animals from ultraviolet rays, although some animals that roam primarily snow-covered terrain remain white all year.

Another survival tactic of alpine animals is a shortened mating and breeding season; they forgo the prolonged formalities engaged in at lower elevations to compensate for the short summers. In addition, there are normally fewer litters per season, although to make up for this there are more young in each. Generally, populations of alpine animals are low.

Some alpine animals have developed physical traits that facilitate functioning in their environment. Animals, such as goats, that command the rocky, steep terrain and mountain precipices have two toes on their front feet that take hold of rocky surfaces, and vestigial toes, or dewclaws, on their hind feet; they land on the entire surface of their well-padded feet to increase surface area. These pads function like suction cups to afford a better grip. Furthermore, these animals are constantly aware of slipping rocks and predators and can bound away without hesitation.

Male and female chamois

Wild sheep and goats are superbly suited to the rigors of life at high elevations. The latter group include the ibex, the markhor, the chamois, the Rocky Mountain goat, the goral, and the serow. The ibex is a stunning creature that can mount sheer rock faces and maneuver over icy surfaces with relative ease. Like most goats, it feeds on coarse grasses, sedges, herbs, and lichens.

Also at ease on steep mountain slopes is the antelopelike chamois. It has a powerful body that enables it to jump 10 feet (3 m) or more straight up a rocky incline and leap as far as 20 feet (6 m).

The Rocky Mountain goat of North America is a large, heavy wild goat with extremely sharp horns. Also an accomplished climber on exposed ridges, it feeds on leaves and twigs of shrubs and other alpine plants. So accustomed is the Rocky Mountain goat to the cold that it sometimes bounds into snowbanks during the summer to cool off.

The markhor, another wild goat, is a sturdy animal, standing 40 inches (102 cm) high with a shaggy beard and mane. Not the skilled climbers that the ibex and chamois are, markhors have, however, been observed resting in trees 12 feet (3.6 m) above the ground.

While the wild goats are found on rough terrain, sheep prefer to roam the more protected and gentler regions, where they can feed on finer grasses. Species include the mouflon, or urial; the argali; the Dall and Stone sheep; the Rocky Mountain bighorn; the barbary sheep, or aoudad, of the Atlas Mountains; and the goatlike bharal, or blue sheep, of Tibet.

Difficult to classify among high-altitude animals is the tahr, which is described as a goat antelope. While its appearance is much like that of a cross between a goat and an antelope, its behavior is similar to that of sheep. Carrying small horns, this shaggy-coated animal is a skilled climber and is found in the most remote areas of the Himalaya; therefore, like many of the sheep and goats, it is out of the range of most predators.

The chiru, a species of antelope found in Tibet, survives the blustery environment by shielding its body in trenches dug out of the cold soil. It also has sacs in its nostrils that help warm the cold air it breathes.

In the Southern Hemisphere, the vicuña, the alpaca, the llama, and the guanaco, all members of the camel family, occupy the high-altitude range of the goats and sheep of the Northern Hemisphere. The vicuña, which has three times as many red blood cells as a human, roams above 10,000 feet (3,048 m). Covered with reddish-brown or golden fur, it is the smallest of the four camelids and stands between 28 and 35 inches (72 and 89 cm) tall. The larger guanaco is 43 inches (110 cm) tall. Both the llama and the alpaca are now domesticated; the latter is highly valued for its wool.

The yak, also called the alpine musk-ox, inhabits the Tibetan Plateau and has also been domesticated to a great extent. Its massive 5- to 6-foot (1.5–1.8-m) frame is superbly designed to carry large loads and climb steep slopes. Yaks are also a precious source of meat, milk, and leather, and their dung can be used for fuel. Their shaggy, unkempt coats hang to the ground and protect the animals from the bitter cold winds that sweep across the plateau.

The snow leopard, one of the more exotic and increasingly rare animals of the Himalaya, preys on young yaks, as well as on the various wild goats and sheep; its primary victims are blue sheep.

Four feet (122 cm) tall and 160 pounds (72 kg), the snow leopard has beautiful gray fur with distinctive black spots. It climbs to up to 18,000 feet (5,486 m).

Wolves and foxes are more common predators at high elevations, even though they are often found below the range of their prey, such as goats and sheep. The animal called the Andean fox or Andean wolf is the most significant predator in the Andes.

Small mammals and birds are most likely to become the prey of these carnivores. Smaller mammals common in high-altitude terrains, with regional differences and variations, include pikas (relatives of the rabbit), hares, and other lagomorphs; and rodents, such as marmots, voles, rats, gophers, squirrels, and weasels. In the Andes, two small rodents, the mountain vizcacha and the chinchilla, are the most abundant small mammals; the latter is prized for its fur.

Although a wide variety of birds are found throughout high-altitude regions, most migrate there during the short summer season; in fact, the black-and-white ptarmigan is the only bird that remains at high elevations all year.

Staying not only close to the ground but also under it is the earthcreeper, which burrows tunnels up to 3 feet (91 cm) long.

Accentors, which resemble buntings, are also ground dwellers and range throughout Europe, Asia, and Africa, while the aptly named wallcreepers in Europe and Asia nest in moss-lined crevices in the sides of cliffs.

In the lower elevations of the Himalaya, up to 16,000 feet (4,877 m), range the white-capped redstart and the red-legged ibis-bill; the snow finch and alpine sparrow venture above 15,000 feet (4,572 m). The snow cock and the snow partridge are found even higher in the Himalaya—up to 19,000 and 20,000 feet (5,791 and 6,096 m).

Hummingbirds are also frequently seen between elevations of 10,000 to 20,000 feet (3,048 and 6,096 m); a species called the hillstar is the most common of this family. Up to 9 inches long (23 cm), this giant hummingbird is far from the diminutive bird of temperate regions.

The chough, one of the most common alpine birds, resembles a crow except for its curved red beak. Traveling in flocks of up to 30 birds, they have been seen at 21,000 feet (6,400 m).

Numerous scavengers roam the skies above alpine regions throughout Europe and Asia. One of the most notable is the lammergeier. It is best known for its habit of dropping bones from as high as 300 feet (91 m) in order to break them so it can get to the marrow inside. The lammergeier has a wing span of up to 9 feet (274 cm) and its appearance has given it its other name, bearded vulture. The massive condor, with wings larger than those of any other bird, must begin each flight by jumping off a cliff; it can then glide for hours on air currents while scavenging for food.

Because of the winds, most alpine insects are wingless. Instead, they are covered with thick hair that protects and insulates them from the elements.

A wide range of insects and arthropods are found up to 16,000 feet (4,876 m) in the Himalaya, including ants, bees, beetles, wasps, aphids, stone flies, and bulky grasshoppers. Butterflies such as the apollo, the swallowtail, and the painted lady are colorful visitors to the region; the diaphanous-winged apollo (*Parnassius acco*) lays its eggs as high as 19,000 feet (5,791 m).

Other insects are the red and black *Pseudabris* beetle of Tibet and the *Adonia* ladybird, similar to the ladybug, which hibernates high on the summits of the Rocky Mountains and Himalaya in masses of 5,000 to 9,000 individuals.

Among the most common insects in sheer number are collembolans, or springtails, also known as glacier fleas or snow fleas. These black bugs blanket snow and ice up to 20,000 feet (6,096 m), giving it a grayish-black tinge.

Some insects live in cold mountain streams; their bodies are designed to give minimal resistance to the frigid currents as they cling to rocks. The same is true of leeches, snails, and mussels.

A European ibex climbs a rocky slope high in the Alps

222   DESERTS

CREDITS

Deciphering Deserts

6 Wind in dunes, Namib Desert, by Günter Ziesler; 7 Sand dune mountain in Gobi Desert, by Ric Ergenbright; 8 COMSTOCK, INC./Georg Gerster; 9 Stephenie S. Ferguson; 10-11 world map by University of Kansas Map Associates (George F. McCleary, Jr., Darin Grauberger); 12 Eastcott and Momatiuk/Woodfin Camp, Inc.; 13 (top) Jeff Gnass; 13 (bottom) R. A. Acharya/Dinodia Picture Agency; 14 Pete Turner; 15 François Gohier; 16-17 Gary Braasch; 18-19 Brian A. Vikander.

Scorched Earth

20 Camel caravan in Sahara, by Kevin Morris/Allstock; 21 Elf owl in saguaro cactus, by George H. H. Huey; 22 George H. H. Huey; 23 Arizona Historical Society Library; 24-25 George H. H. Huey; 25 (top right) map by Les Devenirs Visuels; 25 (bottom right) George H. H. Huey; 26 C. Allan Morgan; 27 (all) C. Allan Morgan; 28 illustration by Les Devenirs Visuels; 29 George H. H. Huey; 30 Emil Muench/Photo Researchers, Inc.; 31 Carl Purcell/Photo Researchers, Inc.; 32 (bottom) COMSTOCK, INC./Georg Gerster; 32-33 Michael S. Yamashita; 33 (bottom) COMSTOCK, INC./Georg Gerster; 33 (top right) Larry Brock/Tom Stack and Associates; 34 Bureau of Reclamation, United States Department of the Interior/Photography by Joe Madrigal; 35 (left) Tom McHugh/Photo Researchers, Inc.; 35 (right) Dr. E. R. Degginger/Folio; 36 Renée Lynn/Photo Researchers, Inc.; 37 (top both) William E. Ferguson; 37 (bottom) Steve Kaufman; 38-39 Richard J. Quataert/Folio; 39 (top right) Warren Garst/Tom Stack and Associates; 39 (bottom right) map by Les Devenirs Visuels; 40 (top) National Anthropological Archives, Smithsonian Institution/Photo no. 75-14014; 40 (bottom) Greg Vaughn; 41 John Cancalosi/Tom Stack and Associates; 42 (top) Edward S. Ross; 42 (bottom) John Cancalosi/Tom Stack and Associates; 43 David C. Fritts/Earth Scenes; 44 (top) map by Les Devenirs Visuels; 44 (bottom) Megan Biesele/Anthro-Photo; 45 Nicholas Devore/Photographers/Aspen; 46 (top) COMSTOCK, INC./Georg Gerster; 46 (bottom) G. C. Kelley; 47 (top) Nigel Dennis/Photo Researchers, Inc.; 47 (bottom) Edward S. Ross; 48 Nelson S. Burack/Lazarus Group; 49 (top) Martha Cooper/Peter Arnold, Inc.; 49 (bottom) Camilla Smith/Rainbow; 50 (top) map by Les Devenirs Visuels; 50 (bottom) Wolfgang Kaehler; 51 Adam Woolfitt/Woodfin Camp, Inc.; 52-53 Robert Azzi/Woodfin Camp, Inc.; 53 (right) Jacques Burlot/Gamma Liaison; 54 (left) S. Compoint/Sygma; 54-55 Noel Quidu/Gamma Liaison; 55 (bottom) A. Tannenbaum/Sygma; 56 (left) COMSTOCK, INC./Georg Gerster; 56-57 Kotoh/Allstock; 57 (right) M. Delluc/Viva/Woodfin Camp, Inc.; 58-59 illustration by Les Devenirs Visuels; 60 Bundesarchiv, Koblenz, Germany; 61 Y. Arthus-Bertrand/Peter Arnold, Inc.; 62 (left) Fred J. Maroon; 62 (right) © Ettagale Blauer/Jason Lauré; 63 (top) National Aeronautics and Space Administration; 63 (middle) Inga Spence/Tom Stack and Associates; 63 (bottom) I.Bich/Sygma; 64 Frans Lanting/Minden Pictures; 65 COMSTOCK, INC./Georg Gerster; 66 (left) Lynn Abercrombie; 66-67 Fred J. Maroon; 67 (right) Lynn Abercrombie.

Frozen Frontiers

68 Adélie penguins in Antarctica, by Eugene G. Schulz; 69 Woman fishing above Arctic Circle, by Harald Sund; 70 Patrick Morrow; 71 Harald Sund; 72 (left) map by Les Devenirs Visuels; 72-73 Patrick Morrow; 73 (right) Wolfgang Kaehler; 74 (bottom) Philippe de Potier/Gamma Liaison; 74-75 James David Brandt/Earth Scenes; 75 (bottom) Patrick Morrow; 76 National Science Foundation-Polar Programs/Carnegie-Mellon Institute; 77 Galen Rowell/Mountain Light; 78 Galen Rowell/Mountain Light; 79 C. Allan Morgan; 80 (both) C. Allan Morgan; 81 (both) Galen Rowell/Mountain Light; 82 Galen Rowell/Mountain Light; 83 Johnny Johnson/Animals, Animals; 84 (both) Galen Rowell/Mountain Light; 85 Wolfgang Kaehler; 86 Wolfgang Kaehler; 87 (top) map by Les Devenirs Visuels; 87 (bottom left) E. R. Degginger/Animals, Animals; 87 (bottom right) M. A. Chappell/Animals, Animals; 88 Fred Bruemmer; 89 (left) Harald Sund; 89 (right) Wolfgang Kaehler; 90 (left) Tom J. Ulrich; 90 (right) S. J. Kraseman/Peter Arnold, Inc.; 91 Wolfgang Kaehler; 92 (left) C. Allan Morgan; 92-93 Boyd Norton; 93 (top right) François Gohier; 93 (bottom right) Tom J. Ulrich; 94 (top) Fred Bruemmer; 94 (bottom) David C. Fritts/Animals, Animals; 95 Wolfgang Kaehler; 96-97 Ted Kerasote/Photo Researchers, Inc.

Lonesome Thoroughfares

98 Storm over Capital Reef National Park, Utah, by Robert Walch; 99 Hairy armadillo in Patagonia, by C. Allan Morgan; 100 François Gohier; 101 David McNew; 102-103 C. Allan Morgan; 103 (top left) Art Wolfe, Inc.; 103 (top right) David McNew; 103 (bottom right) map by Les Devenirs Visuels; 104-105 Loren McIntyre; 105 (right) Art Wolfe, Inc.; 106 map by Les Devenirs Visuels; 107 (both) Keren Su/Allstock; 108-109 Fred J. Maroon; 109 (right) Keren Su/Allstock; 110 Keren Su/Allstock; 111 (top left) Ric Ergenbright; 111 (top right) Kevin Morris/Allstock; 111 (bottom) Ric Ergenbright; 112 (both) Henebry Photography; 113 David Turnley, Detroit Free Press/Black Star; 114-115 Henebry Photography; 115 (right) Ric Ergenbright; 116 (bottom) Wolfgang Kaehler; 116-117 Kevin Fleming; 117 (top) Robert Holmes; 117 (bottom left) Wolfgang Kaehler; 117 (bottom right) Patrick Morrow; 118-119 Henebry Photography; 119 (right) Ric Ergenbright; 120 Louie Psihoyos/Matrix International, Inc.; 121 Louie Psihoyos/Matrix International, Inc.; 122 (left) Neg. No. 265294 (photo by Shackelford) Courtesy Department of Library Services, American Museum of Natural History; 122-123 Neg. No. 276084 (photo by Young) Courtesy Department of Library Services, American Museum of Natural History; 123 (top) Neg. No. 410765 (photo by Shackelford) Courtesy Department of Library Services, American Museum of Natural History; 124 Robert Azzi/Woodfin Camp, Inc.; 125 Michael S. Yamashita; 126 Art Wolfe, Inc.; 127 (top) Erich Lessing from Art Resource; 127 (bottom) COMSTOCK, INC./Bill Ellzey; 128-129 Jeffrey Alford/Asia Access; 130 (top) map by Les Devenirs Visuels; 130 (bottom) Jim Brandenburg/Minden Pictures; 131 Jeff Gnass; 132 illustration by Les Devenirs Visuels; 133 David Muench/Allstock; 134 (left) Phil Schofield/Allstock; 134-135 David Stoecklein/Allstock; 135 (right) Brian Parker/Tom Stack and Associates; 136 (left) Henebry Photography; 136 (right) Adam Woolfitt/Woodfin Camp, Inc.; 137 (top) Ric Ergenbright; 137 (bottom left) Danny Lehman; 137 (bottom right) Carr Clifton; 138 (left) Steve Northup/Black Star; 138-139 Karen Kasmauski/Woodfin Camp, Inc.; 140 Adam Woolfitt/Woodfin Camp, Inc.; 141 UPI/Bettmann; 142 Xinhua-Chine Nouvel/Gamma Liaison; 143 David J. Cross.

Diamonds in the Sand

144 Namib Desert, Atlantic coast, by Nicholas Devore/Photographers/Aspen; 145 Salt crystals in the Atacama Desert, by François Gohier; 146 François Gohier; 147 Loren McIntyre; 148 (left) Mike Jackson; 148 (center) map by Les Devenirs Visuels; 148-149 Günter Ziesler; 149 (right) Mike Jackson; 150 (top) Loren McIntyre; 150 (bottom) Mike Jackson; 151 Loren McIntyre; 152 (left) François Gohier; 152-153 Loren McIntyre; 153 (bottom) Loren McIntyre; 154 (left) François Gohier; 154 (bottom) Mike Jackson; 155 (top) Loren McIntyre; 155 (bottom) Dan McCoy/Rainbow; 156 (left) COMSTOCK, INC./Phyllis Greenberg; 156-157 Jim Brandenburg/Minden Pictures; 157 (right) map by Les Devenirs Visuels; 158 Günter Zeisler; 159 (top) Edward S. Ross; 159 (bottom) Günter Zeisler; 160 Arthur Gloor/Earth Scenes; 161 (both) Edward S. Ross; 162 (both) Günter Zeisler; 163 G. C. Kelley; 164 COMSTOCK, INC./Georg Gerster; 165 DeBeers Consolidated Mines; 166 Anthony Bannister/Animals, Animals; 167 Eric Robert/Gamma Liaison; 168-169 Oryx in Namib Desert, by Jim Brandenburg/Minden Pictures.

Desert Profiles

170 Kevin Fleming; 171 Kevin Fleming; 172 D. Mazonowicz, NYC; 173 Ronny Jaques/Photo Researchers, Inc.; 174 Edward S. Ross; 175 Priscilla Connell/Photo-Nats; 176 Edward S. Ross; 177 William E. Ferguson; 178 William E. Ferguson; 179 Gary Braasch; 180 Buddy Mays/Travel Stock; 181 Mark D. Phillips/Photo Researchers, Inc.; 182 Darek Karp/Animals, Animals; 183 Edward S. Ross; 184 Ric Ergenbright; 185 Robert Holmes; 186 COMSTOCK, INC./Georg Gerster; 187 Ric Ergenbright; 188 Roy Toft/Tom Stack and Associates; 189 Ferrero/Jacana/Photo Researchers, Inc.; 190 Edward S. Ross; 191 Edward S. Ross; 192 Jeff Foott/Tom Stack and Associates; 193 William E. Ferguson; 194 Gary Braasch; 195 Jo-Ann Ordano/Photo-Nats; 196 Robert Walch; 197 George H. H. Huey; 198 David McNew; 199 David McNew; 200 Gary Braasch; 201 Jeff Gnass; 202 Michael Giannechini/Photo Researchers, Inc.; 203 Sam Fried/Photo-Nats; 204 Galen Rowell/Mountain Light; 205 François Gohier; 206 Art Wolfe; 207 François Gohier; 208 Jeff Gnass; 209 François Gohier; 210 Wolfgang Kaehler; 211 Stephen J. Krasemann/Photo Researchers, Inc.; 212 Ben Osborne, Oxford Scientific Films/Animals, Animals; 213 C. Allan Morgan; 214 Gregory G. Dimijian/Photo Researchers, Inc.; 215 Galen Rowell/Mountain Light; 216 Stefan Meyers/Animals, Animals; 217 Stefan Meyers/Animals, Animals.

REDEFINITION

President
Edward Brash

Picture Editor
Rebecca Hirsh

Design Director
Edwina Smith

*Finance, Administration,
and Production Director*
Glenn Smeds

Production Assistant
Catherine Rawson

Writer/Researchers
Claudia Bedwell
Debra Greinke
Susi Lill
Elizabeth Thompson
Tony Wassell

Copy Editors
Claudia Bedwell
Debra Greinke

Design
The Watermark Design Office
Alexandria, VA

Illustrations
Les Devenirs Visuels
Paris, France

Color Separation
Colourscan Overseas
Co. Pte. Ltd.,
Singapore

Susan Arritt is a free-lance writer who brings to this volume her extraordinary firsthand experience of having lived alone for a year in a log cabin in the southeastern portion of the Colorado Plateau, in northern New Mexico. She has written and edited extensively on the natural sciences and was a writer for the United Nations International Fund for Agricultural Development, in Rome.

The index for this book was prepared by Roy Nanovic. The editors wish to thank Dr. Carl A. Fox, Executive Director, Biological Sciences Center, Desert Research Institute, Reno, Nevada, for overseeing the Desert Profiles.

For other editorial contributions, the editors wish to thank the following individuals and organizations: Brent Bingham, Photo Effects; Ellen Gerth; Michele Italiano-Perla; Corinne Martinez; Janice Olson; Kathryn Pfeifer; Allan Savory, Center for Holistic Resource Management, Albuquerque, New Mexico; Elizabeth Simon; David Thomson; Vance Titus; University of Kansas Map Associates (George F. McCleary, Jr., Darin Grauberger); Alta S. Walker, U.S. Geological Survey, Reston, Virginia.

The editors also wish to thank the Utah Wilderness Coalition for allowing them to use the Wallace Stegner quotation from its book, *Wilderness at the Edge*.

FOR FURTHER READING

Bagnold, Ralph A., *Libyan Sands: Travel in a Dead World*. London: Michael Haag Limited, 1987.

Campbell, David G., *The Crystal Desert: Summers in Antarctica*. Boston: Houghton Mifflin Company, 1992.

Evans, Howard, and Mary Alice Evans, *Australia: A Natural History*. Washington, D.C.: Smithsonian Institute Press, 1983.

George, Uwe, *In the Deserts of This Earth* (English translation). New York: Harcourt Brace Jovanovich, 1977.

Limerick, Patricia Nelson, *Desert Passages: Encounters with the American Deserts*. Niwot, Colorado: University Press of Colorado, 1989.

National Geographic Society, *The Desert Realm: Lands of Majesty and Mystery*. Washington, D.C.: National Geographic Society, 1982.

Van Dyke, John C., *The Desert*. New York: Scribners, 1901.

Wagner, Frederic H., *Wildlife of the Deserts*. New York: Harry N. Abrams, Inc., 1980.